Dante, Mercy, and the Beauty
of the Human Person

Dante, Mercy, *and* *the* Beauty *of the* Human Person

EDITED BY

Leonard J. DeLorenzo

AND

Vittorio Montemaggi

 CASCADE *Books* · Eugene, Oregon

DANTE, MERCY, AND THE BEAUTY OF THE HUMAN PERSON

Cascade Books
An Imprint of Wipf and Stock Publishers
199 W. 8th Ave., Suite 3
Eugene, OR 97401

www.wipfandstock.com

PAPERBACK ISBN: 978-1-5326-0583-3
HARDCOVER ISBN: 978-1-4982-4608-8
EBOOK ISBN: 978-1-4982-4607-1

Cataloguing-in-Publication data:

Names: DeLorenzo, Leonard J., editor | Montemaggi, Vittorio, editor

Title: Dante, Mercy, and the Beauty of the Human Person / Edited by Leonard J. DeLorenzo and Vittorio Montemaggi.

Description: Eugene, OR: Cascade Books, 2017 | Includes bibliographical references and index.

Identifiers: ISBN 978-1-5326-0583-3 (paperback) | ISBN 978-1-4982-4608-8 (hardcover) | ISBN 978-1-4982-4607-1 (ebook)

Subjects: LCSH: Dante Alighieri, 1265–1321. Divine commedia—criticism and interpretation. | Paradise—Poetry | Dante Alighieri, 1265–1321—Appreciation. | Dante Alighieri, 1265–1321. Paradiso.

Classification: PQ4390 D45 2017 (print) | PQ4390 (ebook)

Manufactured in the U.S.A.   07/10/17

In gratitude to Pope Francis

For calling us to rediscover ourselves
and one another in mercy

Contents

Part 2: Transformations

Part 3: Beatitude

Contributors

John C. Cavadini is McGrath-Cavadini Director of the McGrath Institute for Church Life and Professor of Theology at the University of Notre Dame. His publications include *The Last Christology of the West, Explorations in the Theology of Benedict XVI* (ed.), *"Who Do You Say That I Am?": Confessing the Mystery of Christ* (ed.), and *Mary on the Eve of the Second Vatican Council* (ed.).

Leonard J. DeLorenzo is Associate Professional Specialist in the McGrath Institute for Church Life, with a concurrent appointment in the Department of Theology at the University of Notre Dame. His publications include *Witness: Learning to Tell the Stories of Grace That Illumine Our Lives* and *Work of Love: A Theological Reconstruction of the Communion of Saints.*

Kevin Grove, CSC, is Assistant Professor of Systematic Theology at the University of Notre Dame. His publications include *Basil Moreau: Essential Writings* (ed.) and numerous book chapters and journal articles.

Jessica Keating is Director of the Human Dignity and Life Initiatives in the McGrath Institute for Church Life at the University of Notre Dame, where she is also a doctoral student in systematic theology. Her popular articles have appeared in such publications as *America Magazine* and *Church Life*, and she is currently working on a book about renewing the consistent ethic of life.

Robin Kirkpatrick is Emeritus Professor of Italian and English Literatures, and Life Fellow of Robinson College at the University of Cambridge. His publications include *Dante's* Inferno: *Difficulty and Dead Poetry*, *Dante's* Paradiso *and the Limitations of Modern Criticism*, and a complete translation with commentary of Dante's *Commedia*.

Jennifer Newsome Martin is Assistant Professor in the Program of Liberal Studies with a concurrent appointment in the Department of Theology at the University of Notre Dame. Her publications include *Hans Urs von Balthasar and the Critical Appropriation of Russian Religious Thought*, and her articles have appeared in *Modern Theology*, *Spiritus*, *Church Life*, and *Christianity and Literature*.

Christian Moevs is Associate Professor of Italian at the University of Notre Dame. His publications include *The Metaphysics of Dante's* Comedy. He is also coeditor of the Devers Series in Dante Studies.

Vittorio Montemaggi is Associate Professor of Religion and Literature in the Department of Romance Languages and Literatures, with a concurrent appointment in the Department of Theology at the University of Notre Dame. His publications include *Reading Dante's* Commedia *as Theology: Divinity Realized in Human Encounter* and *Dante's* Commedia: *Theology as Poetry* (ed.).

Cyril O'Regan is the Catherine Huisking Professor of Theology at the University of Notre Dame. His publications include *The Anatomy of Misremembering*, *Theology and the Spaces of the Apocalyptic*, *Gnostic Apocalypse*, and *The Heterodox Hegel*.

Stephen C. Pepper, CSC, is Campus Minister and serves in the Department of Theology at King's College, Wilkes-Barre, Pennsylvania.

Matthew Treherne is Head of the School of Languages, Cultures and Societies, Codirector of the Leeds Centre for Dante Studies, and Senior Lecturer in Italian at the University of Leeds. His publications include *Dante's* Commedia: *Theology as Poetry* (ed.) and *Reviewing Dante's Theology* (ed.).

Acknowledgments

This exploration of *Dante, Mercy, and the Beauty of the Human Person* is a quest to rediscover the importance of community, which, appropriately, began in the context of a communal gathering. The first conversation about pursuing this exploration occurred between the editors of this volume and Jessica Keating, one of the contributors. A special debt of gratitude is owed to Jessica for her crucial role in bringing this work to life. Shortly thereafter, Kevin Grove, CSC, joined the conversation, and from there each of the contributors joined in too. Without this genuine experience of scholarly and spiritual community, this volume would not have arisen. On an institutional level, this sense of community was enhanced in the production of the volume by interaction between the McGrath Institute for Church Life and the Devers Program in Dante Studies.

Before there was a collection of essays, there was first a lecture series and a course at the University of Notre Dame, both under the same title as this volume. We are grateful to the Institute for Scholarship in the Liberal Arts for awarding us a grant for the lecture series. These initiatives would also not have been possible without the advice and cosponsorship of the Office of Campus Ministry, the Department of Theology, the Congregation of Holy Cross, and the Devers Program in Dante Studies. These partnerships were coordinated through the McGrath Institute for Church Life, which was the primary host for the lecture series and source of consistent support throughout this entire process. We are especially grateful to the McGrath-Cavadini Director of the institute, John C. Cavadini—also a contributor to this volume—for his generosity in supporting this project, as well as for the efforts of Valerie McCance and Brett Robinson for coordinating, publicizing, and broadcasting the lecture series. From there, our gratitude extends to Medi Ann Volpe, who was instrumental in connecting us with our present publisher.

We are also deeply grateful to the students who participated in the interdisciplinary course that accompanied the lecture series during Lent and into Easter of 2016. Their eager engagement of this unique pilgrimage through the text and in community energized this project from the very start. We wish to thank them each individually: Nicholas Acampora, Daniel Anderson, Kevin Barrett, Benedict Becker, Robert Browne, Clare Carmody, John Connors, Domenic Digiovanni, Grace Enright, Lucia Enright, Megan Ferowich, Thomas Gallagher, Monica Golbranson, Madeline Hagan, Megan Jones, Laura Machado, Jose Martinez, Josiah Ponnudurai, Andrew Pott, Stephanie Reuter, Kim Sammons, Madeline Running, Katherine Sisk, Maggie Skoch, Katherine Smith, Kathryn Thompson, Patrick Tinsley, John VanBerkum, Molly Weiner, Catherine Williams, and Sarah Witt.

Introduction

W hat if reading Dante's *Commedia* were a kind of pilgrimage? That would mean that both the destination and the mode of travel would be significant, and that the reasons why one sets off on this journey in the first place would be worthy of attention. Even those with a cursory knowledge of the poem know that Dante ends up gazing upon the "love that moves the sun and other stars" after beginning in a "dark wood" midway through life's journey. With one hundred cantos and the whole cosmos in between, it seems that there is quite a lot of distance between darkness and light, confusion and clarity, sorrow and joy. And yet, that great distance is as if nothing when considering that the journey Dante makes occurs as much within him by increments of love as it takes place outside him by his footsteps. If Dante's *Commedia* were a kind of pilgrimage for the reader, too, then it would be a pilgrimage in a similar manner—one in which the reader moves toward something and also becomes someone in the process. Moreover, it would be a pilgrimage within and toward community, just as Dante himself moves from isolation to guidance to something perhaps best described as "mutual indwelling."

This volume is the work of readers who venture to allow the reading of the *Commedia* to be a spiritual pilgrimage. Those who composed the essays collected here were willing to join with others in moving through the *Commedia* as pilgrims. While the contributors are themselves scholars, these essays are not primarily intended for the scholarly field as conventionally conceived. At the same time, each of the contributors offer their distinctive scholarly expertise to the project of reading the *Commedia* in and as community, with the hope of finding something that we often lose, of clarifying something that is often obscured, and of reclaiming something that we all too often forget: the beauty of the human person revealed in the light of mercy.

None other than Pope Francis provided the keynote for this pilgrim quest when, already looking forward to the Jubilee Year of Mercy in May of 2015, he offered these words to the President of the Pontifical Council of Culture to be shared with the Italian Senate as it observed the 750th anniversary of Dante's birth:

> The *Comedy* can be read as a great itinerary, rather as a true pilgrimage, both personal and interior, as well as communal, ecclesial, social and historic. It represents the paradigm of every authentic voyage in which humanity is called to leave behind what Dante calls "the little patch of earth that makes us here so fierce" (*Par.* 32.51) in order to reach a new condition, marked by harmony, peace and happiness. This is the horizon of all authentic humanism.
>
> Dante is therefore a prophet of hope, a herald of humanity's possible redemption and liberation, of profound change in every man and woman, of all of humanity. He invites us to regain the lost and obscured meaning of our human journey and to hope to see again the bright horizon which shines in the full dignity of the human person.[1]

Pope Francis is inviting an embodied reading of the text. He suggests that the fullness of what the "supreme poet" heralds is only available to those who read personally and interiorly, communally and ecclesially, socially and historically. Readers cannot stand safely outside the text if they are to glimpse the final horizon of the poem's vision. What is in play is nothing less than the possibility of remembering who we are and who we are called to become in and through mercy. Just as Dante journeys, so too are his readers meant to journey, and in so doing learn to see and love one another anew.

This present volume is the fruit of an intentional effort to read the *Commedia* as pilgrims, in community, with the hope of rediscovering the beauty of the human person. In the early months of 2016, the contributors to this volume collaborated to offer a series of lectures alongside a communal reading of the *Commedia* that commenced on Ash Wednesday and concluded on Divine Mercy Sunday. Participants from the University of Notre

---

1. Pope Francis, "Message of His Holiness Pope Francis for the 750th Anniversary of the Birth of the Supreme Poet Dante Alighieri"; cf. Francis, *Lumen Fidei*, no. 4.

Dame, the surrounding community, and across the country and even in several foreign countries made a pilgrimage through the poem as they read two cantos each day, gathered together in discussion groups, and composed their own reflections on their personal and shared pilgrimage.[2] Many who made this pilgrimage were first-time readers of the *Commedia*, others had read the poem in part, while others still were well-versed in Dante's work or even, in the case of several pilgrims, Dante scholars. Regardless of previous experience or expertise, all walked together on a common way, meeting up with others as the journey progressed, seeking to discover with each other, in each other, and for each other the glimmers of our redeemed humanity. Dante does not and cannot deliver such a gift himself but he does open a path for us to journey toward receiving such a gift together.

One of the participants in the communal pilgrimage from Lent to Easter in 2016 reflected on her journey with others through the *Commedia* in this way:

> The *Comedy* is not the story of how Dante gets to heaven but of how God brings the human person home. It is the light of God who illuminates us, Christ who moves us, and Mary who guides us. . . . The journey of introspection begins by surrendering the illusion of autonomy. I struggle to surrender the belief that I can grasp this paradise—or that humanity is entitled to it. . . . It is grace that awakens Dante to the woods, that brings Virgil to him, and that ultimately sets him in motion as part of the divine *Comedy*. Thus every beautiful movement begins with the bestowal of mercy. We have only to utter the fiat that Dante murmured to Beatrice and then follow by our own movement.[3]

The interweaving of the first person voice—"I" and "we"—testifies to how this particular reader moved into and through the text rather than standing outside of it, where she could safely observe and measure. How often does one's disinterested position become that "little patch of earth" that makes us so fierce toward one another? And how often is it that the antidote to this sickness is the humility to submit to journeying with others, alongside them, willing to become something and someone different from who you were before?

The essays presented herein therefore began as lectures composed for a community of pilgrims who gathered in liturgical time to read the *Commedia* together—setting out together on a common journey in hopes

---

2. For more on this lecture series, see http://icl.nd.edu/events/dante-mercy-and-the-beauty-of-the-human-person/.

3. Excerpt from Kathryn Thompson, University of Notre Dame, class of 2017.

of reaching something like a common home. What changed between then and now is that the essays have—as a further stage in the pilgrimage—been revised to read more academically, and recast for a different medium and a different audience. You will, however, still find a certain spoken quality to these essays, because they were originally and always intended to be contributions to a dialogue among pilgrim-readers. In other words, those of us who have written these words invite you, who read these words, to join us in setting out on the ongoing journey of rediscovering our human beauty together, in the light of mercy.

The itinerary of this volume, which is proposed as an initial direction to which others might certainly be added and preferred, follows something of a thematic trajectory rather than a strictly chronological one that goes through the *Commedia* from beginning to end. The first essay comes from Vittorio Montemaggi, who welcomes us with joy into this journey together. His essay offers us, as if from an initial vista, the opportunity to look out over the whole terrain in order to anticipate, in hope and longing, the demanding but delightful journey set before us. Montemaggi portrays a pilgrim path that opens with the cry of mercy and ends in the spontaneity of human encounter. We are likewise invited to always begin anew in humble admiration when we read the *Commedia*, wondering at the depths and heights of our human dignity that Dante wants to help us remember.

After this initial invitation, the volume proceeds according to three general sections. The first section—"Bearings"—includes essays that assist readers of the *Commedia* to set their faces in the direction of the pilgrimage's end. At the beginning of this section, John Cavadini offers a reading of the *Inferno* that follows how Augustine presents the "Earthly City" as an ironic mimicry of the "Heavenly City" in *City of God*. What Dante presents, according to Cavadini, is the ongoing unmasking of sin in the infernal realm, where all of sin's disguises are removed and the absurdity of the sin itself—principally, lying—is laid bare. Even here, though, the presence of mercy is the hermeneutic key since there would be no perspective to see hell for what it is if not for the true light of the human person shining down from the heavenly realm, glowing most brilliantly in the eucharistic sacrifice.

The second essay comes from Kevin Grove, CSC, who offers something of an introduction to the purgatorial nature of Dante's entire journey through the first two *cantiche*, principally from the perspective of the threshold of the Earthly Paradise. When the reader stands with Dante at this critical juncture atop Mount Purgatory, desire, memory, and speech are redressed and remade for the purpose of journeying into true growth and glory. Grove observes how the dawn of mercy is both devastating and healing in one swift stroke.

The third essay in this first section belongs to Christian Moevs, whose considerations of the metaphysical dimensions of the *Commedia* challenge readers to refine and elevate our typical modes of spatial and temporal thinking. Moevs draws out Dante's lament at the tragedy of losing ourselves by looking for our desire as something to grasp and possess. In so doing, Moevs enables us to listen afresh to Dante's laudation of the gift of receiving ourselves again as the fruit of divine desire, in which light and being are one.

The second set of essays falls under the heading of "Transformations," and points readers to how the *Commedia* dramatizes shifts in being and action necessary for journeying as the poem depicts. Matthew Treherne opens this section with a reminder to readers that we always come to any text, but especially Dante's, in the midst of life already in progress. The unfolding drama of the reader herself is perhaps too often neglected when considering who we are as readers of the *Commedia*, and yet from the very first line of the *Inferno* Dante opens his journey to the respective journeys of his readers. The personal and communal must always be intricately connected for the *Commedia's* readers if they are to truly become pilgrims and not just observers.

Leonard J. DeLorenzo continues the theme of "Transformations" as he focuses attention on the middle of the *Purgatorio* to try to understand what, exactly, the penitent souls are doing and why. Reflecting on the communal praying of the "Our Father" on the first terrace of purgatory, DeLorenzo ventures to discern how the movement practiced there might serve as an interpretive key for the movement of the whole *Commedia*. From the pattern of movement that the penitents exhibit, a vision of the meaning of the saints in beatitude emerges and, with them, a way of understanding how Dante's pilgrimage begins, in the order of grace.

Stephen C. Pepper, CSC, concludes the section with an essay that critically distinguishes between gazes locked into fixation and gazes opened up to fascination. The course of treatment for those being capacitated for the full flourishing of beauty in the dignity of the human person has to do with changing the way that we look at each other. Pepper reminds readers that what we are looking for and what we are willing to see is every bit as important—if not more important—as what appears to us.

The third and final section of this volume focuses on "Beatitude," with three essays situated much more on the side of journey's end, helping us see what according to Dante constitutes the mutual indwelling of humanity and divinity embodied in the heavenly community. Jennifer Newsome Martin attends to transcendent vision in the *Paradiso*, where the narrative shuttles toward the nearly unbearable luminosity and the impossible distances of astronomical imagery. Echoing the recalibrations to spatial thinking according to the properties of light that Christian Moevs initiates in his essay, Martin contends that the *Paradiso* requires a new way of seeing, one that reaches toward the perfection of form and proportion. Once again, as in the previous essay, what one sees and how one sees bear directly upon one another.

Jessica Keating explores memory, specifically tracing how Dante presents memory as failed, redeemed, and sanctified in the three *cantiche* of the *Commedia*. Returning to a note that John Cavadini introduces earlier, Keating elucidates the eucharistic memory as both the path and the goal of human memory once sick in sin but, in Christ, bound for communal perfection. What Keating helps readers of the *Commedia* to find is that our own memories find their source and summit in that love that first remembers us.

The third essay of the final section comes from Cyril O'Regan, who reads in the *Paradiso* the healing of rivalries through the charitable exchange of praise. Looking at the figures of St. Francis and St. Bonaventure, St. Dominic and St. Thomas Aquinas, O'Regan sees how particularity is celebrated and union is achieved when Dante orchestrates a mini-drama of chiasmic praise that has the children of each spiritual tradition heaping praise upon the "rival" tradition's founder (Bonaventure sings of Dominic, Thomas Aquinas of Francis). Here we glimpse that the final horizon of the human person—and the beauty of which it is an expression—lights up when the will to self-possession opens to the mutual exchange of gifts.

Following the ten distinct yet unified essays outlined above, this volume enjoys the benefit of an eloquent afterword—a rich essay in its own right—from a leading scholar and experienced pilgrim of Dante's poem. All of us—authors and readers—owe a special debt of gratitude to the afterword's author, Robin Kirkpatrick, who not only wrote something new for this volume but who also wrote the translation of the *Commedia* used throughout this work.[4] Though his contribution to this volume is therefore apparent on just about every page, a great deal of his influence on the approach we have undertaken abides, implicitly but significantly, beneath the surface. Kirkpatrick's teaching, scholarship, and contemplation of the *Commedia* at the intersection of religion and literature present interpretive perspectives that help us see how we might become both vulnerable and

4. All excerpts from Dante's poem in the pages to follow come from Kirkpatrick's 2006–2007 translation of *Inferno*, *Purgatorio*, and *Paradiso* (due to considerations of space, throughout the volume most excerpts of the *Commedia* are quoted in translation only). Alongside his three-volume translation, Kirkpatrick's commentary to the *Commedia* accompanying it, is one of the most important resources available for theological and spiritual reflection on the *Commedia*. See also Kirkpatrick, *Dante's* Paradiso *and the Limitations of Modern Criticism*; and Kirkpatrick, *Dante's* Inferno: *Difficulty and Dead Poetry*.

courageous before Dante's work: readers who are boldly confident that they have something meaningful to bring to the *Commedia*, and radically open to the piercing and surprising meaning the *Commedia* brings to us.

Confidence and openness are twin dispositions that all readers of the *Commedia*—no matter how experienced or not—are always challenged to cultivate. Language can aid in this cultivation or stifle connections between a text and a person, between one person and another. The language of this introduction, as well as the tone of the volume as a whole, is crafted with the explicit hope of building connections and perhaps even community. To some readers, this language might well seem unconventional or perhaps even inappropriate for a work on Dante generated in the academy. Scholarly writing on the *Commedia* does not often embrace perspectives that explicitly explore the spiritual significance of Dante's work. And, even in academic theology, it is often assumed that a more neutral rhetoric with respect to spiritual journeying can more productively convey scholarly meaning. At the same time, and by the same token, the fruits of scholarship are not always given the possibility of reaching readers who might be interested in exploring their broader, non-scholarly implications, especially in connection with questions of spiritual consequence. This volume consciously attempts to pursue such possibility, with confidence and openness.

Along the lines just suggested, the present volume can thus be seen as an experiment and as an invitation: an experiment as to whether the possibility spoken of at the end of the previous paragraph is indeed a viable one; and an invitation to readers to help us carry out such exploration. We intend such exploration to be open-ended. We certainly hope you will join us in our journeying. But, equally certainly, we do not wish to suggest that the particular readings offered in this volume provide, individually or as a whole, the only possible ways of pursuing this kind of journeying. Neither do we wish to presume that the validity of the readings offered here ought to be measured by the extent to which readers will agree with them. We simply hope that the experiment and the invitation of this volume might be welcomed by you as a genuine attempt to enrich interpretation of the *Commedia* by adopting perspectives not usually adopted, at the intersection of scholarship and spiritual seeking.

To our knowledge, and for the reasons outlined in this introduction so far, this is the first volume of its kind. At the same time, it consciously builds on recent scholarly developments that illuminate our understanding of the theological dimensions of Dante's work.[5] Moreover, the volume owes its existence to a particular context at the University of Notre Dame that is uniquely suited for the kind of experiment and invitation that this volume represents. Such context is defined by an intersection of resources that allows for the coming together of academic theology, Dante studies, and reflection on connections between scholarship and ecclesial living. Hosted by the McGrath Institute for Church Life, the initiatives in which this volume originates found their primary context precisely at a point of interaction between academic life and the life of Church. In the case of these initiatives, the scholarly dimension of such interaction was defined, primarily, by conversation and collaboration across the Department of Theology and the Devers Program in Dante Studies. With this capacity to bring together the scholarly and the pastoral, it would be difficult to think of another set of resources that could allow for such a concentrated and extensive response to Pope Francis's invitation to read Dante in conjunction with the Jubilee Year of Mercy.

The Jubilee Year of Mercy had, on Francis's own definition, a specifically Marian dimension, significantly expressed in its formal inauguration on the Feast of the Immaculate Conception. In this sense, too, the context provided for our initiatives by Notre Dame—a scholarly community ultimately formed in Marian inspiration (and whose most recognizable symbol is its golden dome with Our Lady standing atop)—proved spiritually fruitful. As if to enhance the significance of this, it so happened that in 2016, Ash Wednesday—the liturgical moment we had chosen for the formal opening of our pilgrimage with Dante—fell on February 11, feast day of Our Lady of Lourdes (remembered at Notre Dame by its famous "Grotto") and anniversary of the birth of Blessed Basil Moreau (founder of the Congregation of Holy Cross). We offer these observations not as mere spiritual curiosity, but in recognition of a further, important connection with the *Commedia*. Dante's poem, too, was ultimately formed in Marian inspiration (see, for instance, *Inferno* 2 and *Paradiso* 23.88–89). One way of engaging spiritually

---

5. Alongside the work of Robin Kirkpatrick, referred to above, see, for instance, Hawkins, *Dante's Testaments*; Honess and Treherne, *Reviewing Dante's Theology*; Montemaggi, *Reading Dante's* Commedia *as Theology*; Montemaggi and Treherne, *Dante's* Commedia: *Theology as Poetry*; Moevs, *The Metaphysics of Dante's Comedy*. For other examples of work that speaks of and invites a more personal journeying with Dante, see Dreher, *How Dante Can Save Your Life*; and Luzzi, *In a Dark Wood*. Given the nature of this volume, the reader will find relatively little bibliographical reference, as compared to more conventional scholarly writing. The works just listed will provide helpful bibliographical points of reference for any reader interested in pursuing further their exploration of existing scholarship relative to the readings offered here.

with the *Commedia* is to see it as an opportunity for deep reflection on Marian devotion.

That said, in whichever way readers choose to respond to this volume, we hope that the encounter will prove a fruitful one. As mentioned above, we do not write on the assumption that in order to be fruitful the encounter needs to be based on agreement, either of spiritual presupposition or of Dantean interpretation. Indeed, in this respect, we believe that the best way to be true to the spirit of the Year of Mercy is to think of our journeying as open-ended. Intellectual openness can, in this sense, be seen as a scholarly analogue to how, in spiritual terms, we might think of the all-embracingness of divine mercy. This means that we embark upon our journeying on the understanding that it can be a transformative one for us, in and through the way in which readers will contribute to enriching, refining, or correcting what this volume presents. At the same time, we offer this volume to you in the hope that you too will be able to find in it resources for renewed spiritual recognition of human personhood as a mystery in which is manifest a truth we all share. Whether you are reading the *Commedia* and this volume as part of conscious spiritual journeying or not, we hope the reading will offer you an occasion for renewed, courageous, open-ended exploration of that which makes us what we are.

Leonard J. DeLorenzo

Vittorio Montemaggi

1

Encountering Mercy

Dante, Mary, and Us

Vittorio Montemaggi

I would like to begin by expressing joy.[1] It is a true, humbling joy to reflect on Dante and on his *Commedia*, communally, in response to Pope Francis's invitation to encounter Dante anew in conjunction with the Year of Mercy. I use the word "encounter" deliberately to introduce one of the central notions I wish us to reflect on together. I use it on the understanding that encounter is personal and particular. It involves our whole selves. By it we are surprised, challenged, called into question, acknowledged, transformed.

The language of encounter was significantly used by Francis in his homily on the Feast of the Immaculate Conception, for the Mass accompanying the opening of the Holy Door in St. Peter's.[2] On that occasion, Francis spoke of God encountering each and every one of us as mercy. In this significant theological and spiritual sense, mercy is not an abstract concept.

1. I also wish to express infinite gratitude, for inspiring conversations, to Leonard DeLorenzo, Thomas Graff, Kevin Grove, Jessica Keating, Maria McMahon, Griffin Oleynick, Janet Soskice, Lesley Sullivan Marcantonio, Kathryn Thompson, and to Stacey Noem and the Master of Divinity students at Notre Dame who took part in seminars on possible connections between Dante's *Commedia* and pastoral ministry. I also wish to acknowledge the connections between the present essay and my *Reading Dante's* Commedia *as Theology*, where readers can find more detailed exploration of some of the central ideas suggested here, as well as more detailed bibliographical reference relative to these.

2. Pope Francis, "Extraordinary Jubilee of Mercy."

It is, indeed, personal and particular. It involves our whole selves. By it we are surprised, challenged, called into question, acknowledged, transformed.

In his exhortation to read Dante in conjunction with the Year of Mercy—which he sent to the Italian Senate on the occasion of its official celebration of the 750th anniversary of Dante's birth in May 2015—Francis does not specifically use the language of encounter. He does, however, encourage us to recognize in Dante a fellow traveler on "the way to true knowledge, to the authentic discovery of self, of the world, of life's profound and transcendent meaning." As we saw in the introduction above, Francis also speaks of Dante as "a prophet of hope, a herald of humanity's possible redemption and liberation, of profound change in every man and woman, of all of humanity. He invites us to regain the lost and obscured meaning of our human journey and to hope to see again the bright horizon which shines in the full dignity of the human person."[3] One way of interpreting these words is that what is at stake for us in reading Dante is the possibility of a renewed recognition and appreciation of ourselves as beings who encounter and are encountered: beings whose journey is characterized by interactions with others, the world, and God that surprise us, challenge us, call us into question, acknowledge us, transform us.

The light illuminating our journey, according to Francis's reading of Dante, is that of the human person. It is, indeed, the human person who is at the forefront in Dante's *Commedia*. The human person failing, learning, and succeeding to journey toward God—and doing so, primarily, in and through encounters with other human persons. Human encounter is, in Dante's *Commedia*, the form that reflection on divinity takes. It is the form that our encounter with God takes. It is also, therefore, the form taken by our encounter with mercy. This is all but explicitly stated at the very beginning of the poem. The first words spoken by Dante in the poem are *miserere di me* (*Inf.* 1.65)—"have mercy on me"—and they are addressed by him to the Roman poet Virgil, who we later learn has come to rescue Dante in the dark wood at the request of Beatrice, who had been called to this task by St. Lucy, who had in turn been summoned for this by the Virgin Mary.

Marian inspiration is indeed at the spiritual heart of Dante's *Commedia*. To say this is both obvious and unconventional. It is certainly no secret that Mary plays a role of crucial importance in the *Commedia*. More often than not, however, this is something that is not given due attention in readings of the poem. Yet Mary is the beginning and the end of the Dante's journey. As already mentioned, we learn in *Inferno* 2 that it is Mary who

---

3. Pope Francis, "Message of His Holiness Pope Francis for the 750th Anniversary of the Birth of the Supreme Poet Dante Alighieri."

initiates Dante's journey. And the terms with which Dante tells us this are significantly connected to mercy. Mary is the form that God's mercy takes for Dante. She breaks harsh judgment and allows for Dante to be rescued in the dark wood (see, especially, *Inf.* 1.94–96). Later, the journey through purgatory is punctuated by Marian examples of virtue, as the constant point of reference for the refashioning of the human person toward the Earthly Paradise, and beyond that the Empyrean. In the Empyrean, as we shall see, it is Mary's intercession that ushers into Dante's full union with God—or, as Dante puts it, the love that moves the sun and other stars. If Dante's *Commedia* tells the story of the healing of our estrangement from God toward the regaining of our true radiance, it is mercy as encountered in Mary that, according to Dante, makes the journey possible.

It is often said that Christ is conspicuously absent from the *Commedia*; that Dante's poem does not offer us much by way of direct representation of, or reflection on, Christ. This is not entirely accurate. As suggested by Dante's vision of the Trinity in *Paradiso* 33, Christ is ever present in the *Commedia*. He is present in and as the human person. The journey toward God is the journey toward the realization of our own divinity, which is to say that it is the journey toward our becoming transparent to Christ's presence in—as—us. Human encounter, for Dante, is how the journey takes place—in and through the gradual realization that Christ is the truth of each human person, and that it is as the truth of each human person that we can fully appreciate the truth of Christ.

Which is to say, that to be open to the truth of Christ is to open ourselves up toward all other human beings with an embrace that excludes no one. This is how our divinity can best be realized. And in this we once again find profound resonance between Dante's *Commedia* and the way in which Francis invites us to think of mercy in connection with the Jubilee.[4] It is in our ability to open our embrace out in this way that we can most profoundly encounter divine mercy itself. And, as suggested by Francis, Mary is herself the prime human example we have of that open embrace.

We shall return later in more detail to what Dante tells us about Mary at the end of his journey. And to prepare for that we shall focus in some detail on the beginning and the midpoint of Dante's story. But before we do that, I would like to offer some other more general points for reflection. Indeed, as should already be clear, the aim of the present essay, as the first in the volume, is to offer considerations that can hopefully be of overall relevance for thinking about our journey as a whole.

---

4. See Pope Francis, "Misericordiae Vultus."

The first thing to say, in the latter respect, is that if human encounter is a central dimension of the *Commedia*, this is not only because it speaks *of* human encounter—it is also because it speaks *as* human encounter. Dante's portrayal of human encounter—that is, the story told by his poem—is the way in which Dante wishes to encounter us: the way in which he wishes to surprise us, challenge us, call us into question, acknowledge us, transform us. We might not be used to thinking about literature or human encounter in this way. But there can be little doubt that Dante wishes for his text to be a particular moment of encounter between himself and each one of us reading it. And there can be little doubt that, in and through this encounter, Dante wishes for his text, therefore, also to be an encounter with divinity, with the mercy by which our own dark woods might be transformed into a lush earthly paradise, and ourselves healed from our estrangement from God toward the regaining of our true radiance.

It might thus be fair to say Dante wishes for our encounter with him also to be an encounter with divinity itself, with the mercy that heals us. The primary aim of Dante's story is *not*, as often assumed, to *describe* the afterlife. It is, rather, to tell a story about the afterlife the can fruitfully invite introspection, and through introspection allow us to encounter divinity in the depths of our being, in the being of others and of the cosmos as a whole. Arguably, the primary question that we are invited to engage with in reading the *Commedia* is: "What have I learned about myself in reading this?"[5]

This is not necessarily the primary question we generally bring with us when we read literature. Yet we fail to read the *Commedia* as fully as it is offered us, if we give up the opportunity for engaging with it as occasion for self-understanding. And the best way for us to make the most of this opportunity offered to us is to read Dante not just individually but together. Not just in the poem, but in our reading of it too, human encounter is one of the truest ways we have transformatively to learn about ourselves.

There can indeed be little doubt that Dante wishes for his poem to be transformative for us. And I certainly would not be expressing joy at our communal encounter with and through Dante if I did not believe that the *Commedia* can successfully deliver what Dante wished it might. But it is important not to take this for granted. Strong as the wish to celebrate Dante's poem might be, it is also important to recognize that there are dimensions of it that raise questions that complicate the picture I have been presenting so far.

---

5. This was the primary guiding question in the materials prepared for the reading groups that formed in the initiative that gave origin to the present volume of essays. See http://icl.nd.edu/events/dante-mercy-and-the-beauty-of-the-human-person/.

First and foremost: how can we trust that the *Commedia* can provide us with a spiritually nourishing encounter with mercy, when it is the work of a human being who seems to take it upon himself to play God, populating his invented afterlife with other human beings, and consigning a number of them to the damnation of his *Inferno?* This hardly seems to be the work of a merciful human being, let alone one with whom we can encounter divine mercy itself. What are we to make of this? What are we to make of the fact that Dante does not seem to be very merciful—that he categorically seems *not* to open up his embrace without excluding anyone?

There are no easy answers to these questions. There is, however, another aspect of Dante's poem that is generally not taken as seriously as it might, and that can provide us with interesting food for thought in relation to them. In cantos 11 and 13 of *Purgatorio*, Dante tells us he is keenly aware of his pride. Yet we are accustomed to think of Dante as a poet who—exceedingly confident in his own powers—wishes to offer as comprehensive a picture of reality as possible. And there is currently a tendency in scholarly readings of Dante's poem to consider even his confession of pride, ultimately, as a rhetorical construction to captivate our good will toward him. Is this accurate? There is, of course, no way of knowing for certain what Dante's intentions were in writing his poem. It is, ultimately, a question of trust—or lack thereof.

In the latter regard, it is fruitful to keep in mind two things Dante tells us in his poem that are not often reflected upon in conjunction with reflection on his pride and his poetic practice. The first is that Dante tells us in *Paradiso* 22.106–8 that he often cries and beats his breast because of his sins. The second is that in *Paradiso* 23.88–89 Dante tells us that he calls upon the lovely name of Mary every morning and every evening. I believe this is as close as we get in the *Commedia* to catching a glimpse of Dante's compositional practices, and in my *Reading Dante's* Commedia *as Theology: Divinity Realized in Human Encounter*, I explore in more detail the literary, theological, and spiritual implications of this. Ultimately, however, I can offer no definitive justification for my belief other than that my experience of reading Dante so far has led me to perceive in these statements Dante at his most genuine. Be that as it may, however we wish to interpret these statements on Dante's part, it is important to recognize what is at stake here.

What is at stake is nothing other than the whole of our relationship with Dante. Whether we believe Dante is genuine in recognizing his sins and in expressing his devotion to Mary, it is important to realize that our interpretive decision in this regard has implications for our understanding of the *Commedia* as a whole. If we choose not to believe Dante is genuine, we are in effect closing off our embrace to him, at least in the sense of preferring suspicion to trust, accusation to mercy. If we are prepared to trust Dante, some richer perspectives open up before us together with our embrace toward him. One of these—and I think it is the most significant—is that one of the sins for which Dante feels he is in need of forgiveness is the *Commedia* itself. Keenly aware of his pride, Dante is arguably aware of the spiritual danger of playing God in crafting a poem in which he takes it upon himself to judge fellow human beings. Dante's daily invocations of the name of Mary can thus be seen, from this perspective, as one of the animating principles of his writing—a hopeful trust in mercy and in the possibility that his writing can be a source of goodness and not of division.

Seen in this light, Mary is thus not just the beginning and the end of the journey described in the poem. She is the beginning and the end of Dante's writing of it—the mercy Dante hopes to encounter in crafting a text that he knows is dangerously presumptuous but that he also hopes can itself be occasion for our own encounter with nothing other than divine mercy itself.

There is certainly a profound spiritual tension here, which seems in fact somewhat paradoxical and self-contradictory. Or, perhaps: is it precisely in this spiritual tension that Dante opens up for us the space for encountering him most genuinely and, in and through that, encountering mercy itself?

Human beings are finite, vulnerable, fallible creatures. This side of the Empyrean, then, no human encounter can be perfect that does not—like that between Mary and her son—already fully partake in the light-love-joy that the Empyrean is. To expect otherwise would not only be unrealistic but lacking in true respect of our nature. It would be an exercise in pride. By highlighting his own pride, by telling us of his tears for his sins, and by telling us he prays Mary's name every morning and every evening, Dante could thus be seen as offering us a concrete opportunity for humility. We are asked to trust him, open our embrace to him, not despite but because of his limitations. Just like divine mercy does with each one of us because of our own limitations, as Francis has reminded us in the Jubilee Year. In other words, Dante could thus be seen to help us to become, as much as we are capable of in our finitude, mercy itself—or as Dante might put it, to be perfectly at one with the love that moves the sun and the other stars.

Moreover, to predispose our being thus toward our encounter with Dante, is to offer ourselves a concrete opportunity, in humility, for self-knowledge, for recognizing in the human encounters of the *Commedia* our own imperfections. It is thus also to realize in the space opened up by our encounter with Dante, a space that can be filled by nothing other than divine mercy itself, by which our wounds might be healed.

In order to reflect on this in more detail, let us turn to the text of the *Commedia* itself and, more specifically, to three passages that, taken together, present a microcosm of the *Commedia* itself. (They are provided here in their entirety to encourage direct encounter with them.)

> At one point midway on our path in life
>
> I came around and found myself now searching
>
> through a dark wood, the right way blurred and lost.
>
> How hard it is to say what that wood was,
>
> a wilderness, savage, brute, harsh and wild.
>
> Only to think of it renews my fear!
>
> So bitter, that thought, that death is hardly worse.
>
> But since my theme will be the good I found there,
>
> I mean to speak of other things I saw.
>
> I do not know, I cannot rightly say,
>
> how first I came to be here—so full of sleep,
>
> that moment, abandoning the true way on.
>
> But then, on reaching the foot of a hill
>
> which marked the limit of the dark ravine
>
> that had before so pierced my heart with panic,
>
> I looked to that height and saw its shoulders
>
> already clothed in rays from the planet
>
> that leads all others, on any road, aright.
>
> My fears, at this, were somewhat quieted,
>
> though terror, awash in the lake of my heart,
>
> had lasted all the night I'd passed in anguish.
>
> And then, like someone laboring for breath
>
> who, safely reaching shore from open sea,
>
> still turns and stares across those perilous waves,
>
> so in my mind—my thoughts all fleeing still
>
> I turned around to marvel at that strait
>
> that let no living soul pass through till now.

And then—my weary limbs a little rested—

I started up the lonely scree once more,

the foot that drives me always set the lower.

But look now! Almost as the scarp begins,

a leopard, light, and lively, svelte and quick,

its coat displaying a dappled marking.

This never ceased to dance before my face.

No. On it came, so bothering my tread

I'd half a mind at every turn to turn.

The time, however, was the hour of dawn.

The sun was mounting, and those springtime stars

that rose along with it when Holy Love

first moved to being all these lovely things.

So these—the morning hour, the gentle season—

led me to find good reason for my hopes,

seeing that creature with its sparkling hide.

Yet not so far that no fear pressed on me,

to see, appearing now, a lion face.

This, as it seemed, came on and on towards me

hungrily, its ravening head held high,

so that, in dread, the air around it trembled.

And then a wolf. And she who, seemingly,

was gaunt yet gorged on every kind of craving—

and has already blighted many a life—

so heavily oppressed my thought with fears,

which spurted even at the sight of her,

I lost all hope of reaching to those heights.

We all so willingly record our gains,

until the hour that leads us into loss.

Then every single thought is tears and sadness.

So, now, with me. That brute which knows no peace

came ever nearer me and, step by step,

drove me back down to where the sun is mute.

As I went, ruined, rushing to that low,

there had, before my eyes, been offered one

who seemed—long silent—to be faint and dry.

Seeing him near in that great wilderness,

to him I screamed my "*Miserere*": "Save me,

whatever—shadow or truly man—you be."

(*Inf.* 1.1–66)

In the first three lines of the *Commedia* no one other than Dante appears to inhabit the scene. Yet the poem already presents us with at least two instances of human encounter. Most sharply, there is the encounter of Dante with himself. In the dark wood, Dante finds himself again—he (re-) awakens to his own humanity. The humanity he finds, though, is not simply his. It is in the midst of "our" path in life, the life he shares with us, that Dante becomes self-conscious. In encountering himself, Dante encounters humanity as a whole.

Dante encounters himself as lost. Not the easiest of beginnings. Yet already, in itself, progress. To know oneself as lost is already to know one could, in principle, be otherwise. Immediately after telling us how death-like his experience of the dark wood is—even in memory alone—Dante informs us that "since my theme will be the good I found there, I mean to speak of other things I saw" (*Inf.* 1.8–9). These are somewhat scandalous words. Dante had told us he was in a death-like state of anguish. And he is going to go on in the rest of the *Commedia* to present us, among other things, with one of the most detailed accounts of human failure ever to have been crafted. And in these lines here he tells us that what he wishes to speak of is, quite simply, goodness. We are thus immediately challenged by Dante's text. His story is the story of goodness. As dark as some of it undoubtedly and terribly is, what Dante wishes to do is to open up a space for us in which goodness might be found.

In the *Commedia* Dante essentially wishes to speak of goodness: not lost humanity, but humanity encountering the good anew. Dante's telling us this refines our perception of the human encounters with which the poem opens. The Dante who finds himself at the beginning of the *Commedia* is not just the character who awakens in the dark wood. It is also the poet, who by fashioning himself as character enters into a journey of conscious self-discovery, toward goodness. And, in his wish to invite us to share in this journey, the humanity Dante goes on to encounter is not just a general, abstract one, but the particular one of each individual human being who reads the *Commedia*. It is also my humanity, and yours.

Having awakened to his and our humanity, Dante is able to start journeying out of the dark wood. He starts ascending a hill, whose summit is illuminated by the rays of the sun. Progress is impeded, however, by the sudden appearance of three beasts. The pilgrim's first encounter with other living creatures in the *Commedia* is not with human beings. He is still with no immediate human company other than his own. Indeed, whatever their particular allegorical meaning, the beasts can be seen to externalize metaphorically the inner dispositions of character which prevent Dante from making progress on his journey toward divinity, symbolized by the sun.

Next, at lines 49–60, Dante gives us an image as theologically significant as anything else offered us in the poem. In speaking of the she-wolf here, Dante is doing nothing less than setting out the central theological principle underlying the exploration of the relationship between humanity and divinity presented in the *Commedia*. The image reveals the reason Dante is unable to go beyond the beasts is that he does not properly understand how God relates to God's creation. At the beginning of his journey Dante is thinking of the summit of the hill, and the possibility it symbolizes of being at one with the divine, as one would of a material possession: a thing, object, or idea a human being can desire, reach, acquire, and possess—and consequently lose. Dante is thinking of God as part of creation, as being merely one of the things that are. This is not what God is. If it were, God could not have created all there is out of nothing. And this, as Dante will learn on his journey, would be a contradiction. If one is not thinking of the ground of all existence, itself not existing in any particular way but, as being itself, bringing and sustaining everything into existence, one is simply not thinking of God, no matter whatever else one holds about particular aspects of divinity.

Inferno 1.49–60 offers us a precise diagnosis of Dante's spiritual ills. He is yet to properly configure his self in relation to divinity. The divine is here seen as a possession; and the self is still at the center of the self's own world, in the illusion of self-definition and self-subsistence: it does not conceive of divinity as its own existence. God is there to reach but not to be. Which is to say that the self is still living in pride, yet to undergo the radical decentering of self entailed by humility, whereby one can encounter what is other than oneself—and ultimately God—not as something to possess but as source of meaning and life. To reach such humility, another kind of journey is needed than that which the pilgrim initially attempts to undertake.

At lines 61–66, Dante is thus famously rescued by Virgil. As Roberto Benigni recently pointed out in speaking about Pope Francis's book *The Name of God Is Mercy*,[6] it is certainly very significant that upon finally seeing another human figure in the dark wood the first thing Dante appeals to—echoing Psalm 50—is mercy. Dante, who takes his journey on *our* path in life, is in need of mercy. His instinctive response in first encountering another human being is to seek mercy.

Following their initial encounter, throughout the rest of *Inferno* 1 Virgil explains to Dante that what he needs to do is to follow him and later Beatrice, on a journey that will bring him to encounter the damned, the penitent and the blessed—to consider, that is, how other human beings have either failed or succeeded in living in proper relationship with God. This is vital. It suggests that ultimately, for Dante, there is an inextricable connection between relating to God and encountering other human beings, and that exploring this interconnection is necessary for understanding human creatureliness.

Dante, then, has to be guided and the journey is to be communal—toward increasingly penetrating insight into the dynamics of human encounter as seen in the light of divinity. Dante is guided through hell and purgatory by Virgil. At the top of Mount Purgatory, in the Earthly Paradise, he meets Beatrice, who guides him through the heavens up to the Empyrean. There she entrusts Dante to Saint Bernard, who intercedes for Dante before the Virgin Mary that he might be united with God, which—in the very last lines of the poem—Dante finally is. Throughout his journey through the heavens, Dante encounters different groups of blessed human beings, each inhabiting the planetary sphere that, in the poem's cosmology, most corresponds to the particular characteristics of their goodness. The blessed do not in fact inhabit the pre-Empyrean heavens Dante sees them in. This is a show put on just for him, so that he may be adequately prepared for transcending space and time in the Empyrean, the light-love-joy which is God, and as which the blessed eternally have their being. This is the very being Dante comes to share in at the very end of his journey.

Let us, now, focus in on two especially significant moments on this journey. The first can be considered the midpoint of the journey, or more specifically its turning point: Dante's encounter with Beatrice in the Earthly Paradise.

---

6. See Benigni, "Il Nome Di Dio È Misericordia."

So now, beyond a drifting cloud of flowers

(which rose up, arching, from the angels' hands,

then fell within and round the chariot),

seen through a veil, pure white, and olive-crowned,

a lady now appeared to me. Her robe was green,

her dress the color of a living flame.

And I, in spirit, who so long had not

been, trembling in her presence, wracked by awe,

began again to tremble at her glance

(without more evidence that eyes could bring,

but darkly, through the good that flowed from her),

sensing the ancient power of what love was.

But on the instant that it struck my sight—

this power, this virtue, that had pierced me through

before I'd even left my boyhood state—

I turned aside (and leftwards) meaning now,

with all the hope and deference of some child

that runs when hurt or frightened to its mum,

to say to Virgil: "There is not one gram

of blood in me that does not tremble now.

I recognize the signs of ancient flame."

But Virgil was not there. Our lack alone

was left where once he'd been. Virgil, dear sire,

Virgil—to him I'd run to save my soul.

Nor could the All our primal mother lost,

ensure my cheeks—which he once washed with dew—

should not again be sullied with dark tears.

"Dante, that Virgil is no longer here,

do not yet weep, do not yet weep for that.

A different sword cut, first, must make you weep."

(*Purg.* 30.28–57)

Much could be said of this passage. I wish simply to draw your attention to one of its most significant features. If the first word spoken by Dante in the *Commedia* is mercy, the first word spoken by Beatrice is "Dante." This is the first and only time Dante's name is mentioned in the *Commedia*. And the speaking of it coincides with Dante being exposed at his most vulnerable. He had been expecting Beatrice to welcome him smilingly. Instead, he is scolded for even daring to set foot into the Earthly Paradise. The reason for this is that while Dante has seen a lot on his journey through hell and purgatory he is yet to apply what he has seen to himself. Having directed his attention outwards toward the damned and the penitent, Dante now has to direct his attention inwards. He needs to recognize his own shortcomings, before Beatrice and before God. There can be no genuine spiritual progress without introspection, and without acknowledgement of failure. Having asked for mercy in the dark wood, Dante is now offered it in the Earthly Paradise, in the form of painful acknowledgement of failure.

This also applies to us. The speaking of Dante's name coincides, implicitly but crucially, with the speaking of our own names. Dante's journey, taken on *our* path in life, is indeed also our own. We return to the idea that to read the *Commedia* is to ask ourselves what we learn about ourselves in doing so. The question of the spiritual value of the *Commedia* is meaningless if not accompanied by introspection.

What follows from this moment of introspection is the possibility of ascending to heaven. There, Dante discovers human encounter at its fullest: the full reciprocity of human beings, open self-givingly to each other in, through, and as the light-love-joy that is God. The encounter with mercy leads, in turn, to full participation in the love that moves the sun and other stars. What ushers Dante into that final union at the end of his journey is, once again, the intercession of the Virgin Mary. The last canto of the poem famously opens with St. Bernard's prayer to the Virgin on Dante's behalf— taken by many to be one of the summits of human art.

"Virgin and mother, daughter of your son,

greater than all in honor and humility,

you are the point that truth eternally

is fixed upon. And you have made the nature

of the human being proud. Its maker, then,

did not disdain to make himself this making.

Love, in your womb, was fanned to fire again.

And here, in this eternal peace, the warmth of love

has brought the Rose to germinate and bloom.

You are, for us, the noon-time torch of love.

You are, among those mortals there below,

the clearest fountain of their living hopes.

You are, in dignity and power, Our Lady.

All who, in wanting grace, do not seek help

from you, might wish to soar yet lack the wings.

Nor in your kindness do you give your aid

to those alone who ask, but often run,

before they ask, to them in generous freedom.

In you is pity, in you compassion,

in you all-giving power. All good in you

is gathered up that creature form can bear.

This man is one who, from the deepest void

in all the universe, has seen thus far,

and one by one, all lives in spirit mode.

To you, a suppliant, he comes, and asks

that, by your grace, he gains the strength to rise

in sight more still to greet the final peace.

I never burned for visions of my own

more than I do that he might see. To you

I offer all my prayers—praying my prayers

are not too few—that you should free this man

from all the clouds of his mortality,

so highest happiness be shown to him.

Our Queen, to you, who may do what you will,

I also pray you keep him (he has seen so much!)

healthy in all his heart intends.

Watch, and defeat the impulses of man.

See! Beatrice with so many saints

closes her hands in prayers along with mine."

The eyes—which God both loves and venerates—

attentive to these orisons, made clear

how welcome to her were these holy prayers

and then turned straight to eternal light

in which (we're bound to think) no creature's eye

inwardly travels with such clarity.

And drawing nearer, as I had to now,

the end of all desires, in my own self

I ended all the ardor of desire.

Now Bernard, smiling, made a sign to me

that I look up. Already, though, I was,

by my own will, as he desired I be.

My sight, becoming pure and wholly free,

entered still more, then more, along the ray

of that one light which, of itself, is true.

(*Par.* 33.1–54)

Again, there is much that can be said about Dante's words. Once again, though, I would simply like to focus on one of the most significant aspects of the passage. I would like to focus not on the prayer itself but what immediately follows it—at lines 40–54. After traveling through the entire cosmos, after having encountered a multitude of human beings, and after one of the most beautiful prayers ever uttered, all we get is the spontaneity of human encounter itself. We reflected on the first word spoken by Dante and on the first word spoken by Beatrice in the poem. We are here struck by the lack of words. Words are no longer necessary, just the recognition of truth in each other's eyes and in each other's smile. This is what Dante has learned on his journey.

Indeed, one of the most fruitful ways of thinking about the *Commedia* as a whole is to think of it as a journey toward the possibility of that spontaneous moment of recognition. To ask what accounts for the possibility of

Mary ushering Dante into full divine union in this way is to ask ourselves about nothing less than the meaning of Dante's *Commedia* as a whole. A simple set of gestures which finds its full meaning in all the human encounters that have preceded it on Dante's journey.

Having suggested earlier that a primary question the *Commedia* invites us to engage with is "What have I learned about myself in reading this?" I would like to end with the suggestion that it might be fruitful to accompany that question with reflection on Dante's journey as a journey toward the full spontaneity of human encounter. Dante's encounter with mercy takes the form of human encounters leading to the simplicity of recognizing in Mary the way to light, love, joy. To reflect on the simplicity of that recognition is to reflect on Dante's journey as a whole. It is, perhaps, as close as our encounter with Dante can get. And, whether or not we share in Dante's vision of divinity and of the cosmos, if we give ourselves the opportunity of encountering Dante in this way, we are also giving ourselves a wonderful opportunity of encountering anew ourselves, each other, the world, and the mystery in which all that is has its being.

PART 1

Bearings

2

The Kingdom of Irony

Augustine, Sin, and Dante's *Inferno*

John C. Cavadini

T he structure of Dante's *Inferno* may seem familiar to the careful theological reader.[1] Hell, envisioned in its lower levels as a city of the damned, is presented as a community whose human relationships are distorted, and often inverted, by the effects of sin. This City of Dis, as Dante portrays it, is in many ways merely an amplification and eternal continuation of the fallen state of human community in this life, inasmuch as each punishment seems to correspond closely to the sin it represents as committed in the world above (see *Inf.* 8.67–69; 28.139–42).[2] The city thus formed, although rendered by Dante with an original theological poetics, bears a striking resemblance to that one described by Augustine throughout *City of God* as the "city of this world."[3] This city, formed by the sin of pride and the lust for domination, is a community that Augustine can only describe with

1. Editors' note: we are grateful to Gregory Cruess and Kathryn Thompson for their assistance in editing this essay.

2. For a careful consideration of the manner in which the punishments of the sins are, in some manner, continuous with the sins themselves, see Freccero, *Poetics of Conversion*, 106–9. This collection of essays, itself a very sophisticated reading of Dante's *Commedia*, has been influential upon the prolonged meditations which appear now in the following pages. On Dante and Augustine more generally, see Marchesi, *Dante and Augustine*; Brilli, *Firenze e il profeta*; and Lombardi, "Augustine and Dante."

3. The "city of this world" is first mentioned in the preface to the first book of *City of God*, but it recurs as a major theme throughout the entire work. The following pages will indicate many further instances of Augustine's use and elaboration of the concept.

a pointed irony intended to reveal it for what it truly is. Beginning with his
conception of the "city of this world," the present essay will then turn to a
consideration of the manner in which Dante's depiction of such a community in his *Inferno* illustrates the consequences of a city characterized above
all by this pride. Descending ever lower into hell, Dante brings us face to
face with the consequences of preferring ourselves and a lie to the truth of
God's merciful gift.

Augustine's Sense of Irony

The prologue to Augustine's great work *City of God* abounds in ironies that
he seems to relish, and even to celebrate, as he sets them before the reader's
eyes. In the opening lines, he remarks:

> I know how great is the effort needed to convince the proud of
> the power and excellence of humility, an excellence which makes
> it soar above all the summits of this world, which sway in their
> temporal instability, overtopping them all with an eminence not
> arrogated by human pride, but granted by divine grace.[4]

The "long and arduous" *City of God* famously begins by displaying the
irony that humility, the virtue of accepting the lowliness of one's state in
relationship to God, is said to "soar" and even to "overtop," not just any old
height but, "all the summits of this world"—that is, as Augustine explains,
all the claims and achievements built on "human pride." It is, he says, "hard
to convince the proud" of this reality. For how can there be any "power" and
"excellence" (*virtus*) in something that has been, by that very pride, relegat-
ed to a status that seems so lowly, so utterly insignificant, and so completely
unworthy of mention that it appears to have no claim on reality? Ironically,
the proud, who aspire to be at the summit of things, do not see the reality
of the "power" and "excellence" of humility which overtops them. Rather,
they have contempt for it; otherwise it would not be so "hard," so "long and
arduous" a task, to convince them.

The irony of humility overtopping pride is actually an irony intrinsic
to pride itself. Although pride "swells," as Augustine puts it, in its attempt to
arrogate to itself what is God's and thereby lusts after domination of others,
ironically it cannot itself escape domination by that very lust for domination
itself. He comments at the end of the prologue that, although his treatise is
to be on the subject of the "most glorious City of God," he must comment
on another city:

4. Augustine, *City of God*, 1.pref.

> Therefore I cannot refrain from speaking about the city of this
> world, a city which aims at dominion, which holds nations in
> enslavement, but is itself dominated by that very lust of domina-
> tion. I must consider this city as far as the scheme of this work
> demands and as occasion serves.[5]

The irony of this passage is understated, but it is nevertheless present. The "city of this world" includes—as Augustine has already hinted but
will amply demonstrate later—especially empires and those who run the
empires, those who are at the "summits of the world." These empires (as he
will tell the story later) dominate history and, in their attempt to dominate
others, make themselves the center of attention. Here, however, Augustine
relegates them all to something that, ironically, is not itself going to be visible except in the treatment of a prior reality, namely the "most glorious City
of God." This is the case both in terms of the prologue's mention of them and
in terms of the history of the cosmos. That is what Augustine calls the "city
of this world."

The ironies attaching to the "city of this world" are not an accident of
Augustine's compositional strategy but are irreducibly constitutive of the
city's identity, for it is a kind of identity that is no identity, a city that is not a
city, a community that is no community. It can never be seen as itself, therefore, except by contrast with something that has its own solid identity—a
true communion. In book 14 of *City of God*, Augustine famously comments
on the two cities: "This is assuredly the difference that sunders the two cities
of which we are speaking: the one is a community of devout human beings,
the other a company of the irreligious, and each has its own angels attached
to it. In one city love of God has been given first place; in the other, love of
self."[6] Later on, as he closes the same book, he comments that "we see then
that the two cities were created by two kinds of love: the earthly city was
created by self-love reaching the point of contempt for God, the Heavenly
City by the love of God carried as far as contempt of self."[7] "Self-love reaching the point of contempt for God" is what Augustine calls "pride." As he
comments a few paragraphs earlier, "what is pride except a longing for a
perverse kind of exaltation? For it is a perverse kind of exaltation to abandon the basis on which the mind should be firmly fixed, and to become, as
it were, based on oneself, and so remain."[8] The proud, he says, are called in

5. Ibid.
6. Ibid., 14.28.
7. Ibid.
8. Ibid., 14.13.

Scripture "self-pleasers" (*sibi placentes*)[9] and they subscribe to the baseless fiction that they can make themselves happy, that they are self-sufficient for their own happiness, or, in other words, that they are their own "supreme Good."[10] Though it seems like an exaltation, pride is a "perverse" exaltation. "By aiming at more," Augustine wryly comments, "a man is diminished, when he elects to be self-sufficient and defects from the one who is really sufficient for him."[11]

The same applies for the communities that the prideful create. The irony of a "city" whose very constitution is "self-love" is easily grasped: it is inherently not a community at all. "The earthly city," Augustine points out, "is generally divided against itself by litigation, by wars, by battles, by the pursuit of victories that bring death with them or at best are doomed to death. For if any section of that city has risen up in war against another part, it seeks to be victorious over other nations, though it is itself the slave of base passions; and if, when victorious, it is exalted in its arrogance, that victory brings death in its train."[12] Victories that are not really victorious, exaltations that are not really elevations, community that is no community, intrinsically centrifugal and only by circumstance and violence centripetal: that is why this community, the "city of this world," can only be seen by contrast with real community. There is, at the bottom of this so-called "city," nothing but perversion and, that is to say, nothing at all. The irony of this "city" is irreducible. It can only truly be seen in the moment that its pretensions to community are unmasked. Augustine explains that "when it is condemned to the final punishment it will no longer be a city," for it never was truly a city, and could only be seen by contrast with what is truly a city.[13] And yet it will not be annihilated, for that would imply that there was something to annihilate in the first place. It is the moment of unmasking that will be permanent, for that is the only way that this city can actually be seen.

One can take as a kind of synecdoche for this Augustine's comments on the state of the damned. What Augustine highlights the most is the irony of their state. Exploiting the irony inherent in the language of the book of Revelation, he calls it a "'second death,' because the soul cannot be said to be alive in that state, when it is separated from the life of God, nor can the body, when it is subjected to eternal torments.[14] And this is precisely the

9. 2 Pet 2:10; Augustine, *City of God*, 14.13.

10. Augustine, *City of God*, 12.1.

11. Ibid., 14.13.

12. Ibid., 15.4.

13. Ibid.

14. See also *Inferno* 1.117.

reason why this 'second death' will be harder to bear, because it cannot come to an end in death."[15] This is perhaps the ultimate irony. It is a death that is seen to be death precisely, and ironically, because it cannot end in death. It is a life that is continually unmasked as life.

> For in that final and everlasting punishment . . . we correctly talk of the "death of the soul" because it no longer derives life from God. But how can we talk in this case of the death of the body, since it is deriving life from the soul? For otherwise it cannot feel the bodily torments which are to follow the resurrection. Is it because life of any kind is a good thing, while pain is an evil, and for that reason the body cannot be said to be alive, when the purpose of the soul is not the body's life, but the body's pain?[16]

Pride is thus ultimately the commitment not to reality but to a fiction. This comes out most explicitly in Augustine's description of the pride of the first being to commit the sin of pride, the Devil. In his exegesis of John 8:44 ("He was a murderer from the beginning and did not stand fast in the truth"), Augustine comments that the passage means not that the Devil was created a murderer by God but that "from the moment of his creation the Devil refused righteousness."[17] He "did not stand fast in the truth . . . because he refused to be subject to his creator, and in his arrogance supposed that he wielded power as his own private possession and rejoiced in that power. And thus he was both deceived and deceiving, because no one can escape the power of the Omnipotent. He has refused to accept reality and in his arrogant pride presumes to counterfeit an unreality."[18] This "unreality" could also be called a fiction, the fiction of his own self-sufficiency. The Devil can only persuade people to follow him by lying and presenting this unreality as a reality. "The Devil is not only a liar; he is the *father of lies*,"[19] and those who join him—his city, the "city of this world"—must continually dissemble.

These dissemblings can be very persuasive. The angel of darkness can parade as an angel of light. Let us return then, one final time, to the prologue of *City of God* before finally turning to Dante, in order to grasp this point most fully. Here is how it begins:

> Here, my dear Marcellinus, is the fulfillment of my promise, a book in which I have taken upon myself the task of defending

15. Augustine, *City of God*, 19.28.

16. Ibid., 13.2.

17. Ibid., 11.13.

18. Ibid.

19. John 8:44; see Augustine, *City of God*, 14.3.

the glorious City of God against those who prefer their own gods to the founder of that City. I treat of it both as it exists in this world of time, a pilgrim among the ungodly, living by faith, and as it stands in the security of its everlasting seat.[20]

We have already seen how "long and arduous" a task this will be because of the great effort needed to convince the proud of the excellence and strength of humility; that is, of reality. As we now see, pride is an addiction to a counterfeit reality, a fiction, which is actually very good at concealing the fiction. How good? Augustine argues that

> the King and Founder of this City which is our subject has revealed in the Scripture of his people this statement of the divine Law, "God resists the proud but he gives grace to the humble." This is God's prerogative; but man's arrogant spirit in its swelling pride has claimed it as its own, and delights to hear this verse quoted in its own praise: "To spare the conquered, and beat down the proud."[21]

Pride "swells" by delighting to arrogate to itself what is God's prerogative, which is the gift of grace and mercy to those who are humbled by its conquest of them. The Roman Empire, here representing the "city of this world," sets itself up as a kind of chimerical mirror image, an inverse enantiomer, of the City of God. Rather, in fact, it is the text of Virgil's *Aeneid* which gives us the clue and allows Augustine to make the "city of this world" temporarily visible *as* "the city of this world" in his own text, represented by the Roman Empire. Here, however, the Empire is seen not on its own terms, but as a "deceived and deceiving" mimesis, using Virgil's text to achieve this analysis and depiction.[22] This is a point that Virgil's work could not have made on its own, and yet it is one which Augustine could not make as effectively apart from this quotation from Rome's national epic, counterpoised with a verse from Scripture and set up here as a kind of counterpart or anti-Scripture.

Virgil as Guide from *City of God* to *Inferno*

Virgil is a convenient link here to move on to *Inferno*, though in many ways one can feel that one is not leaving behind *City of God*. This is not only because Virgil appears in the first canto of *Inferno*—just as he appears in the

20. Augustine, *City of God*, 1.pref.
21. Ibid., quoting Jas 4:6 and Virgil, *The Aeneid*, 6.853.
22. Augustine, *City of God*, 11.13.

very first chapter of *City of God*—and there helps Dante, as an element in his text, to represent the "city of this world." It is also because Virgil identifies himself in a way that immediately links him to *City of God*, telling Dante that he lived in the time of the "false and lying gods," a poetic quotation of *City of God* 2.29.[23] It is thus the Virgil of *City of God* who identifies himself here. But that is not all, for Dante, just as much as Augustine, offers to our eyes and ears the same celebration of irony in abundance that meets the reader of *City of God* and continues its presence throughout the *Inferno*, connected directly to an evocation of sin.

The text starts out as a perfectly respectable allegory which, in fact, announces itself as a perfectly standard allegory with standard allegorical furniture: the path of our life's journey; the dark wood of error and emergence from it; the beams of Truth, itself unseen just as the sun itself is unseen here; and finally the mountain of the soul's ascent to Truth. If we hadn't gotten the message before Virgil appears, the mountain is unmistakably characterized in his question to Dante the pilgrim as "the mountain of delight, the cause and origin of every joy"[24]—a description which could not possibly be true of any literal mountain (*Inf.* 1.77–78). In response to Virgil's question as to why he does not climb the mountain, Dante points out the third of the three beasts that caused him to abandon hope of ever climbing up the mountain (see *Inf.* 1.53). Whatever particular sins the three beasts represent, it is obviously an unholy trinity, such as the cares, phantasms, and concupiscence that block the mind's road to God in Bonaventure or the triple sin of 1 John 2:16 that structures the *Confessions* of Augustine.[25] These are three hypostases of sin, consubstantial in the original essence of all sin, which is pride. And yet pride itself remains invisible because, if we are following Augustine, it is not an essence but a kind of anti-essence. It is made visible, rather, as a kind of warping of the nice friendly moralistic allegory we thought we were all about to enjoy.

---

23. After quoting again from Virgil, *Aen.*, 1.278, to ironically illustrate the superiority of "the one true God" through what had been written about the old Roman gods, Augustine argues: "You must not regret the loss of those false and deceitful gods; abandon them in contempt and spring out to genuine liberty."

24. Translation adjusted from "that lovely hill? The cause . . ."

25. See in this regard Bonaventure, *The Journey of the Mind to God*, 4.1. In Augustine's *Confessions*, the triple sin of *libido*, *curiositas*, and *superbia* structures the account of his own enthrallment to sin (described in bks. 3–5) and the progress of his conversion and healing (narrated in bks. 6–8). For both Augustine and Bonaventure, the identification of these obstacles helps clarify the difficulty of the soul's ascent to God and makes possible its narration. For a further discussion of the theme in relation to Dante and other possible influences, see Freccero, *Poetics of Conversion*, 49–54.

It is the encounter with the unholy trinity of sin (and, by implication, with pride) which blocks the ascent and makes it necessary for Virgil to inform Dante that in order to go up he must first, ironically, go down. His hope restored by Virgil's account of the gracious favor of heaven, it is a further irony that he begins his journey by passing under the sign that instructs him to abandon hope. As John Freccero pointed out years ago in *Dante: The Poetics of Conversion*, it is an irony that the text of the inscription over the gate of hell is read simultaneously by the fictional characters in the text, the pilgrim Dante and his guide Virgil, and the actual readers of Dante's *Commedia*, you and me.[26] At this point, fiction and reality coincide perfectly, and the allegory is, as it were, warped.[27] Somehow, there is no longer a simple correspondence between obviously allegorical fictional elements and the realities to which they correspond, but rather there is a way in which the fiction is offered as a direct and immediate vision of a reality to which we would have no other access since our vision is blocked by pride.

Falling in Pride: The Infernal Descent

Pride causes us to feel or to accept what is actually a lowering of ourselves as an exaltation of ourselves. It is, if we are to follow Augustine's guidance, an addiction to an illusion, to a fiction. Ironically, the fictional depiction of the punishment of sins offers an antidote to this addiction as the reader is invited to contemplate fearsome images of the sins themselves, shorn of the illusions that pride tenders to us. I would suggest that the Augustinian character of this literary strategy is visible from the punishment depicted in the very first circle (Virgil's own) where he describes the punishment in this way: "we are all lost yet only suffer harm through living in desire, but hopelessly" (*Inf.* 4.41–42). The shades whose portrait Dante paints the most are those of the so-called "virtuous pagans," and their features are described in ways that evoke the classical ideal, Stoic in origin, of *apatheia* or passionlessness. In aspect they had "no sorrow in their countenance, nor joy," their eyes both "firm and grave," and therefore carrying "authority" (*Inf.* 4.84, 112–13). The gathering of poets, philosophers, and virtuous rulers and warriors represents the best of the classical world, and yet the neither sad nor joyous gathering of these "ancient heroes" has something artificial about it (*Inf.* 4.119). In fact, they are in hell, the other side of the evil river as Cato will say of his wife Marcia in the *Purgatorio*, not in a true Limbo but damned

26. See Freccero, *Poetics of Conversion*, 93–109.

27. For an insightful account of the uncertainty which this warping creates and its function in the text, see ibid., 25–28.

(see *Purg.* 1.88–90). They are part of the "blind world" whose denizens have no self-perspective (*Inf.* 4.14). The seemingly virtuous citizens of the first circle are not sad, but they *should* be sad since they have lost everything.

In *City of God*, Augustine reserves some of his choicest and harshest language for his analysis of the virtue of *apatheia*, which he names as such in book fourteen:

> If [the earthly city] has any citizens who give an appearance of controlling and in some way checking [the] emotions, they are so arrogant and pretentious in their irreligion that the swelling of their pride increases in exact proportion as their feeling of pain decreases. Some of those people may display an empty complacency, the more monstrous for being so rare, which makes them so charmed with this achievement in themselves that they are not stirred or excited by any emotions at all, not swayed or influenced by any feelings. If so, they rather lose every shred of humanity than achieve a true tranquility. For hardness does not necessarily imply rectitude, and insensibility is not a guarantee of health.[28]

Dante's depiction of the virtue of *apatheia* as infernal, indeed as its own punishment, recalls passages such as this from *City of God*. It is, in a sense, the depiction of pride at its purest—original sin unmixed with any actual sin and therefore without distraction for the reader. The prideful are depicted as dispassionately bearing the eternal loss of God, fully committed to the fiction that they are their own final Good.[29] Only God can truly bear the loss of God, and yet even he cried, on our behalf, when he was abandoned by his Father on the cross (Matt 27:46). The comparison is especially apt because the emotions of Christ are given as a contrast to the pseudo-virtue of *apatheia* in the same chapter of *City of God*.[30] But it is hard "to convince the proud of the power and excellence of humility," the reader who, perhaps, is attached to the "great heartedness" of these heroes even when it is seen as an infernal greatness. So we descend into the second circle of hell where not only unexpiated original sin, but actual sin, is punished.

In the second circle, the lustful are punished with a tempestuous wind in a dark place that "moans as oceans do impelled by storms, surging, embattled in conflicting squalls" (*Inf.* 5.29–30). "The swirling wind of Hell [never rests]. It drags these spirits onwards in its force. It chafes them—rolling, clashing—grievously" (*Inf.* 5.31–33). The ones who are battered here

---

28. Augustine, *City of God*, 14.9.

29. Cf. ibid., 12.1.

30. Ibid., 14.9.

are "condemned for carnal sin," having "made reason bow to their instinc-tual bent" (*Inf.* 5.38–39). In Dante's depiction of the second circle's punish-ment, it is easy to see it as a depiction of the sin itself. If it were not obvious enough, the Virgil in Dante's text—just as the Virgil in Augustine's text—gives the clue that enables one to see reality not only through the fictional depiction of the punishment but rather through the fiction that lust creates around itself. It is this fiction that blocks a true understanding of what a hellish thing the sin actually is.

Virgil instructs Dante to speak to Paolo and Francesca by telling him to appeal to "that love that draws them on," a description, at one and the same time, of the lust which glues them together for all eternity and of the hellish hurricane that impels them (*Inf.* 5.78). This helps us understand the utter, but for all that not innocent, poignancy of Francesca's story. "Love," she says, "who so fast brings flame to generous hearts, / seized him [speak-ing of Paolo] with feeling for the lovely form, / now torn from me. The harm of how still rankles. / Love, who no loved one pardons love's requite, / seized me for him so strongly in delight / that, as you see, he does not leave me yet" (*Inf.* 5.100–105). The violent language in the metaphors mir-rors the violence of the wind that will not release them, and yet the irony is that Francesca does not see it. To make matters worse, Dante himself buys into the confusing use of language: "Alas, how many [gentle] thoughts, have led them through such sorrow to their fate?" he says, and then tells Francesca that her "suffering saddens me! Sheer pity brings me to the point of tears." He then asks her to tell him "the how and why—that Love, in sweetness of such sighing hours, permitted you to know these doubtful pangs" (*Inf.* 5.112–20).

It is clear that the pilgrim Dante buys into Francesca's self-delusion. Not even he sees the irony that her words describing her love do not depict something gentle and generous but instead something that describes at once the punishment of the sin and the sin itself. Perhaps it is a dim awareness of the closeness of the illusion and the reality, the efficacious deceptiveness of the mimesis of pride, that causes Dante to faint "as though I were to die" at the end of the visit to the second circle (*Inf.* 5.141). But hopefully the reader is beginning to acquire better vision or at least a hermeneutic of suspicion toward the self-justifying rhetoric of the prideful—that is, of themselves. For who could not recognize in the rhetoric of Francesca their own justification of lustful feelings through the mystique of the language of romantic love?

The City of Dis on the Foundation of Lying

In the interest of time we must take our leave of upper hell, where the sins of incontinence are depicted through the depiction of their punishments, and follow the pilgrim Dante into lower hell, where the sins of malice are depicted in the punishments we see. Lower hell is styled as a city, the City of Dis, thus recalling Augustine's characterization of the community of the prideful as a city, "the city of this world," the community that is no community and can be made visible only in its unmasking. In the City of Dis we again encounter an abundance of ironies, not the least of which is, perhaps, the placement of some of the sins lower or higher than we might have expected. The sin of flattery, for example, is punished in the eighth circle, while the sin of tyrannous killing is punished in the seventh circle (and in the first ring of the circle, at that). True, it is probably no picnic to be immersed in a stream of boiling blood, and one may imagine that it is subjectively a worse punishment than to be plunged into excrement as are the flatterers. Nevertheless, flattery is punished lower in the *Inferno*. Hypocrisy, in a similar way, would seem not to be as great a sin as violence against the neighbor, but it too (as well as counterfeiting) is lower.

I would like to suggest that the sins are ordered in this way because the lower you get in hell, the closer you get to the act of lying which is constitutive of the "city of this world," which persuades people to join, and which creates the community that is no community. Fraud (punished in the eighth circle) and betrayal (the most serious form of fraud punished in the ninth) are sins of representation, of communication, of deliberate illusion. There is no circle that punishes "liars," because the entirety of hell is founded on a lie—namely, that pride will exalt you—and the fraudulent are those who have most predicated their identity on this lie.

Some of the most horrifying images in *Inferno* thus come from the eighth and ninth circles, because here the beauty of the human person, made in the image of God, and the good of human solidarity, intended by God from the beginning, are shown as disfigured and marred by a commitment to pride under the guise of fraud. Pride, in the Augustinian sense as the idea that one can pass oneself off as one's own final Good and as completely self-sufficient, is the ultimate fraud. Not only does it disfigure the human person, but also it creates a city that is dark and stinks to high heaven. Fraud batters not just individual people but also the social bonds between them, which are turned to excrement by flattery and to darkness by bribery. The grafters, one of the demons guarding them says, "cash on the nail, and 'no' becomes 'for sure'" and so immerse themselves in a society that is like a sticky mass of pitch, the bonds among people reduced to a kind of substantial darkness, as "dense" as the darkness of the ninth plague of Egypt (*Inf.* 21.17, 42).

In one of the scenes of comic relief in *Inferno*, a grafter from Navarre bribes one of the demons with the promise of other sinners to torture, ironically so that he can slip back under the pitch. He is performing the sin for which he was damned and in the process shows us that the punishment of the sin is the sin itself, for there is only darkness left when truth becomes a function of cash. The sinner looks like an otter when he is originally caught by the demon guard—his human form diminished by his fraud—just as the image of God is defaced by the fraud of divination to the point where Dante weeps to see it so disfigured (*Inf.* 20.21–22).

The irony of the pride of the sin of divination can also be seen in the depiction of the sin. One hardly becomes more Godlike but rather less human; one distorts one's own humanity to walk backwards, imagining that he is walking forward (see *Inf.* 20.10–15). What does a society of thieves look like? It looks, as Dante says, like a pit of snakes if you see it truly, deprived of the perverse mimesis that pride would make of it. Being the master of other people's good seems to elevate you, but in reality, in clasping the fraud that is pride to yourself, you are making yourself one body with a serpent and thereby losing your human form altogether. Dante apostrophizes the reader to emphasize the most horrific scene:

> If you are slow, my reader, to receive,
>
> in faith, what I'll say now—no miracle.
>
> I saw it all, and yet can scarce believe.
>
> While, eyebrows raised, I stared at these three men,
>
> a reptile hurled itself with all six feet
>
> at one, front on, and took a total hold.
>
> It clenched the belly with its middle claws.
>
> With each anterior it seized an arm.
>
> It sank a forked fang deep in either cheek.
>
> Along each loin it slithered out a leg,
>
> then stuck its talk between the two, to take,
>
> now upwardly, a grip around the buttocks.
>
> Ivy in tangles never barbed to tree
>
> So tight as this ferocious awfulness,

linking its limbs in tendrils round that trunk.

As though the two were formed of warming wax,

Each clung to each and, mingling in their hues,

Neither now, seemingly, was what it was.

(*Inf.* 25.46–63)

To commit the sin of thieving fraud is to echo the primal sin of pride as an attempt to steal from God. It is like making yourself available for sex with a serpent, so that you become one flesh with the serpent. The horror of the image is that it is also an image of the society that is formed by the prideful, a perverse image of the communion between Christ and his bride, the Church. This is similar to the way the sin of simony, the buying and selling of the Holy Spirit as though God were a commodity, is imaged earlier in the text as an inversion of the mystery of Pentecost, with the flames of the Holy Spirit (who cannot be bought) dancing on the feet of the sinners (*Inf.* 19.22–30). Their form is distorted by being turned upside down, a position that prohibits any true social interaction but pushes the sinner ever downward, instead of (as he had hoped) ever upward in the ecclesiastical hierarchy.

Sin Unmasked and Eucharistic Vision

It is in the ninth circle, though, that we get the most compelling, if also most horrifying, depiction of the "city of this world," the community that is no community, where the sin of betrayal has turned the bonds of human communion into ice that freezes each one off from the other. We encounter an image of the way in which the sin of pride, as the commitment to the fiction of being one's own self-sufficient Good, is intrinsically fragmenting and can never create true communion, despite the illusions of communion created by the empires, built up as they are by the lust for domination. For this is the circle of the emperor of the despondent kingdom, the ultimate betrayer, Lucifer, whose pride has frozen the warmth of fellow feeling in all of the citizens of his empire (*Inf.* 34.28).

Dante's depiction of the punishment of each sin has been an analysis and depiction of the sin, a depiction of the "city of this world" by unmasking the "city of this world" and showing it as a communion that is no communion, and a peace that is no peace. The sacrament of this anti-communion, its "bestial sign," is the image of the cannibalism of Count Ugolino (*Inf.* 32.133). "You need to see," he tells Dante, "I was Count Ugolino. This is

Ruggieri, the archbishop, there. I'll tell you now why we two are neighbors" (*Inf.* 33.13–15). There could be no more ironic evocation of the word "neighbor" than this one. *Love thy neighbor? No thanks, I prefer to eat my neighbor.* To return to John Freccero, I accept his interpretation of this "bestial sign" as an inverse image of the Eucharist, perhaps the most infernal thing one can imagine.[31] It is the sacrament not of communion but of cannibalism, and, in the image of eternal cannibalism, we see the truth of the "city of this world." Here, neighbors are no neighbors, but rather there is simply the communion that is no communion, the city that is no city—nothing at all but dog eat dog.

Each of the damned thus exist as a kind of microcosm of the "city of this world," the community that is no community, since body and soul (intended to be a kind of harmonious communion that constitutes the human person) live on in an eternal state of war: "What war, then, can be imagined more serious and more bitter than a struggle in which the will is so at odds with the feelings and the feelings with the will, that their hostility cannot be ended by the victory of either—a struggle in which the violence of pain is in such conflict with the nature of the body that neither can yield to the other?"[32] With these words, Augustine reminds us that it is a state of complete disintegration of the human being, whose soul was supposed to be integrated with the life of God and whose body integrated into the life of the soul.

Oddly enough, the farther we get to the bottom of things, the more familiar they become, despite the fact that disintegration becomes ever more apparent. Who is not familiar with the society that has horrifyingly become a city of snakes: where one can trust no one; where nothing can be taken at face value; where even the most sacred bonds of kinship and friendship—can be betrayed? Who does not recognize this "mass of evils" that even perverts friendship:

> The much more bitter fear, that [the friendship of our friends] be changed into treachery, malice and baseness. And when such things do happen (and the more numerous our friends, the more often they happen) and the news is brought to our ears, who, except one who has this experience, can be aware of the burning sorrow that ravages our hearts? Certainly we would rather hear that our friends were dead, although this also we could not hear without grief.[33]

31. See Freccero, *Poetics of Conversion*, 163.

32. Augustine, *City of God*, 19.28.

33. Ibid., 19.8.

This passage from book 19 of *City of God*, where Augustine is once again taking up his rhetorical cudgel against the idea of *apatheia*, shows us just how familiar the ninth circle of hell is to us, if we are honest and have not tried to cultivate the passionlessness that is only one more prideful illusion. But in the ninth circle, Dante reveals this familiar scene for what it is: an inversion of the communion of which the Eucharist is the efficacious sign. That is the reason we can see it for what it is, in the light afforded by the perspective of the Eucharist, of which the "city of this world" is the prideful perversion. Because there is the Eucharist, we can afford—we can just afford—to look at this earthly city all around us without the sugarcoated, rose-colored blandishments of pride and yet not despair, not abandon all hope, and not get caught. Ultimately, because of the Eucharist, we can "take our leave of so much ill" (*Inf.* 34.84).

For even as the "banner of the king of hell approaches," as the first verse of the last canto describes the entry into the bottom ring of the ninth circle, this inversion of the traditional Good Friday hymn announcing the veneration of the cross invites us to be on the lookout for the cross, somehow, even in this infernal world (*Inf.* 34.1). It is funny how the hair of the Devil's body, frozen in the ice, serves the pilgrim and his guide as a way out of hell, a way to climb down to the center of the earth, and then, ironically, as "a ladder"—so many "steps" or "stairs"—that permits one to ascend (*Inf.* 34.82, 87, 119). The body of the Devil, who is frozen in the ice and able as an emperor to create only a community that is no community and to rule with his freedom immobilized, is the image of the cross because it is the image of the triumph of Christ. It is the image of Christ's self-emptying love which caused him to mix himself into this world of sin and sinners, to experience all of the desolation and horror that we experience in this fallen world, and thus to find the "hidden path" out of it (*Inf.* 34.133). This is Christ's own love that is not represented directly in hell because in fact it *is* hidden in this world. As Augustine says in book 18 of *City of God*, it is hidden "in the shadows," the shadows cast by empires, by the lust for domination and the pride which it is so difficult to convince of the power and excellence of humility.[34]

The cross is represented in the ability of the reader to see the whole of this evil, and its illusions, *as* somehow a whole, as a reality which can only be depicted in its unmasking as a reality. This is to see, in the revelation that the Devil is "a liar" and "the father of lies," the lie that Love is not real and that only power is real, that humility is self-defeating and that pride elevates.[35] It

---

34. Augustine, *City of God*, 18.1. For a complementary investigation of Augustine's theology of the two cities and the love which alone allows them to be seen as they truly are, see Cavadini, "Spousal Vision," 127–34.

35. Cf. John 8:44; Augustine, *City of God*, 14.3.

is the lie that there is no way out and that you will be trapped here forever, that in your desolation you are truly alone and there is no one who cares or who can help you. By clinging to the cross—the victory of Christ—you will always see through this lie. It turns out that the joke is on the Devil, and the ultimate irony is not a function of pride but of love. It is the power and excellence of the humility of Christ's love that ironically exposes the powerlessness of the supposed strong man, who cannot keep anyone in hell who clings to this irony and so sees the way out. Such a person will, with repristinated vision, emerge to see "the lovely things the skies above us bear" (*Inf.* 34.138). They will see all of creation from the perspective of the love that created it and thus emerge to see once more and maybe now for the first time truly, "the stars" (*Inf.* 34.137–39).

3

Becoming True in the *Purgatorio*

Dante on Forgetting, Remembering, and Learning to Speak

Kevin Grove, CSC

Introduction: Mercy and the *Commedia*

This essay examines the relationship between mercy and memory in Dante's *Commedia*, beginning from the Garden of Eden, the Earthly Paradise of the *Purgatorio*. This starting point—though at first glance *in medias res*—reveals a pivotal turn in the text. Dante is at the very threshold of salvation, lacking but one final encounter with Beatrice—and therein, with mercy and memory—which may prove to be more dramatic and demanding than any circle of hell or terrace of purgatory traversed thus far. Beginning a reading from this particular moment allows for a synthetic approach to the *Commedia* that is both literary and theological, a look both backward and forward from the mountaintop after having passed through hell, ascended through purgatory, and in anticipation of straining higher yet unto the stars of the heavenly paradise.

Mercy permeates the *Commedia*. Famously, the first words to issue from the mouth of the pilgrim Dante are a cry for mercy. "*Miserere*, save me" (*Inf.* 1.65), exclaims Dante in the dark wood, desperately entrusting himself to the unknown shadow of a man who approaches, and hoping for refuge and guidance. What begins as Dante's fearful, interior, and isolated monologue becomes dialogic, and mercy, however nondescript, takes its first narrative form in Dante's poetic hero, Virgil. Given that mercy grounds the possibility of and conditions for the pilgrim's journey, it is surprising that it is only at the end of two canticles that Dante receives a full explanation about why this journey was necessary for him at all. I will further suggest that wrapped up in that moment at the top of Mount Purgatory is also why such a journey might be beneficial to the reader.[1]

In the Garden of Eden at purgatory's peak, Beatrice, the merciful mediator of Dante's entire journey, says,

> I went, then, to the doorway of the dead,
>
> and, weeping, my entreaties there were borne
>
> to one who, since, has brought him to these heights.
>
> (*Purg.* 30.139–41)

Mercy would come for the beloved by a journey that starts from the doorway of death and tends toward heaven. Beatrice's tone resonates with ritual pilgrimages of penance in Christianity that commence with awareness of death. Ash Wednesday, the beginning of the liturgical season of Lent, is perhaps the most prominent example. A whole people begins from the doorway of the dead a pilgrimage toward Easter, toward God, that starts with the most humbling admission that humans are sinners and are going to die. As a minister imposes ashes, recipients hear either "Remember that you are dust, and to dust you shall return" or "Repent and believe in the Gospel."[2] These two phrases simply and clearly set forth two distinct aspects of the theology of mercy that contextualize what we see in Dante. The first phrase, "Remember you are dust and to dust you shall return," draws the hearer back to the first chapters of Genesis, where God forms a human being from the clay of the earth.[3] The dust is both a reminder of mortality, and at the same time the glorious power of the Creator. If from dust humans were created and held in being, one is meant to imagine what might be re-created in the same humans by some dust well worn. The second phrase, "Repent and believe in the Gospel," is both an acknowledgment that the one receiving ashes has sinned and that the Good News of Jesus Christ implies somehow the re-creation of just such a sinner. Both of these aspects of mercy—God as source and sustainer of being and mercy as the re-creative act of forgiveness of the sinful person in

---

1. See also *Inferno* 2.

2. "'Blessing and Distribution of Ashes,' Ash Wednesday," 71–72.

3. Gen 2:4–25; the second creation account. All English Scripture citations are from the NRSV unless otherwise noted. Michael Coogan, ed., *New Oxford Annotated Bible* (Oxford: Oxford University Press, 2001).

Christ—are present in the single gesture of the imposition of ashes. Mercy is equally correlated to being made and being made new, re-created, and drawn out such that the image of God is brought forth and one takes up his or her place in the body of Christ.

From the vantage point of Dante's Earthly Paradise in the *Purgatorio*, we see in clear relief that Dante's entire journey is a mercy from above, a formation meant to save him and make him new. Indeed, we catch glimpses of this merciful formation in the sacred geography of the *Commedia* itself. As Virgil explains to Dante at the end of *Inferno* 34, earth fled from Lucifer's proud fall, producing the gaping pit of hell in the northern hemisphere, and yet simultaneously pushing forth the mountain of purgatory in the southern hemisphere.[4] Thus, in an act of salvific tectonics, the way down to hell miraculously provided the way up toward heaven.[5] Having descended through the frozen pit of hell, Dante actually begins to climb, guided by Virgil, up the mountain of purgatory alongside sinners whose movements reform them from the earthly habits of sin they knew.

Purgatory, though a rigorous place, is a profoundly hopeful one. The journey up the mountain's slopes leads to the *Earthly* Paradise, the Garden of Eden. One makes a return, as it were, to the place from where it all once fell apart. The structure of the Earthly Paradise is one of a terrain between two rivers, Lethe and Eunoe, a river of forgetting of sin and a river of remembering of good things. Between the rivers grows the Tree of Knowledge of Good and Evil. This is the place where Dante at long last meets his beloved Beatrice. We shall return to treat the rivers, the tree, and the confession that Dante makes in due course. We must first treat Beatrice, the lifeblood of Dante's poetry and journey.

---

4. Virgil recounts:
Falling from Heaven, when he reached this side,
the lands that then spread out to southern parts
in fear of him took on a veil of sea.
These reached our hemisphere. Whatever now
is visible to us—in flight perhaps from him—
took refuge here and left an empty space. (*Inf.* 34.121–26)

5. Kirkpatrick notes: "Satan's fall, then, positively contributes to the development of providential purpose, establishing the realm in which human beings first enjoy their relationship with God and then, after the Fall and atonement, eventually come to be purged of their sins" (Kirkpatrick, "Canto 34," in *Inferno*, 447).

Beatrice: Memory and Mercy

Though she does not dominate each and every canto, the person and figure of Beatrice nevertheless is critical for the evolution of both Dante's poetry and theology.[6] In the radiance of her life and the drama of her untimely death, Beatrice ultimately provides the poetic raw material with which Dante would craft his emergent vision of love poetry.

The reconciliation episode between Dante and Beatrice in the Earthly Paradise marks one of the climaxes of this poetic evolution; yet, its dramatic tension and pathos are largely unintelligible without first appreciating the personal, poetic, and spiritual complexity which characterized Dante's love for Beatrice while on earth, which he immortalized in his *Vita Nova*.[7] Composed in a prosimetrum style, the *Vita Nova* weaves together Dante's past works of poetry with prose self-commentary and plot to produce an artificially continuous narrative. What Dante ultimately constructs is a highly stylized love story about Beatrice: of trembling at his first encounter with the young Florentine girl at age nine; her beatifying salutation to him nine years later; a series of romantic mishaps by which he falls out of favor with Beatrice, her early death which inspired both a flood of tears and guilt for his now wavering devotion to her; and a resolve to dedicate his future poetry in selfless devotion to her blessed memory, "to say things about her that have never been said about any woman" (*Vita Nova* 31.2).

6. Beyond those who cite Boccaccio's biography (*Trattatello in laude di Dante*) and various para-textual documents that identify Dante's Beatrice with Beatrice Portinari or at least with a living woman of Dante's time, and beyond those who find the demure and illusive Beatrice of the Vita Nova and the almost too divine Beatrice of the Commedia as indications of pure allegory and poetic abstraction, Dante himself cites both the historical and allegorical Beatrice as complementary and necessary along his journey to God. In fact, at the very summit of Dante's praise of the heavenly Beatrice's beauty, he cannot help but recall: "Not since the day that I, in our first life, / first saw her face until this living sight, / has song in me been cut so cleanly short" (*Paradiso* 30.28–30). The expansiveness of "*questa vita*," specified by Kirkpatrick as "in our first life," can contain both Dante's memories of love for Beatrice, and his own artistic praise of her perfection and role as beatifier in the afterlife. Ultimately, as Jaroslav Pelikan writes in *Eternal Feminines*, both history and allegory in her "are one, in pointing beyond Beatrice to God" (Pelikan, *Eternal Feminines*, 75).

7. As Andrew Frisardi argues in his introduction to the *Vita Nova*, not only does the intensity of the reconciliation scene in the Earthly Paradise depend upon its context in the *Vita Nova* narrative, but so too does Beatrice's status as an embodied—and not merely abstracted—character in the *Commedia*: "Without the *Vita Nova* the reappearance of Beatrice in the Earthly Paradise, in canto XXX of *Purgatorio*, and her increasingly radiant smile throughout *Paradiso*, would lack personal context and therefore would be far easier to dismiss as allegorical abstractions. The libello . . . establishes Beatrice as Dante's pole star and beatifier" (Dante Alighieri, *Vita Nova*, xx).

And so we arrive at the *Commedia*, Dante's inimitable poetic achievement once boldly prophesied in the *Vita Nova*. Just as Dante's poetry has matured, so too has his depiction of Beatrice. Her appearance in the Earthly Paradise of the *Purgatorio* is a scene at once marvelous, beautiful, commanding, and terrifying. Dante recounts,

> So now, beyond a drifting cloud of flowers . . .
>
> seen through a veil, pure white, and olive-crowned,
>
> a lady now appeared to me. Her robe was green,
>
> her dress the color of a living flame.
>
> (*Purg.* 30.28, 31–33)

Beatrice's face is veiled from Dante. She is wearing a dress the color of living flame. If the love of his life was extraordinary when he saw her in a church as young man, now indeed she is literally otherworldly in her radiance. And Dante's response to this vision is very interesting. It is a flashback, a remembering, of what he once was and what she once drew out of him. He says:

> And I, in spirit, who so long had not
>
> been, trembling in her presence, wracked by awe,
>
> began again to tremble at her glance . . .
>
> sensing the ancient power of what love was.
>
> But on the instant that it struck my sight—
>
> this power, this virtue, that had pierced me through
>
> before I'd even left my boyhood state—
>
> I turned aside (and leftwards) meaning now,
>
> with all the hope and deference of some child
>
> that runs when hurt or frightened to its mum,
>
> to say to Virgil: "There is not one gram
>
> of blood in me that does not tremble now.
>
> I recognize the signs of ancient flame."
>
> (*Purg.* 30.34–36, 39–48)

This is an extraordinary moment for Dante. First, he is certainly recalling how he saw Beatrice as a young boy. Commentaries are clear that Dante intended resonances even in the wording and repetition of sounds in these verses that would recall his own little book the *Vita Nova*.[8] As a poet, certainly, he is building on what he once was. But this is more than Dante the poet footnoting himself. This is about who he was then and who he is now. As a boy he saw and fell in love with Beatrice. As these lines so beautifully capture, the source of his trembling love and admiration is articulated in terms of a great virtue: "this power, this virtue, that had pierced me through before I'd even left my boyhood state" (*Purg.* 30.41–42).[9] In other words, this divine virtue that emanates from Beatrice and which pierces Dante's heart with wonder, fear, and trembling as an adult is that same holy power which struck him as a child, and once inaugurated his journey as a love poet.[10] The phrasing implies that Dante has strayed far from the goodness of that virtue. In this moment, he does not dwell on it for long, but the memory of

8. Kirkpatrick writes, "With its abrupt arrival at the phrase '*donna m'apparve*' ('a lady now appeared to me') (30:32)—which appears almost *verbatim* in the *Vita nuova* 1—the passage changes character and begins to revert to the idiom of Dante's earlier style. In particular, the passage at 30:34–9 recalls those phases of the *Vita nuova* when the poet was under the influence of Cavalcanti's melancholic understanding of love, and love was, as here, a power that shook the self-possession of the lover to the point of fear and trembling" (Kirkpatrick, "Cantos 30 and 31," in *Purgatorio*, 487).

9. The generic term "virtue" is justifiably multivalent, and here Dante is applying it to the figure of Beatrice in a unique and cogent way. Ruth Chester states that the most recognizable forms of "virtue" are human virtue and divine virtue. Human virtue describes the "acquired, moral modes of action and structuring principles of human character," consonant with Dante's Aristotelian definition in the *Convivio* (IV.xvii.7) of virtue as an "*abito elettivo consistente nel mezzo*," which Chester translates, "a habit of choice that keeps to the mean." Thus, repetition lies at the heart of purgatorial cleansing, insofar as it effects this transition "from an individual event to a fixed disposition." Divine virtue is then described "as the creative, informing power of God imprinting upon the celestial heavens who, in turn, contain inferior types of virtue, which then go on to inform the sub-lunar world" (Chester, "Virtue in Dante," 211); it is this latter informing virtue which capacitates virtue in creation to begin with, giving form and individuality to matter, and a unique mode of exercising one's creaturely virtue. Chester, however, offers a third way to understand virtue in Dante in relation to Beatrice which he describes as a kind of "mediated virtue," which originates in the *Vita Nova* and which now returns again to claim Dante's love, fear, and devotion. She explains that this mediating power is "the morally ennobling quality originating in Love itself, which passes through the figure of the beloved (Beatrice) to the lover by means of her beauty and goodness." Beatrice's "*l'alta virtù*" ("this power, this virtue") of *Purgatorio* 30.41 thus is both a habitual activity of beauty and goodness, and yet simultaneously a miraculous means of inspiring virtue in others. Chester continues: "Part of the special quality of Beatrice herself is that she creates this state of morality which was not pre-existing in those who saw her, emphasizing her miraculous, more-than-human nature" (ibid., 213).

10. This same "power" can been seen also in Dante's adolescence, and on the cusp of his poetic career: "And passing along the street, she turned her eyes in the direction of where I stood gripped by fear, and thanks to her ineffable benevolence and grace . . . she greeted me with such power that then and there I seemed to see to the farthest reaches of beatitude" (*Vita Nova*, I.12).

that love that struck him so deep as to be a virtue was still in Dante and its recovery makes him tremble.

Like anyone who has grown too shrewd, realist, or jaded to believe in such ideals, Dante shifts. He changes his focus to one he knows and one with whom he has become comfortable. He goes back to his classical guide Virgil to seek advice and comment on how much this experience has affected him. The ancient wisdom, the poet, is here supposed to give an interpretive key. And proving how indebted to Virgil Dante has become, he quotes Virgil as he describes what is happening in him as he sees this person, Beatrice. In the last line of what I quoted above, Dante turns toward Virgil and as he does prepares to say, "I recognize the signs of ancient flame" (*Purg.* 30.48). There is nothing more haunting he might have said at that moment. Those are the words in Virgil's *Aeneid* of the love-struck Carthaginian Dido.[11]

On the one hand, Dante's quotation is a great honor, that just before Virgil disappears, Dante's last words to Virgil should be Virgil's own. It is in some ways a hat tip of honor among equals. But on the other hand, there is a deep subtext about love going on here. For Dido, at the point she says that line, had fallen madly in love with Aeneas. And in the course of book four of the *Aeneid*, this love was Dido's *undoing*. She neglected the glorious city she was building in Carthage, she failed to convince Aeneas to stay, she attempted to manipulate him, and watched with lament as he sailed away. The end of that story is that Dido takes her own life on a burning pyre. It is a tragic classical tale and a story that love wrongly ordered can bring total destruction. And the gods in that tale—Mercury, Venus, and others—do not help the situation, but exacerbate the conflict between the lovers that leads to separation and death.

So when Dante trembles and quotes Dido from the *Aeneid* as Beatrice appears, he is not recalling the happiest of memories. Rather, he is recalling a beautiful but torrid North African love affair that brought about the undoing of the lover. The allusion invites an unsettling, open question: what would be the end of Dante's love of Beatrice? He has known that deep of a love—as powerful as Dido's—so strong it could well completely undo him.

We should recall that Dido sits in the second circle of hell with Francesca, Paolo, Achilles, Paris and other souls who are now characterized eternally by the inconstancy of their desire. There, Dante not only pities them but openly weeps at Francesca's account of tragic love and loss, saying, "Francesca, how your suffering saddens me! / Sheer pity brings me to the point of tears" (*Inf.* 5.116–17). Indeed, Dante is so emotionally invested in the tale that he faints at its climax, "as though [he] were to die" (*Inf.*

11. Virgil, *Aeneid*, 4.23.

5.141). He is claiming that such an experience of tragic, romantic love is a feeling to which he—and perhaps his readers—can relate. And so, at the edge of the bank of the river of forgetting, a drama opens. Is Dante too going to be undone by his love for Beatrice?[12] And if not, what is going to change, and how?

The first subtle change is Dante's orientation—he is described as turning left as he quotes Dido (*Inf.* 30.43). Directions are important—all but a couple of times in the *Inferno* Dante and Virgil go left; nearly always in the *Purgatorio* the two go right. Thus, when he turns left to Virgil, to the guide he's had thus far, he finds nothing: Virgil has disappeared, his advice now an anachronism at the threshold of Paradise. It is the other direction he must turn now, not only with his glance but with his life. At Virgil's disappearance, Beatrice reveals herself to Dante, and begins her rebuke. Look, she explains,

> I am, truly, I am Beatrice.
>
> What right had you to venture to this mount?
>
> Did not you know that all are happy here?
>
> (*Purg.* 30.73–75)

Recall above that I laid out two aspects of an encounter with mercy. Here we see that Dante's encounter with his Beatrice is no simple encounter with the image of attraction—even to goodness—that he had as a boy. Beatrice here represents allegorically the very being of God the creator. "I am," she says. And repeats, "Truly, *I am* Beatrice." The resonance of her unveiling her name is with Moses in the account of Sinai in Exodus 3. The Lord there says, "I am who am" (Exod 3:14). Literally: the one who is with you and will be with you. The Lord then clarifies by a second addition when the Lord tells Moses that "I am" is also the God of Abraham, Isaac, and Jacob (Exod 3:15). Notice that Beatrice's speech of self-revelation traces a similar

---

12. Insofar as Dante's identification with Dido portends an equally tragic outcome in Dante's encounter with Beatrice, it is interesting to note that this undoing is anticipated in *Inf.* 5 when the poem describes Dante as *quasi smarrito* or "almost lost" as a result of his pity for the lustful souls. The adjective *smarrito* also famously describes Dante's condition of being lost at the beginning of the poem: "I came around and found myself now searching / through a dark wood, the right way *blurred and lost*" [*mi ritrovai per una selva oscura, / ché la diritta via era smarrita*] (*Inf.* 1.2–3). The textual relationship invites the possibility that a significant reason Dante finds himself lost in the dark wood to begin with is this very inconstancy to Beatrice, an infidelity that now in the Earthly Paradise and at the cusp of the Heavenly Paradise he fears will leave him again lost and undone. See also *Inf.* 5.142.

trajectory. The "I am" comes first, and the connection to a personage Dante knew, "Truly. *I am* Beatrice," follows.

At this point, I suppose we could accuse Dante either of a tremendous heresy or a tremendous Christology.[13] He has, in a qualified way, made Beatrice into God. Yet, in Dante's metaphysics, as Christian Moevs has argued, "God, as the ultimate subject of all experience, cannot be an object of experience: to know God is to know oneself as God, or (if the expression seems troubling) as one 'with' God or 'in' God."[14] And it is in that claim that we have hope that Dante is going to take a different road from that of Dido. His love for Beatrice is not going to be that of his un-doing, but of his re-doing. We can be assured of it because Beatrice presents herself in a theophanic way. *I am*, truly, *I am* Beatrice means that she is no lover in the ordinary sense, but one whose very existence and therein love is revealed as communion with God as source and sustainer of being. This love could never bring about a suicide—a choice of total solitude. This is the love of the whole Christ.

What is lovely is that the divine really is closer to Dante than his interior inmost being. Beatrice's presentation of what Dante became is not about the reliving of each peccadillo or sin; it is a setting forth of what sin is, using Dante as an example. Sin erodes the very potentialities for which Dante was created and which he certainly even exhibited at different points in his life. Beatrice begins this by saying of Dante,

> This man through all his new life, fresh and young,
>
> in virtual power was one who might have proved,
>
> in all of his behavior wonderful.
>
> Yet there, on earth, the richer soil may be,
>
> the more—untilled or sown with evil seed—
>
> its vigor turns to wilderness and bane.
>
> (*Purg.* 30.115–20)

The warning here is actually a bit terrifying. It is not that the better or more successful one becomes, the holier one is. Rather, the richer the soil, the better the person, the correlatively more tempting it is to turn to

---

13. This, in fact, was a concern for counter-reformation censors of Dante's work. Dante uses the word beatitude in connection with Beatrice eleven times in the *Vita Nova*. Censors replaced them all with the word "happiness" (Scott, *Understanding Dante*, 357n8).

14. Moevs, *The Metaphysics of Dante's* Comedy, 5.

wilderness and bane. And to that young and talented man Beatrice recounts
her role when she was on earth:

> I, looking on, sustained him for a time.
>
> My eyes, when bright with youth, I turned to him,
>
> and led him with me on the road to truth.
>
> (*Purg.* 30.121–23)

So while Beatrice was alive, her glance and movements did indeed bring out
of Dante what was true and good. There is a real power and goodness to the
embodied-ness of human love. Yet, Beatrice continues that upon her death
and entry to her second life, things changed for Dante:

> Then, on the threshold of my second age,
>
> I changed, took different life, and he at once
>
> drew back and yielded to another's glance.
>
> Risen from body into spirit-form,
>
> my goodness, power, and beauty grew more strong.
>
> Yet I to him was then less dear, less pleasing.
>
> He turned his steps to paths that were not true.
>
> He followed images of failing good
>
> which cannot meet, in full, their promises.
>
> And when I prayed that he might be inspired,
>
> seeking to call him back—by dreams and other ways—
>
> all that came to nothing. He paid little heed.
>
> (*Purg.* 30.124–35)

This must be a devastating critique for Dante. There, at the moment
he sees once more his beloved, she explains that her relationship was meant
to make him true. And he, of his own will, chose the paths of falsehood.
Beatrice tried, through prayers and even dreams, not to bring Dante guilt or
shame but to "inspire," literally to breathe a spirit into him. And we should
note that the account is of Dante's rejection of that spirit. And so Beatrice
does the unthinkable. She says,

> He fell so far that every other means
>
> to save this man, by now, came short, unless

he saw, himself, those people who are lost.

(*Purg.* 30.136–38)

And we return to the line with which we opened: Beatrice says,

I went, then, to the doorway of the dead,

and weeping, my entreaties there were borne

to one who, since, has brought him to these heights.

(*Purg.* 30.139–41)

Devastating for Dante, yes, but a most powerful testament to mercy. Beatrice, when she was alive on earth, drew Dante by her glance. Alive in heaven she has been in his dreams, prayed for him, and knows his ways. She reveals that the goal of the entire project, of this journey, is to save Dante's soul. It is here cast in terms of his relationship to the truth. The truth is not that which Dante even can express as the greatest poet of all time. It is that thing which by his practicing, Dante becomes. This journey is meant to make him True. Beatrice is saying that Dante's life of sin has made him false, a lie to his own self. It is not who he is; it is not who he was created to be; it does not set him free but it ensnares him as he saw it do to others through nine circles of infernal entrapment. No, the journey to God is one of becoming true, free, and new. Dante now has reached that moment.

Conversion: The Word, Words, and Learning to Speak

This brings us to Dante's conversion. It is a remarkable affair in so many ways and I want to call attention not merely to Dante's experiencing mercy, but how he—the poet—has both to lose his words and then to learn to speak. This is Dante's confession in the truest sense of the word. Augustine defines confession as the act of uniting oneself to God.[15] Similarly, in Dante's metaphysics, conversion not only renews true speech or true actions, it ultimately leads one to *become* true, insofar as one is united with, in, and as truth itself.[16] This is the beginning of a conversion at once existential, episte-

15. Augustine, "Exposition on Psalm 75," vol. 4:75.14.

16. On humanity's self-transformation and self-knowledge in and as truth, Moevs writes, "As intellect en-trues itself in itself (*s'invera*) more and more, it comes to know itself as encompassing, or spawning, more and more of the contingent universe. In perfect self-knowledge, it knows itself as a dimensionless point of awareness spawning all experience. . . . To achieve this pure reflexivity of conscious being is to become (one with) the ultimate ontological principle . . . it is to find oneself in the Empyrean"

mological, and metaphysical, such that, as Moevs explains, one knows both one's fullest self and knows God in and through becoming deiform: "To see God is to see the power to see that is God: it is to see *as* God. In Christian terms it is to become deiform, assimilated to an angelic intelligence. To know God is, as the inscription on the great temple of Apollo at Delphi commanded, to know oneself."[17]

For Dante, it takes an entire *cantica* to enter fully into this vision. For now, the mediator of his divine conversion is Beatrice. Beatrice is a tougher confessor than any earthly minister. She addresses Dante—her face still veiled—from across the stream of Lethe, and demands of her past admirer,

> "You, who are there beyond the sacred stream,"
>
> turning the sword point of her words on me
>
> (the edge had seemed quite keen enough),
>
> so, without lapse continuing, she began,
>
> "Say, say, if this is true. To such a charge
>
> your own confession needs to be conjoined."
>
> (*Purg.* 31.1–6)

The text plays on what it means to speak and have words. It is not just that Beatrice is speaking words; she is, for Dante, a speaker of the Word: a Christ-figure. As Beatrice is fully configured to Christ, in her speaking the Word speaks. And when such a word cuts, if we recall the way that it appears in the letter to the Hebrews, it is alive and active and does so with a vigor that is sharper than any two-edged sword (4:12). It is the very Word of God that is going to work on Dante here at the scene of his conversion. And he has the good humor, in light of his saying that Beatrice has directed the sword-point of her words at him, to say that a single edge of the two-edged sword would have been completely sufficient to accomplish these purposes.

Dante the poet, the master of words, is being purified by the Word, uncomfortable though that may be. The consequence is humbling. When Beatrice commands Dante to speak, to confess—was what she said true?—he loses his words. The poet, the wordsmith, the *terza rima* mind, comes up blank. It is not so much that Beatrice needs confirmation or that she is uncertain. Or, it is not even that Dante disagrees with her formulation. Both she and Dante recognize the situation perfectly. The trouble with Dante groping for words and coming up short is that speaking the truth (that is,

---

(Moevs, *The Metaphysics of Dante's Comedy*, 7; see also 173).

17. Moevs, *The Metaphysics of Dante's Comedy*, 173.

being true) in this final and God-like way is not something he has been used
to doing. In fact, much of his life has been speaking differently.

And so Dante continues,

> My natural powers by now were so confused
>
> that voice began to move but then gave out
>
> before it cleared the larynx and the throat.
>
> She bore this for a little while, and then she said:
>
> "Respond to me. Your memories
>
> have not been struck through yet by Lethe's stream."
>
> (*Purg.* 31.7–12)

He has not forgotten what he has done; he has forgotten who he is. That is
what makes this word of truth so hard to utter. Truth in the way of becoming True does not come to Dante so easily. When he finally is able to get out
a word, it is the most feebly spoken word in all of the *Commedia*:

> Fear and confusion, intermixed in me,
>
> drove from my lips a "yes" so hard to hear
>
> it needed sight to make it understood.
>
> (*Purg.* 31.13–15)

It is an extraordinary expression, of a word so hard to hear that it needs
sight to make it understood. The deliberate confusion of sensory perception
shows even Dante's difficulty at producing this tiny yes—so small that it is
like noticing a little bit of floating dust only visible when it is illuminated by
a ray of sun.[18]

There is profound precedent for considering this moment of speech-
less conversion. One recalls another most famous garden scene, in which a
very similar thing happens. This is the moment of Augustine's conversion
in his *Confessions*. What Dante does and does not take from Augustine is
open to much debate. Nevertheless, the resonances here are strong enough I
think it foolish not to point them out. For Augustine also was a wordsmith,
a rhetorician, whose care for meaning, beauty, and movement in language
place him in the company of the greatest of late classical Latinists.

But at the moment of his conversion, Augustine finds himself, like
Dante, in a garden, in a place of re-creation.[19] And there the rhetorician loses

18. Compare to *Paradiso* 14.109–17.
19. Augustine, *Confessions*, 8.19–8.12.30.

words. He chokes up with tears so much so that he is unable to communicate with his friend Alypius and removes himself from his presence. Augustine, crying, loses his words and under a single tree that alludes to the Garden of Eden, he throws himself down upon the ground. He has become an *infans*, a baby without words.[20] And in order to take up a life in Christ, he will have to learn to grow up and to speak anew. For Augustine, he heard a child's voice in the distance saying, "Take up and read, take up and read."[21] The words he needed to learn to speak were those of Scripture. And the passage from Paul to which he opened told him not merely to cast off his sins but literally to put on Christ (Rom 13:13–14). Augustine was being made true, when he spoke the Truth in Christ—in this case, Scripture.

Dante's conversion has this sort of christological tone. As soon as he has uttered the little yes of his sin, at the edge of the garden he loses control, tears stream, sobs come, and his voice becomes slack and slow. He needed words. And what Beatrice does is engage him in a conversation. And it is a tough one in which his speaking, as he says, is labored and difficult.

And she asks him,

> In your desire for me . . .
>
> which then was leading you to love the Good
>
> beyond which we cannot aspire to reach,
>
> what ditches or what chains across your path
>
> did you discover that led you to strip
>
> the hopes you had of getting further on?
>
> What easements, profits, gain or benefit
>
> displayed themselves to you on other brows
>
> that you preferred to flounce within their sight?
>
> (*Purg.* 31.22–30)

Dante through his tears, speaks the truth:

> Weeping, I said: "Mere things of here and now
>
> and their false pleasures turned my steps away

20. I am grateful to Janet Martin Soskice for this insight. In "Monica's Tears: Augustine on Words and Speech," she writes, "In the garden, and it is partly Eden, the great wordsmith is once again deprived of his words, once again in fans. It seems that God's early gift to this 'salesman of words,' as he describes his early profession, is to deprive of speech" (Soskice, "Monica's Tears," 452).

21. Augustine, *The Confessions*, 8.8.19–8.12.30.

the moment that your face had hid itself."

(*Purg.* 31.34–36)

And with that, Dante said the one and most important thing in any confession: I desired you, yet I sought you in things that were not you.[22] This is the human problem—our problem. And this has been on Dante's mind from the very first canto of the *Inferno* before he ever enters the gates of hell.

Three Desires: A Scriptural Retrospective

One further aspect of theology helps interpret the mythology of the poem, revealing the significance of Dante's confession of wrongly turned desire. At the opening of the epic, Dante, midway through the journey of his life in the dark forest encountered three beasts: a leopard, a lion, and a wolf. Robin Kirkpatrick describes them as pleasure, pride, and greed.[23] Yet, these three beasts' identities are difficult to ascertain, and I suggest that a proper theological anthropology helps us to do so.

The relevant moment is in the Garden of Eden, when the Genesis writer describes the fruit on the Tree of the Knowledge of Good and Evil. Eve looks at the tree and sees that it—in the words of a single verse of Genesis—"was good for food, and that it was a delight to the eyes, and that the tree was to be desired to make one wise" (3:6). What is remarkable about this scriptural text is that it captures a way of describing three desires that would have been intelligible across ancient Near Eastern civilizations. The first, taking them in the order that Genesis puts them, is the desire of the flesh—the fruit of the tree was good for food. In other words, those human desires that relate to physical embodiment: food, drink, sex, etc. The second phrase in that tightly packed bit of scripture is "delight to the eyes." This, the desire of the eyes, is for ownership of things of the world: anything that one might see with his or her eyes and seek to have, control, or use. And finally, the third desire was for that which would make one wise. This desire was called pride of life, or sometimes worldly ambition, and the wisdom coming from the tree would augment that in a very important manner.

These three desires—the desire of the flesh, the desire of the eyes, and pride of life—are present in Genesis's description of the first man and the first woman *before* they ever sin and disobey God's command not to eat. That the desires exist is a good thing and readers of the text can only hold that they were created as good. The narrative account of the first sin is not

22. See also Augustine, *The Confessions*, 10.27.38.

23. Kirkpatrick, "Canto 1," in *Inferno*, 318–19.

that food, drink, sex, possessions, and ambition are bad. It is that they some-how got out of balance, become ends in themselves—allegorical leopards, lions, and wolves. And since that time—both in the Bible and in human history that includes Dante—individuals struggle with the integration of the same three desires. The extremes are flopping back and forth between com-plete self-denial and total self-indulgence. One does whatever feels good sometimes at the expense of what is good (desire of the flesh), one wants more than one's fair share (desire of the eyes), and one's life runs the risk of becoming all about oneself once in a while (pride of life).

This treatment of desire within a Christian anthropology does not stop here with the naming of these three desires in Genesis. In the New Testa-ment before Jesus ever calls disciples, performs miracles, or preaches, he goes out into the desert to face three desires (Matt 4:1–11). Christ went out to face his own human desires. While he was there, the tempter came and asked him to make stones into bread because he was hungry—to feed the desires of his flesh. Jesus refuses the temptation. Food is not bad, but it could not be stronger than his desire for God. The tempter also took Jesus up onto a very high mountain and showed him every kingdom on earth—every desire the eye could wish to control. Again, he did not accept the offer of the tempter, for he would have had to put his possessions before God his Father. In one final flourish, the tempter took him to Jerusalem, to the seat of prayer itself, and told him to throw himself off of the high parapet of the temple and to let God save him—to have so much pride in his life that he would make God serve his own pride. But again, he did not do it. The text suggests that uniquely in human history we see one whose actions are a claim on having reintegrated those three desires toward their end in God. Jesus does not suppress or eliminate any of the three desires, just puts them in a different relationship to God.

These three desires are further refracted through Evangelical counsels. When Jesus preaches his Sermon on the Mount, he then carries on to de-scribe how it is that people might live out this blessedness (Matt 5:1–11). He gives instruction on three practices and how to do them with integrity rather than in the manner of the Pharisees and the hypocrites. It is worth consider-ing, if the desire of the flesh—for bodily satisfaction—is overpowering at times, what is a way to reverse that in a positive manner? The answer is to fast, to discipline one's own consumption in such a way that another might eat. What would it mean to invert an overwhelming desire to own things, to control what is around us, or to own the kingdoms of the earth? The answer is to give alms, to take what one has and share it with those in need. And finally the opposite of letting one's world become all about oneself is, of course, prayer. For anyone who truly prays, "Thy will be done" and intends what those words mean places the will of Another before that of oneself. It is a three-pronged approach of reintegrating three human desires. Notice that each of these inversions of desire is not to make the one who undergoes them hungry, poor, and grouchy. Each of them turns the practitioner outward, other-ward, in Christian terms toward the body of Christ.

It is worth noting that this formulation for desire has been refracted across the Christian tradition—from the First Epistle of John (1 John 2:16) through Augustine, Aquinas, and other modern thinkers like John Paul II and Martin Heidegger.[24] Yet it is worth specifically mentioning that one might commit oneself to a long-term course of integrating the three desires. This provides the ground for religious vows: a commitment to fleshly control is chastity. Not succumbing to the desire to own all things but to share what we have in common or with those in need is poverty. Putting the will of others before that of oneself is called obedience. Not only, then, human life, but "religious life"—priests, brothers, and sisters—is built around this system of trying to work out these three desires.

Inferno 1	Genesis 3:6	Human Desires	Christ in the Desert	Ascetic Practices	Religious Vows
Leopard	Good for Food	Desire of the Flesh	Turn Stones into Bread	Fasting	Chastity
Lion	Pleasing to the Eyes	Desire of the Eyes	Own Kingdoms of Earth	Almsgiving	Poverty
Wolf	Gaining Wisdom	Pride of Life	Throw Self off Temple	Prayer	Obedience

Sacramental Mercy: Forgetting Sin and Remembering Good Things

Returning now to the *Commedia*: when Dante admits at the edge of the garden that he has desired God in things not God, he has just finally made the most extraordinary confession. He cannot manage on his own; he cannot maintain as oriented to their final end in God the desires of his physical

24. 1 John 2:16: "For all that is in the world—the desire of the flesh, the desire of the eyes, the pride in riches—comes not from the Father but from the world." See Augustine, *The Confessions*, 10.27.38–10.39.64; on Thomas Aquinas, Grove, "Desires, Counsels, and Christ"; John Paul II, *Vita Consecrata*; Heidegger, *The Phenomenology of Religious Life*.

flesh, or of his eyes to control and own, or certainly of his pride. In short, Dante comes to the Christian conclusion that he is what he desires; he is what he loves. There is a thematic echo of an act of ritual contrition: "In choosing to do wrong and failing to do good, I have sinned against you whom I should love above all things."[25] It took a pit of hell and a mountain of purgatory to get Dante to this point. But we can see now that the labor of such a journey pays off.

Beatrice turns her gaze to a mythical creature called a Griffin, another allegorical figure of Christ. After this, Dante can be drawn through the river of Lethe, the river of forgetting. This mythical body of water existed first in classical literature, depicted as an otherworldly place of forgetting and oblivion. In book 10 of Plato's *Republic*, the river of Lethe lies along the "plain of Forgetting" in the afterlife, and mediates each soul's journey to reincarnation as a completely new identity.[26] For Dante, Lethe is much more like a sacrament of mercy and healing. He has just gone through the work of remembering things very painful to him, but not so as to dwell upon their pain. He will not, as the *Paradiso* will show, forget himself or his history, but he will forget the shame of sin. The love cast here and there on other things is obliterated in that stream. It is a holy forgetting. And when he reaches the other side he hears a song so sweetly sung that he cannot even describe it. *Asperges me*; O wash me, Lord.[27] The first words of Dante's new life are not those of his own poetic creation but the psalm of praise spoken for him by the rest of the body of Christ. Others speak for him; these words are shared.

Sin had kept him from seeing Beatrice's face. It had kept him from the truth. She unveils her face. He now looks at her eyes. Desire wrongly cast had obscured Paradise. He now stands in Paradise's midst. But mercy, Dante comes to find, is not the completion of his journey, but the way. For there are things in that Paradise which he does not understand, including fanciful creatures from revelation's pages. The most important example is the Tree of Knowledge of Good and Evil. This is the very site at which human desire went awry. In the midst of an extraordinary cast of charac-ters, the Griffin—a half-eagle and half-lion that evokes the two natures of

25. "The Rite of Penance," 546.

26. Plato, *Republic*, 621a–c. Plato lauds Er for his wisdom not to drink deeply of the river like all the other souls, who consequently forget their past identity and soon are reborn into new lives. Er instead comes back to life in his own body, lying on his funeral pyre. "In this way," Plato concludes, "his story was saved and not lost. And so it can be our salvation, since if we believe it we shall pass the river of Forgetting in the right way, without polluting our souls."

27. *"Asperges me,"* is taken from Psalm 51:9 and used as an antiphon for ritual sprin-kling with water in the Latin Catholic Church.

Christ—is praised for not eating of the tree, unlike Adam, while the tree suddenly swells with new foliage (*Purg.* 32.52–60), and only to be stripped of its bark, flowers, and verdant growth soon after by an eagle (*Purg.* 32.109–14). Dante is still unable to make full sense of this. Indeed, though he confesses that Beatrice's mark has been placed upon his very mind, there is much even in her speech that he does not at present understand. Now that mercy has set free Dante's heart, *Paradiso* will indeed have to supply what continues to be missing for his mind.

There are in fact two rivers in the geography of the Earthly Paradise, both flowing from the same source in the will of God. Lethe is the river of forgetting; Eunoe is the river of the memory of good things. And before Dante makes his exit to learn the perfected logic and music of heaven, he is led once more to drink. This time he is not led there alone but with others. The memory of good things—the things that last—is one that constitutionally is shared.

Dante closes his *Purgatorio* by saying,

> I came back from that holiest of waves
>
> remade, refreshed as any new tree is,
>
> renewed, refreshed with foliage anew,
>
> pure and prepared to rise towards the stars.

(*Purg.* 33.142–45)

Conclusions: Praxis in Mercy and Memory

I wish to add a consideration from practical theology by way of conclusion. Like the rest of this essay, it concerns speaking, remembering, and mercy. Because I read Dante not only as a theologian, pilgrim, and sinner, but also as an ordained priest, I find that Dante shows forth one particular moment that I wish all the world could come and witness, but the nature of the moment necessarily forbids. It is that moment in the act of sacramental confession when a sinner has recalled that which hurts or has hurt not in order to dwell in details of any sin, but that the shame of sin might be erased. And drinking the mercy of a dispensation given by Christ, a Church promises pardon and peace through the prayer of a minister. In that moment, a movement between two rivers, in a fleeting encounter that is often only of speaking and not of sight, a holy freedom transpires. In speaking truth, one becomes True again. In Christ, one's loves are once again aright, never condemned but set free to gain their noble purpose. The waters of forgetting and the waters of good things gush over the penitent in the form of mercy. And it is very often there, in that quiet instant of freedom and truth, that I wish the world could start to comprehend the good which God has fixed in humans, and sets again free if they will not clench it bound.

Such a moment might require a journey through hell and a hike up the Mount of Purgatory, but I do wonder what would happen if a contemporary reader might accompany Dante not merely literarily but also spiritually on this most marvelous adventure. The top of the Mount of Purgatory gives a vantage and a perspective on why one might bother at all. For the newness, the mercy, Dante found there was not in spite of his faults but right through them. Without words, the poet learned again the Word. Having chosen falsehood, he learned himself to be true. And earthly loves that had become leopard, lion, and wolf dissolved as forgotten misunderstandings of a love that is real and true. The tree that became humanity's downfall was also its only hope. Dante forces the reader, from this mountain, to consider what he or she would have to leave behind, and one's truest self they would need remember in order to be prepared to journey higher unto the stars.

4

Dante: Knowing Oneself, Knowing God

Christian Moevs

The phrase "knowing oneself, knowing God" is an echo of Saint Augustine's famous "perfect prayer": *Deus semper idem, noverim me, noverim te* ("O God, always one and the same, grant that I may know myself, grant that I may know You").[1] The key to Augustine's prayer is that each clause depends on the one preceding it: one comes to know God only through truly knowing oneself, or rather through knowing one's true self, and one comes to such true self-knowledge only through divine grace, through a self-giving or self-revealing of the divine. In light of the recent Year of Mercy, we could call divine grace divine mercy. To know oneself is to know God, because a human being is a form of divine self-giving, of divine self-revelation. One can know oneself only by awakening or surrendering to that self-giving of God.

In the Christian tradition, as in all the great spiritual traditions of the world, the journey to God is a journey into the self, a search for the source or being or ground of the finite self, of the finite ego or thinking mind, a search that leads the mind into stillness, into unlimited consciousness and love. It is to come to know oneself as, or as not other than, consciousness-being-awareness-love, revealed as the ontological foundation of all reality, of all possible experience. The divine cannot be sought outside oneself, as an external reality, because we ourselves embody or are what we seek: we have

1. *Soliloquies* 2.1.1.

65

no being apart from it. Through us, at least potentially, pure consciousness and love, the ground of all reality, is made manifest in or as the world. All true spiritual life is a journey of self-inquiry, of coming to know what one truly is or was made to be.

Thus Augustine famously says in the *Confessions*: "See, You were within and I was in the external world and sought you there."[2] Elsewhere he says, *Noli foras ire, in te ipsum redi* ("Do not go out, return into yourself").[3] This message is at the heart of the Vedic/Upanishadic tradition, too, reiterated consistently by those who have had direct experience of God. A poem attributed to the great Sufi / Hindu poet Kabir says,

> Do not go to the garden of flowers!
>
> O Friend! Go not there;
>
> In your body is the garden of flowers.
>
> Take your seat on the thousand petals
>
> of the lotus, and there gaze on the
>
> Infinite Beauty.[4]

It should not be surprising, then, that for Dante too the journey toward God is a journey into the self, toward the source from which the finite mind or ego arises. There are a number of ways to trace this trajectory in the *Comedy*. One of them is through Dante's play on the word *pome* (*pomo*), which means "apple" or "fruit."

In the *Convivio*, Dante represents the journey of life as a quest moved by desire, a search for fulfillment or satiety that nothing in the world can fulfill. The first movement of human desire, the first effort to find peace in an object of the world, is emblematically a child's desire for a *pome*, an apple. So, like Adam, the human soul begins to seek fulfillment in finite objects of desire, in the garden of the world, desiring then a bird, and then a dress, and then a horse, and then sex (a woman), and then riches, and then more riches, without end, and in the process alienating itself ever more from itself and from its innate or true goal:

> The highest desire in every being, and the first implanted in it
> by nature, is the desire to return to its first cause. Since, further,
> God is the first cause of our souls, and creates them in His own
> likeness, the soul desires first and foremost to return to Him.

2. *Confessions* 10.27.38.

3. *Of True Religion*, 72.

4. Tagore, *Songs of Kabir*, 47 [1.58].

And just as a pilgrim travelling along a road on which he has never before set foot believes every house he sees is the hostel, and, when he finds that it is not, transfers this belief onto the next house, and the next, and the next, until he does come to the hostel, so with our soul. As soon as it starts out along the new, quite untraveled road of this life, the soul is always on the lookout for its ultimate goal, the highest good; and so whenever it sees anything in which some good appears, it thinks that it is the highest good. Since its judgment is at first imperfect, being as yet unschooled either by experience or by instruction, goods of little value seem to it to be of great value, and so it first begins to desire by setting its heart on them. So we see small children desiring above all else an apple; then, when they are somewhat older, desiring a little bird; then, still later, desiring fine clothes; then a horse; then a woman; then riches in small measure; then riches in large measure; then even more riches. This happens because people find in none of these things what they are actually seeking, and think they will find it a little way on. . . . The person who takes the right path reaches his goal and finds rest; the person who makes an error never reaches his goal: his mind wears itself out with effort as he fixes his greedy eyes unceasingly on what lies ahead.[5]

The *Comedy* picks up the *pome* imagery, representing the pilgrim's quest as a search for sweet fruit or apples. In *Inferno* 16, the pilgrim explains to a denizen of Hell that Vergil is leading him toward sweet fruit: *Lascio lo fele e vo per dolci pomi / promessi a me per lo verace duca* ("I leave bitterness behind, and go toward the sweet fruits / promised me by my truthful leader" [61–62]).[6] When he reaches the curtain of fire that surrounds the Earthly Paradise, the pilgrim balks, and refuses to cross through the fire. Virgil tries to reason with him, telling him that the fire will not actually burn him, but Dante obstinately resists, until Virgil tells him that Beatrice is on the other side of the fire. All his resistance instantly undone, the pilgrim turns willingly to follow Virgil, ready to plunge into the fire in order to cross over into Eden. He has been won over by Beatrice's name, and Virgil smiles at him as one does to a child won over by an apple (*come al fanciul si fa chè vinto al pome* [*Purg.* 27.45]). Adam lost Eden by seeking an apple outside himself on the branches of a tree; Dante regains Eden, and union with Beatrice, by seeking an apple—the sweetness, nourishment, beauty, infinity, fulfillment, peace—denoted for him by Beatrice's name, the name *che sempre ne*

5. Dante, *Convivio*, 153–54.
6. All translations from Dante's *Comedy* are the author's own.

la mente mi rampolla, that constantly springs up in his mind (41–42), as the name or image of the true goal of his soul's desire.

Once in Eden, on the threshold of coming face to face with Beatrice, Virgil tells Dante,

> *Quel dolce pome che per tanti rami*
>
> *cercando va la cura de' mortali,*
>
> *oggi porrà in pace le tue fami.*

> That sweet fruit which mortals with so much effort
>
> go seeking on so many different branches
>
> shall today bring peace to all your cravings.

(*Purg.* 27.115–17)

We seek peace, fulfillment, ultimate joy, freedom, infinity in all kinds of things in the world, projecting onto them our heart's desire, but no finite ephemeral thing can deliver what we seek. What we seek is an all-encompassing reality, the infinite freedom, consciousness, being, love that spawns and gives being to all things, and is limited by nothing. It is a reality that manifests itself in or as the world—for Dante, as Beatrice in particular—but it is not of the world. If we awaken or surrender to the truth of our own being, we will know ourselves as manifestations, as embodiments of that reality.

The *pome* motif culminates in *Paradiso* 26, when the pilgrim comes face to face with our archetypal progenitor, Adam. The pilgrim is near the end of his journey and he has just undergone the examination or rather celebration, public manifestation, and praise of the theological virtues now perfected in himself. This is the fruition in him of faith, hope, and love. The theological virtues are transcendent, supernatural virtues: they come from the divine through grace through mercy and orient us to, conform us to, our divine or supernatural end. They are the foundation of, and prepare us for, the beatific vision, the vision of God. As soon as the final "examination" (on love) ends, the pilgrim hears the Sanctus ("Holy, holy, holy . . .") and Adam appears in front of him. How does the pilgrim address Adam? "*O pomo che maturo / solo prodotto fosti . . .*" ("O apple [fruit] who alone / were brought forth ripe . . ." [*Par.* 26.91–92]). Adam is himself the fruit that he sought outside himself as if it were other than himself.

Adam was himself the fruit of the garden of the world, and he thought it was out there in the world, something to seek through the senses, to devour. That is to have lost sight of our true nature, the truth of what we are; it is to be existentially alienated from ourselves. To seek to devour the world through the senses is to lose Eden, or rather, it is to turn the garden of the world into a harsh desert, a place of exile, of ceaseless fruitless striving and frustration and depression: it is like drowning in a dangerous sea, losing one's way in a wild black forest. Which is of course where the pilgrim's journey begins.[7]

Adam makes the dynamic of his self-alienation his Edenic expulsion explicit when he answers the pilgrim's unexpressed question about Adam's past offense. Adam answers,

> *Or, figliuol mio, non il gustar del legno*
>
> *fu per sé la cagion di tanto essilio,*
>
> *ma solamente il trapassar del segno.*

> Now, my son, the tasting of the tree [wood]
>
> was not in itself what caused the great exile
>
> but only the trespassing of the sign [boundary].

(*Par.* 26.115–117)

Il trapassar del segno has a double sense: it means not only trespassing a boundary, a limit, but also violating, transgressing, a sign. The two are one. Through an eclipse of self-knowledge, of consciousness and love in himself, Adam disfigured himself as a sign or signifier of the divine. He did that by going beyond the limit: by fruitlessly seeking more from the senses, from the world, than they can provide. It is like trying to unveil the secret of existence, to encompass infinity, by eating an apple.

Finite things cannot satiate the human instinct for infinity, no matter how much of the world one tries to devour through the senses, how much one tries to expand one's ego or sense of self in space and time. Nor can the world, or science, or explanations, provide a resolution to the mystery of life. As the great philosopher Ludwig Wittgenstein remarked:

> The solution of the riddle of life in space and time lies *outside* space and time.

> (It is certainly not the solution of any problems of natural science that is required.)

---

7. See *Inferno* 1.1–27.

> The facts all contribute only to setting the problem, not to its solution.
>
> It is not *how* things are in the world that is mystical, but *that* it exists.[8]

Seeking the resolution of the mystery of life, ultimate understanding and peace and fulfillment from the world of the senses is to bite into bitter wood (*legno*), not a sweet apple. This is the nature of all human seeking that is born from pride, that is, from the illusion of being an autonomous, self-sufficient thing, simply a finite self or mind or ego.

Those familiar with the *Comedy* may recognize in Adam's reference to *legno* and *trapassar del segno* an evocation of Ulysses' "mad flight" in *Inferno* 26 (a canto parallel to *Paradiso* 26). Ulysses sought to plumb the mystery of life (*divenir del mondo esperto / e de li vizi umani e del valore . . . seguir virtute e canoscenza* ["to become expert of the world / and of human vices and worth," "follow virtue and knowledge"]) by exploring what he could of the unknown world in the few days left to his senses, to his physical life (*d'i nostri sensi ch'è del rimanente, / non vogliate negar l'esperienza, / di retro al sol, del mondo sanza gente* ["do not deny to our senses, in the little time left them, the experience, following the sun, of the world without people"]). So he set out alone in a *legno*, a (wood) ship, with a few companions he had seduced into following him, and sailed out beyond the limit-sign that is the Pillars of Hercules (*dov'Ercule segnò li suoi riguardi / acciò che l'uom più oltre non si metta* [where Hercules signed/marked the limit / so that men would not go further]) into the open ocean, where he shipwrecks in a divinely-ordained whirlwind (*Inf.* 26.90–142).

Ulysses seeks to understand the mystery of life by doing a little more exploring, experimenting, explaining, out in the world in the few days left to his senses. In the meantime, he is oblivious to himself as embodying, as being, the very mystery he seeks to fathom. Wittgenstein condemned the shallow understanding that is so often behind the modern "scientific mentality," "our disgusting soapy-water science,"[9] because it is essentially Ulyssean, it loses the mystery and profundity of existence itself:

> The whole modern conception of the world is founded on the illusion that the so-called laws of nature are the explanations of natural phenomena.

---

8. Wittgenstein, *Tractatus*, 6.4312, 6.4321, 6.44 (pp. 72–73).
9. Wittgenstein and Winch, *Culture and Value*, 49.

Thus people today stop at the laws of nature, treating them as something inviolable, just as God and Fate were treated in past ages.

And in fact both are right and both wrong: though the view of the ancients is clearer in so far as they have a clear and acknowledged terminus, while the modern system tries to make it look as if *everything* were explained.[10]

For Dante and his world, of course, the ultimate answer to the *legno*, to the bitter wood of insatiable hunger, to Ulysses' doomed, solitary wood ship of exploration, is the *legno* (the wood) of the cross, of Christ, of self-sacrifice and surrender. It is to surrender the illusion of the autonomous, finite, self-subsistent "I." Or rather, it is to discover what has been called "the infinite depth of the 'I.'"[11] It is to find out and experience what our "I" ultimately refers to, which is to know for ourselves what Christ's "I" refers to, which is to know Christ, instead of simply knowing about Christ. When Christ says, "I am the way, the truth, and the life" (John 14:6), what does that "I" refer to? We need to find out. We can only find out by knowing the ultimate referent of our own "I." Christ fully knew who he was; we have yet to find out.

Dante's Adam evokes this dynamic, too. He tells Dante that at first he called the *sommo bene*, the supreme good, "*I*"; later God's name became "*El.*" In Italian, this is to go from calling God "I," to calling him "He."[12] It is to go from experiencing God as "I," the "I" of one's own "I," as the ground and substance of one's own being, to conceiving God as other, as alien. For Dante, the ground of all reality is conscious being, self-awareness: it is that self-subsistent infinite power that manifests itself in space-time as conscious beings, and that ultimately says "I" in or through every creature, mortal or angelic, that can say "I."[13] The creature whose "I" refers only to a finite set of thoughts and desires and memories, to a finite ego, to a mortal body, has alienated itself from God, from itself. To be limited by a finite sense of self, to presume that one has any autonomous being apart from the divine, is pride, the ground of all sin, ignorance, and disharmony.

The fundamental point we have been making can also be expressed through the language of sacrament, in particular, the Eucharist.[14] It is no

---

10. Wittgenstein, *Tractatus*, 6.371, 6.372 (p. 70).

11. Tolle, *A New Earth*, 28.

12. In these very lines, Adam refers to himself as "I": *Pria ch'i' scendessi a l'infernale ambasica, / I s'appellava in terra il sommo bene . . .* ("Before I descended to the infernal torment, / the supreme good was known on earth as *I . . .*" [*Par.* 26.133–34]).

13. See *Paradiso* 29.13–18, 142–45.

14. Little, "'The Sacramental Poetics of Dante's Commedia."

coincidence that the great "examinations" on the theological virtues that absorb Dante into the "brotherhood elected to the great banquet / of the blessed Lamb" (*sodalizio eletto a la gran cena / del benedetto Agnello* [*Par.* 24.1–2]) as a "manifest Christian" (52) culminate in the Sanctus. As we noted, the Sanctus is then followed immediately by the appearance of Adam. In the canon of the Mass, the Sanctus introduces the sacrament of the Eucharist, the banquet of the Lamb. Adam, in his created and redeemed state, can thus be understood as himself the Eucharist, the ultimate sign or sacrament. A sacrament is a stable sign, redeemed from the flux of death and change, because it is a sign that participates in, that enacts, the reality it denotes. Simply put, it is what it signifies. As created by God, a human being is a sacrament (indeed, to one who is awake to the divine, the entire world is a sacrament). In a created (and redeemed) Adam, as in Christ, the new Adam, it is pure awareness or being or love that says "I," both denoting the divine and embodying it. The "I" of a perfected human being knows it has no reality apart from, other than, the infinite self-subsistent "I" or conscious act of being that is the ground of all reality. In fulfilling the truth and potential of our nature, in awakening to what we are and were made to be, we ourselves become the Eucharist: we both signify, and share in, the life of God. Our entire being, and our language, become praise, an expression of divine freedom and love, as in fact they do in the "examination" cantos (*Par.* 24–26). It is then God, Christ, who lives and acts and speaks through us: our lives and our speech become revelatory, they re-reveal revelation. To put it in very simple Christian terms: we come to fully know ourselves as created, with no being apart from the Creator.

Part of the power of the *Comedy* (and of medieval thought), is that it grounds this understanding of the human not only in theology, but also in philosophy and in natural science, integrating all the disciplines in one coherent, all-encompassing vision of reality. In *The Metaphysics of Dante's Comedy*, I traced the philosophical/cosmological understanding that underlies the poem, and that generates the full meaning of Dante's fictive journey. It may be worth summarizing a few key points here, to show how the axiom that knowledge of self is knowledge of God is anchored in the very structure of the cosmos, and thus of Dante's journey through it.

Dante's medieval world picture was essentially Aristotelian, with some Ptolemaic and Christian refinements. The earth was a stationary sphere at the center, the theatre of the changing flux and transformations of the four elements: earth, water, air, and fire. Those transformations were governed by the nine heavenly spheres that rotated around the earth, each made of transparent unchanging ether; all the visible heavenly bodies, also made of ether, were embedded in these. One of the sharpest observations of Aristotle concerned "what lay outside" this cosmos; in other words, "where" or "in what" the entire cosmos could be said to exist. Aristotle saw clearly what should be obvious (and usually is not): anything that existed "outside" the universe would by definition (as a thing) be part of the universe, and would not answer any question about "where" or "in what" the universe existed. He thus dispensed with all the pre-Socratic notions about "what" the entire universe was ultimately "made of," or "where it was." For Aristotle, there could be literally nothing—no space, vacuum, essence, element, anything— "outside" the universe. The only reality that could in any sense be said to be "outside" the universe, and ontologically ground it, was consciousness (*nous*), because consciousness is nothing; it is a power to be everything and nothing. Consciousness is a power of awareness that perceives and is all things, but is nothing in itself. *Nous*, said Aristotle, is nothing until it thinks, and when it thinks, it is what it thinks. That is the being of the world. In this deep sense, the world is not "made of" anything, although it is absolutely, immediately, "real." It is a projection within consciousness, which is pure self-subsistent active being, and it has no existence apart from consciousness.

For Aristotle, then, *nous* was divinity, the ultimate ontological principle, grounding all perception, all reality, all being. Aristotle underlined that consciousness is a reflexive principle: it is aware of itself, of its own existence. Awareness is self-awareness. It is not a stretch to connect Aristotle's profound insight with what the Lord told Moses when Moses asked, "Who shall I say sent me?" and God answered, "Tell them: 'I AM sent me to you'" (Exod 3:14). That I AM, the revelation/experience of pure awareness or being as the very foundation of all reality, is the ultimate ground and source of all authority. It is God. In fact, Aristotle's understanding became the foundation of medieval Christian thought.

Note that explanation, for Aristotle and the medieval world, was less a question of one event causing another than of coming to deeper ontological principles: what constitutes the being of something, what does it consist in? Aquinas observes, for example, that it makes very little difference for the concept of creation whether the world always existed or whether it had some starting point, before which it did not exist. What counts is that the entire visible universe is dependent, at every instant of its being, on pure Intellect (consciousness), which is pure Act or Esse (*to be*): that is, on God. In other words, if you removed consciousness, the entire universe would instantly vanish. That is what it means to say that the universe is created. It is radically contingent. At every instant that it exists it is dependent on and a manifestation of consciousness, which is love (the power to give itself to / be all things, and know them as itself), which is the act *to be*. To awaken to the world as created is to awaken to all of reality—and one's own finite self—as a gift, an ever-new self-giving, at every moment it exists. The universe is intensely present, alive, continuous with our own reality, something God "is doing" instant to instant. It is not, to quote Augustine again, a house God built and left standing.[15]

The Christians adopted Aristotle's picture of the cosmos, but "outside" the cosmos, where Aristotle had put *nous*, they put the Empyrean. Among many theologians, the Empyrean became a messy notion, contaminating Aristotle's crystalline understanding with various shades of materiality and attribute. But Dante's Empyrean, the reality that "contains"/gives being to his cosmos, is rigorous: he identifies it precisely with what Aristotle had put there, pure conscious being or God, the "divine mind." So Dante's Empyrean is perfectly immaterial, uncreated, and out of space and time. It is pure intellectual light, the light of perfect reflexive self-awareness, which is perfect love, the power to be and give itself to and know itself as everything that exists, which is perfect joy or bliss (*Par.* 30.38–42). The manifest universe is "girdled" with intellectual light and love; it has no "where" except the divine mind, which is love and the power to form/generate all things. No one can understand that "girdling," how the universe springs from divine consciousness and love, except one who himself girdles it; it is not a question of explanations and concepts (*Par.* 27.106–14). Note that for Dante pure consciousness *is* perfect love, a power to experience itself as other, to give itself voluntarily to finite experience. The world comes into being when consciousness or being sacrifices its freedom and infinity to become finite experience, while of course always remaining itself. Thus love is not an emotion, although it can trigger intense emotion. It is to recognize, experience, the other as oneself. To the extent that one experiences oneself as pure awareness or being, as the principle that gives being to all things, to that extent one experiences all things as oneself. This perfect love is perfect joy, infinite sweetness, a surrender of the finite self into unlimited being.

Just after meeting Adam, in *Paradiso* 27–29, the pilgrim comes to understand the nature of finite reality, and of the world as created. In *Paradiso* 27, Dante addresses the concept of time; in *Paradiso* 28, the concept of space, and in *Paradiso* 29, "how" the manifest spatio-temporal world arises from consciousness or love. Once all that is clear, he finds himself in the Empyrean (in *Paradiso* 30), in a sense encompassing the world, containing it, knowing it as himself.

15. Augustine, *De Genesi ad litteram* 4.12; see Aquinas, *Summa Contra Gentiles* 3.65.9.

How does the world arise from conscious being? As Aristotle understood, there can be no how, in the sense of events or things. Any account of creation that mentions events and things is not an account of creation, but a description of the world. That is why Aristotle said that consciousness is nothing until it thinks, and when it thinks, it is what it thinks. The closest analogy would be how an intelligence generates (and sometimes inhabits) a dream world. No how or where applies.

Then what do time and space consist in? Nothing. The fundamental Aristotelian point, echoed by Beatrice in the *Paradiso*[16] is that there is no intrinsic ultimate unit of either time or space; both are infinitely divisible and continuous. There are no fundamental "building blocks" of either, nothing they consist in. There is nothing the spatio-temporal world is "made of." We may think the world is made of "matter," but Aristotle saw with perfect clarity that any attempt to define matter simply describes a form that "matter" has assumed. Aristotle concluded that matter in itself is nothing, non-existence, simply a principle of continuity in change. Beatrice compares "how" time and space arise (from conscious being) to how mathematics springs from the number one. The number one, by giving rise to the concept of number, contains or generates all of mathematics, already contained in germ within the concept of number itself. Mathematics adds nothing to the number one, but unfolds its implications. In the same way, the world adds nothing to consciousness,[17] but manifests its infinite power or actuality. Space-time is contained within the I AM of consciousness as mathematics is contained in the number one.

In *Paradiso* 28, the pilgrim's attention is absorbed by a burning infinitesimal point of light, and he turns to focus on it directly (*Par.* 28.1–21). Turning is a key image in the Neoplatonic tradition: contemplation is to turn one's attention away from the external world, to focus one's sight or mind within on itself, in a burning point of concentration. This is the essence of meditation or true contemplative prayer, turning the mind's attention on itself, in a dimensionless point of awareness, focused in self-inquiry: "Who am I?" Thus the mind is drawn back to its source in consciousness: love itself, the ultimate ontological ground, of which the finite mind is simply a reflected ray in space and time. Saint Bonaventure, for example, speaks of bringing the mind to a supreme peak or point of love or awareness, focusing

---

16. *Paradiso* 27.115–20, 28.22–39; see my *Metaphysics*, 132–46.

17. Meister Eckhart: "If I had the whole world and God, I should have no more than if I had God alone" (German Sermon 4, in *Meister Eckhart, Teacher and Preacher*, 250).

it in a single point, so that it enters itself, ultimately to pass over through that point into pure Being, "totally transferred and transformed into God."[18]

The burning dimensionless point the pilgrim sees in *Paradiso* 28 spawns a series of nine concentric rings of fire around itself, spinning faster the closer they are to the point. These are the nine orders of angelic intelligences, each corresponding to, and governing, one of the nine concentric spheres of the cosmos. Beatrice's first words about the point are a direct quotation from Aristotle. She says, *Da quel punto / depende il cielo e tutta la natura* ("From that point / depend the heavens and all of nature" [*Par.* 28.37–38]). Beatrice is quoting Aristotle's *Metaphysics*, where Aristotle says that *nous*, the reflexivity of consciousness or self-awareness, is the ultimate ontological principle: "From such a principle depend the heavens and the world of nature."[19] The cosmos depends on the burning point of pure self-awareness, the I AM or pure consciousness that grounds all of reality. There is no "how" to that dependence: space-time, and finite intelligences, are a reflected image or projection of that conscious ground, and have no being apart from it, as a light projects a reflected ring about itself onto mist (*Par.* 28.22–27).

The pilgrim muses that the closer the angelic intelligences, spinning around the point, are to the point that is their source, the brighter they are, perhaps because they more "entrue" themselves in that point (*più di lei s'invera* [*Par.* 28.37–39]). The more a finite intellect enters into itself, the more that it knows itself a dimensionless burning point of pure consciousness, the more it is assimilated to God, to the ground of all reality. Beatrice tells Dante that at this stage in his journey he is in the smallest ring of fire, closest to the point. In the poem's narrative, he has reached the Primum Mobile, the largest and limit sphere of the manifest universe, on the threshold of the Empyrean. The largest sphere, closest to the Empyrean, corresponds to the smallest ring, closest to the point. The point and rings are an inverted image of the cosmos and Empyrean. All of a sudden we realize that we can conceive Dante's journey to God in two equivalent, but opposite ways: (1) We can conceive it as traveling from the Earth, at the center of the manifest universe, through the heavenly spheres, ultimately to pass beyond the limit of the world into the Empyrean. This is to grow in love and understanding, to encompass or experience more and more of the universe as oneself, until one knows oneself as the pure being or consciousness or love that is and contains all things. (2) We can also conceive it as a journey inside oneself, focusing one's awareness on itself through the inquiry, "Who am I?" The

18. Bonaventure, *Itinerarium Mentis in Deum*, 1.2, 1.4, chs. 5–7, 7.4.

19. Aristotle, *Metaphysics*, 12.7 [1072b14].

inquiry leads one ever deeper toward the source of all thought and desire and experience, to the self-subsistent reality from which the mind, and all possible experience, arises. It is to experience oneself as the pure consciousness or love that spawns or generates all things. Turning at the opening of *Paradiso* 28, Dante has shifted from the one perspective to the other. In the projected (reflected) image of our normal experience, the world is at the center, and God at the periphery; after turning (to see as Beatrice does), the pilgrim experiences consciousness or God at the center (within himself), and the world of the senses as a radiated or reflected projection from that source. Among other effects, this shift shakes the frame of reference, the sense of the world as an inert given, and of oneself as an autonomous object in that world.

We have seen that for Dante, theology, philosophy, and science or cosmology are all integrated in one coherent all-encompassing vision of reality. For Dante, it makes sense at every level to say that truly to know oneself is to know God (and all of reality). Is such an integration impossible for us? Can our "scientific" understanding of the cosmos be reconciled with the "spiritual" understanding of reality—and of the human in particular—that underlies the Catholic faith? Since the science under the "spiritual" understanding is largely built on Aristotle, we are asking whether modern science may eventually lead us to think that Aristotle was fundamentally right.

We might offer just a few reflections. We mentioned that Aristotle understood that no naive notion of matter can sustain analysis: any attempt to define what it is simply describes a form it has assumed. Therefore, said Aristotle, it is nothing in itself: matter has no being apart from the principle of form, which is consciousness (hence the medieval axiom: *Forma dat esse materiae* [Form gives being to matter]). Materialism requires some kind of self-subsistent matter, some ultimate building blocks to make the universe out of. For millennia, these were atoms. Atoms have not done well recently: subparticles proliferate, along with anti-particles, and particles can be transmuted into each other, or described as waves and forces, or converted into energy. In fact it turns out that all matter/manifestation is convertible with nothing. As the physicist Heinz Pagels puts it, "Everything that ever existed or can exist is already potentially there in the nothingness of space."[20] The Canadian physicist Mir Faizal has observed that, properly understood, the cosmos came into being from nothing and remains nothing: "Something did not come from nothing. The universe is still nothing, it's just more

20. Pagels, *Cosmic Code*, 244.

elegantly ordered nothing." Any physics of space and time, he says, is simply an approximation to a purely mathematical theory.[21]

What science has not probed is the convertibility or relation between matter-energy-vacuum and consciousness. That is inevitable: science will never probe it. That is because, as Aristotle saw, consciousness is nothing (it is "outside" the cosmos), and by definition science can only talk about things, the cosmos. As Ludwig Wittgenstein observed, the visual field, what is seen, does not include the eye itself. The ultimate subject of experience, what is doing the experiencing (consciousness itself) alone is absent from every description of experience. Nothing can be said about that subject, because it is nothing: the "metaphysical subject" lies "outside" the world.[22] But science has discovered that at a quantum level, one cannot leave consciousness out, because every description of reality is in part determined by the act of observation itself. We may be close to realizing, on scientific grounds, that there is no such thing as "the world in itself" autonomous from consciousness.

That in fact was the conclusion of the chief architects of quantum mechanics. Heisenberg said the smallest units of matter are not physical objects, but "forms, structures, or—in Plato's sense—Ideas, which can be unambiguously spoken of only in the language of mathematics."[23] The principle of being, for Aristotle, was in fact form, not matter. Schrödinger maintained that mind and world coincide: "Subject and object are only one."[24] That is what Aristotle said: consciousness is what it thinks. Max Planck said that the true "I," the "I-awareness" (the true ultimate subject of experience) is entirely independent of all natural causality, and he calls it "one single point in the immeasurable world of mind and matter."[25] That is Dante's image, for what Aristotle said alone lay "outside" the world.

Also relevant is nonlocality, the fact that two entangled phenomena separated by distance can affect each other simultaneously, a consequence of quantum mechanics recently conclusively confirmed at Delft. Locality, position, distance, are in some sense illusory, which suggests that reality is ultimately one, and ultimately dimensionless, as in a point of consciousness, or the parts of a dream world, of a world projected in consciousness.

This is the truth that Dante portrays himself as awakening to, and that he seeks to awaken in us. Consciousness—love itself—is the omnipresent,

21. Baldwin, "Historic Discovery."
22. Wittgenstein, *Tractatus*, 5.631–5.6331 (p. 57).
23. Heisenberg and Heath, *Across the Frontiers*, 116.
24. Schrödinger, *Mind and Matter*, 51–52.
25. Planck, "Where Is Science Going?," 114–15, 118.

indivisible, dimensionless reality in which the world consists. But consciousness is completely free, unbound by time, space, motion, death. It is a dimensionless point; it is an all-encompassing reality. It is each thing, and it is nothing. It is infinite power, infinite love, infinite being, infinite bliss, infinite self-giving. It is a blade of grass, a particle of dust, a human being, an angel. To know oneself as (not other than) that reality is to achieve the goal of the *Comedy*, what medieval theologians called union with God, or *deificatio*, deification.

But how can that revelation, that awakening, dawn? Not through philosophical or scientific explanations, though they have a role. Not through essays, though they too might have a role. Not by simply reading the *Comedy*, or even the Bible. The almanac predicts rain, but none may be had by wringing its pages.

A Catholic could answer: by partaking of the sacraments, the Eucharist, through which we are what we see, receive what we are (to quote Augustine again).[26] We can do no more than prepare for the Eucharist, as in Lent, the liturgical season preceding the dawn of Easter. Because this ultimate awakening or understanding is not something we can do for ourselves. We can only prepare the way, make straight the way of the Lord. Empty ourselves like Mary, so that Christ may be born in us. We can seek to purify ourselves, to repent, to surrender ourselves, to sacrifice our finite attachments and desires, to forgive radically and unconditionally, to bear all joy and sorrow with stillness and equanimity, to treat everyone and everything with equal love, to do all our work as an offering, seeking no reward from it, to serve all anonymously and joyously, with no expectation of outcome or acknowledgment. We can seek to burn with love and longing for the unveiling of that reality, to love God, love, beauty, truth, infinity, more than we love the world, more than we love our finite selves, more than we love our mortal bodies. We can seek to constantly bring the mind back to its source, to still it in the infinite ocean from which it arises, with the persistent focused self-inquiry, "Who am I?" In doing all this, we are simply conforming ourselves to the truth of how things are, to the true nature of reality.

The pilgrim Dante does all this, in one form or another. But ultimately of course, to do all this what is required is the radical—even if gradual—surrender of what thinks it is doing all this, the sacrifice of the very sense of finite agent or self, our sense of being an autonomous doer. The ego is the illusion that blocks the truth, blocks revelation. Only the higher nature in us, the divine in us, can effect that surrender, can take over, subsume, our own sense of self, or even fully control the lower self and its impulses, the

26. Augustine, "Sermon 272."

mind and body and emotions. Only the higher nature can kill the illusion of an autonomous, self-sufficient, finite self, kill our pride or ego. That is why we need to constantly turn back in love, in gratitude, in longing, in praise, toward that higher nature, toward the infinite divine mercy, praying with Saint Augustine,

Deus semper idem, noverim me, noverim te.

PART 2

Transformations

5

Beginning Midway

Dante's Midlife, and Ours

Matthew Treherne

Nel mezzo del cammin di nostra vita
mi ritrovai per una selva oscura,
ché la diritta via era smarrita.

(*Inf.* 1.1–3)

The *Commedia* begins, without preamble, right in the middle of things, *nel mezzo del cammin di nostra vita*. The simplicity of these lines masks the precision with which the moment of the narrative is being situated in time: the pilgrim is halfway through his three score years and ten; the year, therefore, is 1300; the great disaster of Dante's life, his exile from Florence, is yet to befall him. And the fact that the pilgrim's journey is situated so precisely in time will be crucial to much of the poem's narrative: the prophecies of Dante's exile depend on it, as does the anticipation in *Inferno* 19 of the arrival in hell of Pope Boniface VIII, which corresponds to the space held in heaven for the soul of Emperor Henry VII (*Par.* 30.136–38), both still living in 1300.

But the poem is, of course, also presented as a universal journey, taking place not only midway through Dante's life, but midway through our life, *nostra vita*. In important respects, the year 1300 matters not only to Dante but also, as a Holy Year, to his entire Christian community, with pardon for the sins of those who traveled in penitence to the basilicas of Peter and Paul in Rome.[1] Beyond the significance of the Holy Year, the universal call of the *Commedia*'s opening line—*nostra vita*—invites a set of questions about the condition which is evoked. What is it about being midway through life's journey that makes a particular starting point? Is the timing of this moment, midway through Dante's life, at the age of thirty-five, merely accidental? Or is there an important point being made here about being caught up in the middle of things, embroiled in life? And if so, how might the *Commedia* help us reflect on this condition—as one which can be a bewildering dark wood of despair, but which can also be the ground on which a redemptive journey begins?

Prior to writing the *Commedia*, Dante had offered an account of midlife in book 4 of the *Convivio*, where he discusses nobility. Like the opening line of the *Commedia*, the *Convivio* takes the biblical lifespan of three score years and ten, with the midpoint of thirty-five serving as the pinnacle of the period Dante defines as *gioventute*—translated by Christopher Ryan as "maturity"—namely, between the ages of twenty-five to forty-five. In each phase of life within those seventy years—maturity, adolescence (until the age of twenty-five), old age (from forty-five to seventy)—the moral virtues are developed, from the virtues of obedience and bodily grace in adolescence, to the supreme virtues of prudence and justice in old age. The midpoint of the normative life marks a high point in physical development:

> Là dove sia lo punto sommo di questo arco, per quella disagua-
> glianza che detta è di sopra, è forte da sapere; ma nelli più, io
> credo, tra il trentesimo e 'l quarantesimo anno; e io credo che nelli
> perfettamente naturati esso ne sia nel trentacinquesimo anno. E
> muovemi questa ragione: che ottimamente naturato fue lo nostro
> salvatore Cristo, lo quale volle morire nel trentaquattresimo anno
> della sua etade; ché non era convenevole la divinitade stare in
> cosa [in] discrescere; né da credere è ch'elli non volesse dimorare
> in questa nostra vita al sommo, poi che stato c'era nel basso stato
> della puerizia (*Convivio*, 4.23).

It is no easy matter to determine where the high point of this arc is situated, granted the inequality just spoken of. My own view is that in most people it occurs somewhere between the ages of thirty and forty. I also believe that in those endowed with a perfect nature it occurs in the thirty-fifth year. My reason for adopting this view is that Christ our Saviour was endowed with a supremely perfect nature, and he chose to die in his

---

1. See Esposito, *Dante e il Giubileo*, for a discussion of the Jubilee year of 1300 and its significance for Dante.

thirty-fourth year, because on the one hand it was not fitting
that his divinity should be present in something that was in
decline, and on the other it really is unthinkable that he should
not have wished to live his life here below to its climax after
experiencing the lowly condition of childhood.

For those endowed with a perfect nature, then, midlife marks a physical
peak, with the later stages of life bringing about the moral peak, and for
those in extreme old age, a preparation for the return to God.

How does this relate to the midlife moment with which the *Commedia*
begins? There are important points in common with the *Convivio* account:
the association of the pilgrim with Christ, who descended into hell at the
same age, reinforces the notion of the pilgrim's journey as an imitation of
Christ. In terms of the biography of the historical Dante, this moment is
indeed a high point in his political career, the point at which he is elected
prior of Florence.

Yet the emphases in describing the midlife condition of the pilgrim
of the *Commedia* are far removed from those of the *Convivio*'s account of
midlife. The pilgrim's vulnerability is stressed. He is not on any natural arc of
physical or moral development, or if he is, this is not drawn to our attention:
indeed, the *Convivio*'s language of the arc of moral development throughout life is very different from the spatial account of the condition here. The
condition of being in the midst of things instead involves straying from the
proper path, finding oneself bewildered in the dark wood.

What is the cause of this bewilderment, of the pilgrim's straying from
the true path? It is not unreasonable to imagine in the lonely, frightened
pilgrim, far from his urban, civic community, the figure of the exiled Dante.
But the precision of the timing of the journey is important here: he is not *yet*
in exile, but he is approaching the peak of his political engagement. Some
other, inner cause must also be imagined. It is as though, at a point in life
when he is riding on the crest of the wave of his success, some undercurrent
is at work which will cause that wave to crash.[2]

Perhaps the ambiguity of the moment is the key here. Even with some
basic information about Dante's life in 1300, readers can bring a range of
interpretations to Dante's dark wood at the midpoint of his life. On the one
hand, the arrangements for his life are about to unravel; the events leading
toward his exile are about to be set in train; he is about to face circumstances
which will mirror closely his situation in the dark wood, wandering far from

2. Leonardo Bruni cites a now-lost letter from Dante in which he claims that the
appointment to Prior was the beginning of his problems (see Bruni, *Della Vita, Studi e
Costumi di Dante*, 211).

home. The dark wood is, then, an *external* crisis. Or, read differently, there is nothing wrong at this moment. He is the man who has everything—or, at least, nothing is wrong; and yet he is in crisis. In this latter view, the crisis is internally driven.

These different interpretations of a crisis *nel mezzo del cammin* resonate with modern stories of midlife crises. For instance, in his moving 2015 memoir, Joseph Luzzi takes Dante's dark wood as a model for bereavement and his search for meaning and solace thereafter. "We will all find ourselves in a dark wood one day," Luzzi explains, and Dante's poem offers a way to find our way out, painful as that might be.[3]

The dark wood can appear in other forms too—where nothing is wrong, where a life is relatively secure and established, commitments formed. David Mamet's 1982 play *Edmond* offers an example. Structurally owing a good deal to Dante's *Commedia*, it shows an Everyman figure (in this case, a white-collar worker in New York) who undertakes a journey through an *Inferno*-like New York underworld before a purgatorial period in prison and something approaching a redemptive experience, or at least acceptance. He is like "Dante without a Virgil to guide him in New York's special *Inferno*."[4] And the provocation for his journey is not some obvious external crisis, but an apparently whimsical unraveling following a prediction from a fortune-teller. Nothing is demonstrably wrong in his comfortable life.

Edmond's "midlife crisis," with no obvious external cause, represents an extreme version of a phenomenon which continues to have a hold on popular imagination. There is still considerable comic value in the midlife crisis, usually involving a desperate, doomed and entertaining (to the observer) attempt by an affluent person to recapture youthful prowess in order to fight the comfort, boredom, and declining powers of middle age. The notion of midlife crisis is not universally accepted among psychologists, but the idea of midlife crisis still has considerable currency in the media and culture, as a period in life that requires a particular reassessing of priorities, where old habits of living and thinking feel like clothes that you once thought suited you but which now feel entirely wrong.

A flurry of media coverage for a study in 2013 in the United Kingdom about what constitutes a midlife crisis in the twenty-first century offers some evidence for the shape of this idea in the modern imagination.[5] Although

---

3. Luzzi, *In a Dark Wood*, 3.

4. Clive Barnes cited in Dean, *David Mamet*, 169.

5. I cite the study not because of its robustness but as an example of how the midlife crisis can be perceived and presented in the popular imagination—and because the forty signs offered present a particularly detailed account of the midlife crisis, see "Top

the "study" is of indeterminate rigor—it was commissioned and publicized by a company which offers hair transplants to balding men, which perhaps gives cause for some suspicion, and I was unable to gain any information about the methodology used—the results are nevertheless interesting as a narrative of the kinds of things associated with this period in life. The forty most commonly identified signs of a midlife crisis include, as expected, attempts to recapture youth or deny the passing of time ("looking up old boyfriends or girlfriends on Facebook"; dying hair; contemplating plastic surgery; "flirting embarrassingly with people twenty years your junior"). There is fear of mortality (fearing phone calls bringing bad news; reading obituaries; looking up medical symptoms online). There is a desire, too, to engage with new cultural forms (taking up a new musical instrument; listening to new music; wanting to read more). But finally, some of the "signs of a midlife crisis" also involve a desire to make deeper commitments to spiritual and social commitments ("start thinking about going to church"; "want to make the world a better place"; start making philanthropic gifts). And, indeed, books continue to be published presenting the midlife years as an ideal moment to discover renewed purpose, with titles such as *It's Not A Midlife Crisis, It's An Opportunity* (2016), or *Changing Lanes: Road Maps to Midlife Renewal* (2008).

In the Middle of Things

We would certainly be doing Dante a disservice if we limited our understanding of the condition of being *nel mezzo del cammin di nostra vita* to men of thirty-five (in the Middle Ages) or to men or women of whatever age that the twenty-first-century midlife crisis is deemed to begin at. For being in the middle of things seems to matter more broadly for Dante. The pilgrim's own journey is one which constantly confronts him with his own past—whether in the form of those he has known, or his failings, or figures that seem to represent a version of himself, such as Ulysses (*Inf.* 26)—and with reminders of his own, exilic future after his journey through the afterlife is completed. The vernacular language in which the *Commedia* is written—which Dante theorizes more explicitly than anyone before him—is itself in a process of constant evolution—changing, as he puts it in *De vulgari eloquentia*—in a manner no more strange than that by which a man grows from youth to maturity.[6] This association of language change with the

---

40 Signs of a Mid-Life Crisis." As noted, I have not been able to obtain details from the media relations company, nor from the funders of the survey, on methodology.

6. *Nec aliter mirum videatur quod dicimus, quam percipere iuvenem exoletum*

changes undergone by human beings is strengthened further in *Paradiso* 26, where Adam emphasizes that human language has always, even in the Garden of Eden, been subject to change (see *Par.* 26.133–38). The vernacular of the text itself is a marker of "midwayness."

In a profound way the entire narrative of the *Commedia* is itself in the midst of a larger journey. The *Commedia* frequently seems to wish to relate the pilgrim's journey to the broad sweep of providential history. Such redemption history inevitably has a difficult temporal status, both unfolding in time, and existing eternally in the mind of God. Even as the narrative moves forward, it enters into typological relationships with other moments in time, relating, as Hollander puts it, "two historical events or things or persons, each of which has a discrete and particular historical reality in time, so that the relationship between them may express spiritual significance."[7] In the *Commedia*, such typological relationships are clear from very early on in the poem, when the pilgrim protests to Virgil that *Io non Enëa, io non Paulo sono* (*Inf.* 2.32) [I am not Aeneas; I am not Paul]: the negative statement is in effect negated by the fact that the pilgrim does undertake a journey through the afterlife, thereby replicating the journeys of Aeneas and St. Paul. The recurrent motifs of earlier journeys and conversion suggest another, fundamental typology in the *Commedia*: with the Exodus narrative. Through the view of history presented in the *Commedia*, in Giuseppe Mazzotta's terms, Dante "shows us how individual lives and history vitally interact and partake in the paradigmatic story of Exodus."[8] The exegetical methods with which the poem appears to demand to be read suggest a figural relationship across different times. Other aspects of the poem also break any strict sense of sequentiality. For instance, the rhyme structure of the poem also disrupts

---

quem exolescere non videmus (*DVE*, 1.9.8) [Nor should what I have just said seem more strange than to see a young man grown to maturity when we have not witnessed his growing].

7. Hollander, *Allegory in Dante*, 59.

8. Mazzotta, *Dante, Poet of the Desert*, 5. See also Barański, "La lezione esegetica," for an account of how *Inferno* I demands to be read as a narrative which also points outwards from a specific moment in time—that of the pilgrim in the Dark Wood—to God's time: "Dante the character can only escape his problems by coming to realize his own place, and their place, within the divine plans" [*Dante-personaggio può solo sfuggire ai suoi problemi apprezzando il proprio e il loro posto negli schemi divini*] (118). This echoes the principles of biblical exegesis, as Barański explains. The allegorical sense of the pilgrim's journey is present in its Christ-like aspects: like Christ, the pilgrim will journey from Hell to Paradise. Its anagogical sense is evident in Virgil's explanation of arriving at the celestial city (*Inf.* 1.112–29); and the moral sense is implicit in the pilgrim's decision to follow Virgil (*Inf.* 1.130–34). Within the terms of its narrative, therefore, multiple times are brought together, within the event of the pilgrim's journey which, Barański argues, is increasingly presented in *Inferno* 1 as a real, historical event.

the linearity of the reading experience, with what Barolini describes as its "continual dialectic between forward motion and backward glance."[9]

The relationship and understanding of the present moment in relation to past and future is important for Dante's presentation of the spiritual condition of the souls in the afterlife. For the souls in hell, an inability to see themselves in the middle of things—in a relationship between future and past—is part of their damnation. As Farinata explains, events in the distant future and past can somehow be seen, but those close or in the present are not.

> "We see like those who suffer from ill light.
>
> We are," he said, "aware of distant things.
>
> Thus far he shines in us, the Lord on high.
>
> But when a thing draws near to us, our minds
>
> go blank. So if not other brings us news,
>
> then nothing of your human state is known to us."
>
> (*Inf.* 10.100–105)

This is the condition of being caught in the middle of things for those in hell: it entirely closes off the possibility of understanding the present moment, and helps gloss the souls' inability to engage reflectively with their sin, the peculiar density of character which marks their self-presentation to the pilgrim. Erich Auerbach described how in these encounters, "We behold an intensified image of the essence of their being, fixed for all eternity in gigantic dimensions, behold it in a purity and distinctness which could never for one moment have been possible during their lives on earth."[10] The present moment for the souls in Hell is strangely divorced from the past and future: distant from them, but with no route from or to them. They inhabit their past habits and personalities, aware of a future moment when the Last Judgment will close the door of the future (*Inf.* 10.107) and therefore their knowledge will be entirely extinguished, and when the return of their earthly bodies will only intensify their degradation (*Inf.* 13.103–8). In this condition of suspension in distance from both past and future, they seemingly have no capacity to review or reflect upon their former selves, or on the reasons for their damnation.

9. Barolini, *The Undivine Comedy*, 101; Freccero, "The Significance of Terza Rima," which describes "the temporal paradox of terza rima forward motion which recapitulates the beginning in the end" (263).

10. Auerbach, *Mimesis*, 192.

This is all the more striking because *Purgatorio* offers an entirely different model for the human person in the condition of being in the midst of journey. Engaged in a process of moral change, traveling on Mount Purgatory, the souls of purgatory proper are constantly reflecting on their past lives in the context of the present moment, and in preparation for their future blessedness. Purgatory is the realm where the condition of being in the midst of things comes to be understood, not as crisis but as a source of renewal.

Community is at the heart of this condition of being midway. Dante's crisis at the opening of the poem is, of course, framed not only in terms of an individual life, but also in terms of other human lives: he finds ourselves in the midst of *nostra vita—our* life—as well as his life. And his journey from the wood depends, of course, on the intervention of, and interaction with, other human persons—Virgil himself, and St. Lucy, Beatrice, and Mary, as we learn in *Inferno* 2. His journey is one of constant interaction with others; and it is a journey away from isolation in the dark wood (although, as the poem makes clear, toward exile). Similarly, the souls in purgatory live and work in community. The souls of the envious, leaning on each other's shoulder in order to provide support as their eyes have been sown shut, offers perhaps the strongest emblem of this condition. And, as we shall see in the next section, liturgy is one of the fundamental ways in which the shared condition of being midway is inhabited and performed by the souls of purgatory.

In the Middle of Things, Liturgically

The fact that the souls in Dante's purgatory are performing liturgy would have been striking and surprising to late medieval readers. Among the considerable surprises of the opening cantos of *Purgatorio*—the geographical siting of purgatory in the southern hemisphere; the presence of Cato, a pagan suicide, as guardian of Mount Purgatory; the very notion of an antepurgatory—we might count the fact that the penitent souls arriving in purgatory, the first the pilgrim and Virgil encounter, are singing a Psalm (*Purg.* 2.46–48). For the idea of the souls in purgatory singing liturgically had been wholly absent from earlier accounts of the afterlife. Indeed, Aquinas had gone so far as to deny explicitly the notion that they prayed at all: they need our prayers on earth, but they do not pray themselves (*non sunt in statu orandi, sed magis ut oretur pro eis* [*ST* IIa 2^{ae} 83 art. 11 resp. 3]).

The involvement of the souls of purgatory in liturgy marks a particular relationship to others, a particular configuration of the condition of being in the midst of our life. In part this is through the shared performance of liturgy, a central exemplification of the involvement of the souls in each other's lives. Thus the souls arriving at the shore of Mount Purgatory sing in unison (*cantavan insieme ad una voce* [*Purg.* 2.47] [they sang this altogether, in one voice]); and the souls on the terrace of wrath sing in unison, and in the same musical mode, producing an effect of utter harmony: *una parola in tutte era e un modo, / sì che parea tra esse ogne concordia* (16.20–21) [the self-same text and tune from all of them, so that, it seemed, at heart they sang as one]. Prayers emphasize the communion of saints—such as the litany of saints at *Purgatorio* 13.49–51.

By recasting individual moments in time in the light of divine providence, medieval liturgical practice connect with understandings of Christ as bringing together the whole of history within himself. These were expressed variously through descriptions of Christ as "the Lord of History" who, in the incarnation, directed all of time toward the plan of salvation, who contained all of time within himself and who, in taking on the condition of being subject to time, cast the light of eternity onto time itself.[11] The breaking of sequential time, the notion that Christ, while entering into time, also drew all of space and time into himself, is often described using the Greek term *kairos*: where *chronos* describes the sequential passage of time, the *kairotic* temporality of Christ rewrites time and, in Frank Kermode's summary, "in a new way fulfills it."[12] The fulfillment of time in Christ, the manner in which the incarnation was believed to represent simultaneously the assumption of time by the eternal God, and the transfiguration of time within the Incarnate Word, was a fundamental expression of the notion of Christ as God-man, in which human nature was joined to the divine in Christ as the means by which fallen humanity might be reconciled with God. It was a key theological underpinning for medieval exegetical methods, which sought typological meanings in Old Testament events, seeing

11. The phrase "Lord of History" [*dispositor saeculorum*] is Odo of Cluny's (*De Vita Sancti Geraldi*, III, 12 [*PL* 133, 698]). For Christ directing time toward himself, see Baldwin of Canterbury: *Tota dispensatio rerum at temporum ejus moderamine ad hunc finem dirigebatur, et in omnibus quae ad hanc causam conducebant delectatus est, auctor ipse omnium* (*De sacramento altaris*, II, 1; 180) [The entire dispensation of things and of times was directed by him toward this end (the providential plan); and he took pleasure in each detail which served this cause, he, the Creator of all things]. On Christ encompassing all of time and casting the light of eternity on time itself, see Gregory the Great, *Moralia in Job* (XXIX, 2): Christ *intra semetipsum temporum discursus claudit* [encloses in himself all the succession of time]; *dum ipse umbras nostrae temporalitatis suscepit, lumen nobis suae aeternitatis infudit* [in taking on the shadows of our temporal condition, he spreads on us the light of his eternity].

12. Kermode, *The Sense of an Ending*, 47.

them as prefiguring while also participating in the incarnation which made sense of them and fulfilled them.

This fundamental understanding of Christ's presence in human time is also embodied in liturgical practice itself. The shaping of time into overlapping cycles, led to a re-presentation of the sequential narrative of the Bible in the temporale, organized around the nativity and crucifixion of Christ in Christmas and Easter. The lectionary shows this clearly: not only in the annual cycle of the temporale, but also within individual services, readings did not follow a single narrative, but presented alongside one another elements from different historical moments. Thus a reading from the Old Testament was given a particular place in the lectionary, not as part of a sequential narrative, but "predominantly for its prophetic and typological value."[13] The importance of the lectionary in liturgy was emphasized in liturgical commentaries: Rupert of Deutz describes the Bible readings as "the most important of all the things that are said in the office of the Mass" [*principale est omnium quae dicuntur ad missae officium*].[14] The structure of the lectionary, this most central aspect of liturgical performance, thus embedded within liturgical cycles the reshaping of history in Christ.

This reshaping of sequential history can also be seen in the ways in which medieval commentators on the liturgy made it clear that the liturgical cycles themselves represented, as if in microcosm, different moments of historical or sequential time. Each liturgical division of the day corresponded to a division of the year: so that the period from Septuagesima to Easter corresponded to night; that from Advent to Christmas corresponded to the dawn; that from the eighth week after Easter to the eighth week after Pentecost corresponded to the daytime; and that from the eighth week after Pentecost to Advent corresponded to evening.[15] In this way, any single moment in the liturgical year was also part of the daily cycle. Liturgy did not therefore *compress* the sequential passage of time, but rather made different elements in sequential time coincide and interact. This relationship of different moments in the liturgical calendar was, according to William Durand's *Rationale*, one of the most widely distributed liturgical commentaries

13. Van Dijk, "The Bible in Liturgical Use," 221.

14. *De divinis officiis*, I, 37; PL 170, 32. See also Remegius of Auxerre's description of the way in which the Mass, by setting the proper context for the Bible through music and penitence, enabled the faithful to receive the Gospel properly when it was read: *post modulationem suavis cantilenae in spiritualibus rebus populus per compunctionem mentis intentus, salutifera Evangelii verba ardenti affectu suscipiat* (*De celebratione missae*, PL 101, 1247) [after the melody of a sweet song and after having had their mind fixed on spiritual matters through repentance, the salvific words of the Gospel will be taken in ardently].

15. Durand, *Rationale*, III:xi.

in the late Middle Ages, further overlaid by a complex set of relationships, derived from the techniques of biblical exegesis. The daily cycle represented in microcosm the fall of mankind and mankind's redemption;[16] but it also figured the life of every individual, with each stage in a person's life being represented by a different liturgical service.[17] Each of those moments in the cycle was related to moments in the biblical narratives. For instance, the Nocturne brought together a participation in the Passover, the birth of Christ, the arrest of Christ, the Last Judgment, and the darkness of the individual soul in sin.[18]

Fully in keeping with this continuity between Christ and liturgical time was the Eucharist, at the heart of the Mass. The daily Eucharist was not understood as a mere representation of the passion of Christ, but it was held to make the passion present; the body and blood of Christ were truly present in the host.[19] This made the Eucharist unique: it actually participated in the sacrifice of the cross, unlike Old Testament sacrifices, which prefigured the crucifixion, but did not make it present.[20] Thus every day in the liturgy the crucifixion was brought into the present, in a way which was not merely significative, but real. And this real presence drew into itself the many Old Testament sacrifices which prefigured the Eucharist: in the Eucharist, as Peter Damian put it, those sacrifices were completed or fulfilled.[21]

16. *Nocturnum officium tempus miserie, quo genus humanum a dyabolo tenebatur obsessum, representat; diurnum uero nostre redemptionis et liberationis per Christum* (*Rationale*, I, x) [the nocturnal office represents the time of misery, when the human race was held by the devil; the daytime office represents our redemption and liberation through Christ].

17. For example: *prima est infantia, que per matutinas laudes representur. Secunda pueritia, que per primam* (*Rationale*, I, xi) [First is infancy, which is represented by Lauds in the morning. Second is childhood, which is represent by Prime].

18. Durand, *Rationale*, III:i.

19. For examples of this idea, pervasive in medieval thought even across very diverse intellectual contexts, see Radbertus, *In Matthaeum*, IV, 6 (*PL* 120, 212); Baldwin of Canterbury, *De sacramento altaris*.

20. For instance, Baldwin of Canterbury states that the Old Testament types for the Eucharist hid the truth in figural terms, whereas the Eucharist itself makes that truth manifest: *Sicut veritas nunc propalata dudum latebat sub figurarum velamine; sic caligo figurarum radiante veritate nunc manifestatur sicut in lumine* (*De sacramento altaris*, III, 1; 418) [In the past the truth which is now made manifest was hidden under the veil of figures. Today it shines so well that the darkness of figures is dissipated, and they appear in full light].

21. *Quidquid in illis hostiis typice gerebatur, totum in immolatione Agni, qui tollit peccata mundi, veraciter adimpletur* (*Opusculum* III; *PL* 145, 58) [whatever was carried out typologically in those sacrifices is fully completed in the immolation of the Lamb, which takes away the sins of the world].

In these ways, then, medieval liturgy might be said to have been a manifestation of the incarnational entry of God into time, and of the gathering of time into Christ.[22] Liturgy's nature as the spoken performance of written texts further emphasizes the way it constantly engages and shapes time. As an oral performance, it is always subject to the passage of time. Yet as the oral performance of written texts, it also in its nature emphasizes repetition: every liturgical performance was a re-performance of something which had already been performed before, and although it passed in time it also contained the possibility of its future repetition. That it took place in a cyclical structure further emphasized this: liturgy did not have an end point, but was seen as an ongoing manifestation and re-performance of the incarnation.

Any moment of entry into liturgy, then, is in these important senses "in the middle of things;" and so the presence of liturgy in purgatory offers important possibilities for the condition of being midway in life. This can be seen from the first liturgical performance described in *Purgatorio*, in canto 2, where the beginning of the journey of the souls in purgatory is marked by the singing of Psalm 114 (*Purg.* 2.46–48). The souls are at the end of their earthly life's journey, at the start of their journey in the afterlife, and yet they are also in the middle of a different narrative: that of providential history, with the typological relationship fully established between the Psalm's description of the Israelites' release from servitude and the souls' freedom from sin.

The arrival of the souls at the shore of purgatory echoes the opening lines of the *Commedia*. Like the pilgrim in *Inferno* I, the souls are bewildered and lost (*Purg.* 2.52–54), and as the pilgrim had turned to Virgil for help and questioned whether he is a living being or a shade, here the souls turn to the pilgrim and Virgil, awestruck as they realize that Dante is a living human person (67–69). The relationship between an individual's life and all human lives, the condition of being midway through life, are here performed liturgically. Through typology, through singing in unison, through the sign of the cross which angelic pilot makes over the souls, the individual's moment in time is made one with the community immediately present, and with the community of all humanity, in Christ.

---

22. The Eastern Church explicitly identified the Mass as an intervention of *kairos*: it is preceded by the phrase *Kairos tou poiesai to Kyrio* [It is time for the Lord to act]. See Wybrew, *The Orthodox Liturgy*, 6–11 for an account of how the Orthodox Mass makes present the whole of the life of Christ.

Present Things, Created Things

Purgatory, then, shows how the condition of being caught in the midst of life—of an individual life, of *our* life as community and in providential history—can be lived liturgically. And at a key point of *Purgatorio*, the condition of the pilgrim at the beginning of the *Commedia* is revisited in ways which bring to the fore the intimate links between the idea of being midway and understandings of being created. At the point of Dante's longed-for reunion with Beatrice in the Earthly Paradise, in the context of a procession and pageant which seem to bring together all of universal history, the pilgrim is compelled to confess his condition at the point at which the poem had opened, in the dark wood. If this moment marks in some ways a new beginning, with the arrival of a new guide for the pilgrim and his imminent passage from purgatory to paradise, in the site of the beginnings of human history—there is also a powerful presence of what is past. As the text builds to Beatrice's arrival, there is an intensification of classical and Virgilian allusions, fused with the christological. This is perhaps most readily evident as the arrival of Beatrice is announced with the phrases *Benedictus qui venit* and *Manibus, oh date lilia plenis!* (*Purg.* 30.19, 21), placing the words sung at the end of the *Sanctus* directly beside phrases echoing *Aeneid* 6.883. Here, too, then, the new moment of the new beginning is presented as intensely engaged in recollection of the past and anticipation of the future. The same can be said for the pilgrim's confession; for, at a point in the text when Virgil had appeared to declare the pilgrim fully master of himself,[23] Beatrice calls him back to himself as a man with a history. In doing so, she presents an account of his condition in the dark wood. After her death, she explains, he turned to less true paths:

> Then, on the threshold of my second age,
>
> I changed, took different life, and he at once
>
> drew back and yielded to another's glance.
>
> Risen from body into spirit-form,
>
> my goodness, power and beauty grew more strong.
>
> Yet I to him was then less dear, less pleasing.
>
> He turned his steps to paths that were not true.

23. *Non aspettar mio dir più né mio cenno: / libero, dritto e sano è tuo arbitrio, / a fallo fora non fare a suo senno. / Per ch'io te sovra te corono e mitrio* [No longer look to me for signs or word. Your will is healthy, upright, free and whole. And not to heed that sense would be a fault. Lord of yourself, I crown and mitre you] (*Purg.* 27.139–42).

He followed images of failing good

which cannot meet, in full, their promises.

(*Purg.* 30.124–32)

This, then, was the condition, which demanded Beatrice's intervention and needed the pilgrim to undertake this journey. The pilgrim's own confession then restates this:

Weeping, I said: "Mere things of here and now

and their false pleasures turned my steps away

the moment that your face had hid itself."

(*Purg.* 31.34–36)

This is Dante's crisis at midlife: his attachment to things in the here and now rather than to his proper goal, the future good. He is caught in the middle of things, with a past and a future, involved in universal history, yet only able to see that which is immediate. He is like the child growing into early youth described in the *Convivio*, desiring that which is directly in front of him for its own sake—and confusing it for that which is truly desired:

Lo sommo desiderio di ciascuna cosa . . . *è lo ritornare al suo principio. E però che Dio è principio de le nostre anime* . . . *essa anima massimamente desidera di tornare a quello.* . . . *L'anima nostra, incontinente che nel nuovo e mai non fatto cammino di questa vita entra, dirizza li occhi al termine del suo sommo bene, e però qualunque cosa vede, che paia in sé avere alcuno bene, crede che sia esso.* . . . *Onde vedemo li parvuli desiderare massimamente* un pomo; *e poi, più procedendo, desiderare* uno augellino; *e poi, più oltre, desiderare bel vestimento; e poi lo cavallo; e poi* una donna; *e poi ricchezza non grande, e poi grande, e poi più. E questo incontra perché in nulla di queste cose truova quella che va cercando, e credela trovare più oltre.* (Convivio, 4.14, my emphases)

The highest desire in every being . . . is the desire to return to its first cause. Since, further, God is the first cause of our souls . . . the soul desires first and foremost to return to Him. . . . As soon as it starts out along the new, quite untravelled road of this life, the soul is always on the look-out for its ultimate goal, the highest good; and so whenever it sees anything in which some good appears, it thinks that it is that highest good. . . . So we see small children desiring above all else *an apple*; then, when they are somewhat older, desiring *a little bird*; then, still later, desiring fine clothes; then a horse; then *a woman*; then riches in small measure; then riches in large measure; then even more riches. This happens because people find in none of these things what they are actually seeking, and think they will find it a little way on.

The condition of being lost is, then, one in which the world cannot be interpreted properly, in which present things seem to have value only in their immediacy. The way out of that obscurity involves setting the immediate in its nature as created, of perceiving the present moment as related to other present moments. Still midway, but not lost.

The *Commedia* invites us to understand the condition of living human beings as that of being caught in the midst of time—whether or not they are at life's midpoint. When we feel that we too are in Dante's dark wood—whether or not through external crisis—the *Commedia* offers ways to look deeper into that condition of being midway. In this perspective, we are in the middle of things because we are created beings, because our individual lives enter into a broader, universal history. *Purgatorio*'s liturgy shows us one way out of the dark wood: living liturgically, with others, inhabiting and performing a place in providential history. We arrive at any moment in the condition of being midway. It is not, in itself, a regrettable condition at all, although it can seem dark and bewildering—a midlife crisis, there at any moment. But it is an invitation for us, as we read, to reflect how new beginnings must be grounded in this moment to which we have been given, caught *nel mezzo del cammin*, in the middle of things as we are.

6

Hastening to Heal

To Read, Pray, and Move in
the Order of Grace

Leonard J. DeLorenzo

E ven for the first-time reader, the discovery of "movement" as a dominant element in the *Commedia* is predictable and unsurprising—the
poem is about a pilgrimage, after all. What becomes apparent to the reader
who plunges into this poem time and time again, though, is just how much
movement is required of him to continue to grow as a reader who understands not just what is going on but also why it all matters. No moment of
the *Commedia* is a moment unto itself and the connections between moments sometimes slowly and sometimes abruptly become more and more
apparent the more the reader practices both reading horizontally, back and
forth among cantos, and vertically, between the three *cantiche*. As if this
were not already enough, the zigzagging and diagonal connections in the
growing panoply of signifiers and poetic participles adds to the complexity of the poem all the more once the reader hazards to consider how his
own spiritual condition is also pulled into the journey.[1] For a poem that is
predictably and unsurprisingly about movement, this multiplicity of movements can be rather dizzying. With a little bit of stability, orientation, or

---

1. I am grateful to Paola Nasti for articulating so well the multidirectional movement required for reading the *Commedia* in its fullest sense (see "The Art of Teaching
and the Nature of Love," 223).

even resolve, however, dizziness might become puzzlement, and puzzlement is a potentially productive posture for growth.

Puzzling over Words

I dabble in crossword puzzles. Actually, to say I dabble is misleading, because I never really dabble in anything; what I do is develop periodic obsessions. For about two years, crossword puzzles were my thing. As anyone who does crosswords knows, there are forms of logic and certain patterns that only those who have spent considerable time and considerable strain in the world of crosswords learn, especially when moving to more difficult puzzles.

As an avid amateur and dedicated dilettante, I did not always exercise virtue when thwarted by seemingly impenetrable codes of sophisticated puzzles. Will Shortz—the longtime crossword puzzle editor for the *New York Times*—has been the object of my ire and muttering tirades more than once, as if he and his ilk failed in presenting a theme because I could not figure it out. Time and again I would be certain that the puzzle master was without a clue and created an illogical puzzle in which I was mired in confusion trying to decipher one small section at a time without any overall rhyme or reason.

And then it would happen. I would suddenly catch a fresh glimpse of one of those fifteen-word thematic clues that exerts centripetal force upon the many surrounding words, opening to me the logic of the whole puzzle. Suddenly I would not just decipher a bunch of words at once; I would also find new confidence because, at last, I was in on a theme true to the puzzle, not just the scattered themes I tried to force. Will Shortz has been exonerated in my private courtroom innumerable times in just this way.

I experienced something quite like this midway through Dante's *Commedia*.[2] My puzzle concerned one bit of text in one canto of the *Purgatorio* that at first annoyed me, then intrigued me, then as if all at once gave me the glimpse I needed to see something fundamental and, I believe, true about the order of the whole *Commedia* from within the very middle of the poem itself. This certainly was not the only time I had cursed Dante from the shadows of my mind, and each time those cursed shadows were always densest just before the dawn of insight. But what a relief it was this time when light broke upon the scene, inspiring wonder and awe, and conferring confidence, allowing me to say, "I can trust this. This whole thing is speaking truth after all and I'm learning."

2. I am ultimately indebted to Dorothy Sayers for this analogy (see Sayers, *Introductory Papers on Dante*, 128).

The Perplexing Paternoster

The site of my own puzzlement is the beginning of the eleventh canto of the *Purgatorio*. If the verses I found there had been obscure to me, I would have glossed over them, focusing my gaze elsewhere, unperturbed. It was the familiarity of the words that irked me, though, stirring within me the puzzling dissatisfaction that gave rise to the accusatory question: "Why on earth . . . ?!"

At the outset of the *Purgatorio* 11, I stumbled upon these words:

Our Father, dwelling in the heavenly spheres,

not circumscribed by these but through that love

which you bear more, on high, to primal things,

Your name, and all the powers of your might,

be praised by every creature. It is fit

to pay all thanks to Your sweet forming power.

May peace, as in Your realm, come down to us.

For we ourselves cannot attain to that,

if come it doesn't—not with all our wit.

As all your angels make a sacrifice,

singing "Osanna," of their wills to You,

so, too, may men make sacrifice of theirs.

Give us this day the manna each day needs.

Without that, exiled in this grinding waste,

all travel backwards who strive forwards most.

And just as we, to everyone, forgive

the harm we bear, grant generous pardon, too.

And do not look upon what we deserve.

The powers we have (so easily subdued)

do not make trial of through the ancient foe,

but free us from the one who is our goad.

This final prayer is made, O dearest Lord,

not for ourselves (we now have no such need).

We speak for those behind us, who've remained.

(*Purg.* 11.1–24)

The first time I read this I could not help but wonder who exactly Dante thought he was to change the words of the "Our Father." It seemed to me an act of excessive pride, even hubris, to presume the authority to poeticize Christianity's central daily prayer in order to fit it within the poem's frame, for the poet's purposes.[3] I also happened to notice that this was not just an issue of linguistic embellishment since the final tercet of the prayer (lines 22–24) was actually a novel construction that Dante appended to the prayer itself. Were it not for that addition, which puzzled me, I likely would have sped away from my dizzying annoyance at Dante's apparent presumptuousness, dismissing the poet's pride as having reached too far.

Left unchecked, my annoyance might have eventually led to my general disinterest in the poem as a whole, since this feeling resonated with some lingering skepticism I harbored about Dante's authority to orchestrate the eschaton and since I was not sure what, exactly, his theme was or why I should trust it. But that small puzzle of the last tercet touched on my curiosity and spurred me to inquire further. I was curious enough to look around a little bit more to see if I could figure out what was going on and why. As with a crossword puzzle, a seemingly obscure clue would not open itself to me just because I stared at it for a very long time. I would need to get a sense for its setting, its context, to see how it fits in and how it holds together what lies around it. Understanding this portion of Dante's poem required some of the same movement and searching: if I were to understand his *Paternoster* I would need to follow the promptings of curiosity to learn more before foreclosing on judgment. It was my curiosity that led me to zoom out from this portion of the text, looking ahead—horizontally, as it were—to gain some perspective and insight on what troubled me in this specific place.

Zooming out just far enough, we can see that the eleventh canto of the *Purgatorio* is not only in the middle *cantica* of the threefold poem, but also that it approaches the very middle of that middle *cantica*. If we follow that observation to the canto precisely in the middle of the *Purgatorio*—and

3. Much later I discovered that it would have been common practice in Dante's day, when translating the *Paternoster*, to paraphrase or alter it, as a gesture in humility. Famously, Francis of Assisi paraphrased the prayer, but more in terms of commenting on the lines of the prayer as it is rather than adapting or adjusting the words of the prayer itself. Whatever Francis does is not at all irrelevant to *Purgatorio* 11 or even *Inferno* 11 since *Paradiso* 11 features Francis and the vertical reading of the *Commedia* is also part of the poet's intended schema. In any event, my dis-ease with Dante's reshaping of the prayer itself in canto 11 had to do with the reformulating the words of the prayer and especially, as I note below, the finale of the prayer.

therefore the center of the *Commedia* as a whole—we discover that there Dante has allowed Virgil to tell him and us exactly where we are and what is happening. With lucid but cool rationality, Virgil—like the art critic who describes a breathtaking landscape but forgets to be moved by it—offers a description of the *Purgatorio's* schema.

> *Restat*: if I've prepared the ground aright,
>
> the ill we love must be our *neighbor's* harm.
>
> Such "love" is born in three ways in your slime.
>
> Some hope, by keeping all their neighbors down,
>
> that they'll excel. They yearn for that alone—
>
> to see them brought from high to low estate.
>
> Then, some will fear that, if another mounts,
>
> they'll lose all honor, fame and grace and power,
>
> so, grieving at success, love what it's not.
>
> And some, it seems, when hurt, bear such a grudge
>
> that they crave only to exact revenge—
>
> which means they seek to speed another's harm.
>
> This tri-formed love is wept for down below.
>
> But now I'd have you understand the next
>
> which runs, in broken order, after good.
>
> We all, confusedly, conceive a good,
>
> desiring that our hearts may rest in that.
>
> And each will strive to make their way to it.
>
> If love is slack in drawing you to view—
>
> or win—that good, then this ledge, where we're now,
>
> after your fit repentance, martyrs you.
>
> (*Purg.* 17.112–32)

As Virgil tells Dante and Dante thus tells us, in this seventeenth canto we are standing upon the fourth terrace of purgatory, where sloth is purged (lines 130–32). From this middle of the seven terraces, Virgil is recounting the folly of pride (on the first terrace, where we just were, lines 115–17), of envy (the second terrace, lines 118–20), and of anger (the third terrace, lines

121–23). These three vices manifest related yet distinct ways in which an obsessive self-regard comes at the expense of care for others. In other words, while the final four vices concern forms of love made erroneous by disproportion—with deficient proportion characterizing sloth and excessive proportion characterizing avarice, gluttony, and lust—these first three vices concern love failing its purpose, of one's concern curving inward rather than bending outwards.[4]

Notice, pride is born of your wish to keep others down so that you may excel *by comparison*. Envy is spurning the success of others because you are concerned that you will not be as praiseworthy *by comparison*. And anger arises from that urge to cause someone else harm as retribution for a grievance you see as done to yourself—in other words, anger is lashing out at others because you have learned to see them as harming you (your status, your security, your prospects for self-promotion) *by comparison*.

To stand at this midpoint and to see the path of the pilgrimage thus far, we begin to recognize—lucidly, even if only coolly—that the matter of purgation, especially on the first three terraces, concerns not merely individual vices but a whole economy of competition, an economy that locks us in to the logic that the good of others comes at my own expense, and vice versa. These vices we look back on show how would-be neighbors are driven into isolation from one another. This present terrace—for sloth—is for curing the laggardly desire to act on behalf of what is truly good. Taking stock of the Mountain of Purgatory from this middle terrace, we begin to discern a theme: all the various manifestations and consequences of habitual competitiveness are what the purgatorial journey means to remedy, especially in its first three stages.

With this general appreciation for the landscape surrounding us, we are able to return to the eleventh canto, on the first terrace purgatory, with some purchase on the context of Dante's *Paternoster*. Since the final tercet of this prayer is the point from which we zoomed out previously, we can now take the opportunity to zoom in a bit further to attend to the proximate setting of this puzzling element. Looking slightly ahead will benefit us eventually, but first let us gaze slightly before that last tercet, where we find the final petition proper to the "Our Father" which Dante has styled to fit his poem:

4. For more on these characteristics of the seven vices in relation to love, see Balthasar, *Glory of the Lord III*, 58.

The powers we have (so easily subdued)

do not make trial of through the ancient foe,

but free us from the one who is our goal.

(11.19–21)

With these words, of course, Dante is poeticizing those last words of the "Our Father": "And lead us not into temptation but deliver us from evil." What did not occur to me at first is that this is a very peculiar petition to utter in purgatory. In fact upon further reflection, it is seemingly nonsensical and contradictory. "Lead us not into temptation?" Purgatory is that state in which, by definition, the effects of sin are being healed—it is not a state subject to the illusory power of evil, that is, to even the possibility of sinning.[5] The penitent souls—including those whose voices mingle in prayer here—beg remission for the *consequences* of the sins they have committed and the harm they have caused, but they also know themselves to be free from the snares of evil. Sin *has been* forgiven—*their* sins have been forgiven.

---

5. Purgatory is the realm of penance for Dante, not indecision. Purgatory is filled with hope and the pain of longing, even remorse that spurs the desire for what is true and good and beautiful. Once passing through the gates of purgatory proper (canto 11), all movement is progress by way of humility and the strengthening of the will. In ante-purgatory, the souls of those who delayed in seeking penance while living wait to be admitted entrance to the place of true spiritual progress. Indeed, the journey through purgatory is all progress, unto the point at which the penitent decides for himself that he is ready to behold glory. As we learn along with the pilgrim Dante on the fifth terrace for avarice: "The will alone gives proof of purity / when, wholly free to change its sacred place, / it aids and sweeps the soul up, willing well" (21.61–63; cf. 18.115–16; 19.139–41; 23.85–86; 26.13–15). This matter of becoming capable is not predicated on indecision between the sinful choice for vice and the meritorious choice for virtue, but is rather wholly about the journey toward becoming fully capable of virtue, stronger in it, and wholly ready to will it. As Guido Guinizelli confesses about purgatory in a section we will return to later, purgatory is that realm "where no ability to sin is ours" (26.133). In terms of the traditional and innovative dimensions of Dante's view of purgatory, Dorothy Sayers concludes that "the two elements in all just punishment—the purgation of 'culpa' and 'reatus,' amelioration and satisfaction, ethical and legal, internal amendment and external amends—are both there; but in Dante as in [S.T.I., II Q.87, A.7 from] Saint Thomas they are fused and blended together, with the emphasis lying always on the purification of the heart and the eager consent of the will. You pay the price—but you pay it because you want to, and because it is your only means of expressing your love and sorrow: and in paying you grow clean and fit to receive the forgiveness freely offered and to return to that right relationship which nothing but your own folly ever disturbed" (Sayers, *Introductory Papers on Dante*, 84). For a concise, modern explanation of the history and content of the doctrine of purgatory, see Ratzinger, *Eschatology*, 218–33. Consider also Jacques Le Goff's treatment of Dante's purgatory, which he calls "a vast symphony" that systematizes doctrinal fragments and presents them as a coherent and insightful whole in *The Birth of Purgatory*, 334–55.

They *are already* free "from the one who is our goad" (11.21). So what are they doing praying *these* words, offering *this* petition?

It is necessary to recognize the oddity of this petition in order to rightly approach that puzzling final tercet of the prayer, the one that Dante appended to the "Our Father." This tercet is Dante's response to the peculiarity of the previous petition. Dante includes a coda within the prayer itself as he imagines, in full, what it would be like for these penitents souls—in purgatory—to pray the Christian's central daily prayer:

> This final prayer is made, O dearest Lord,
>
> not for ourselves (we now have no such need).
>
> We speak for those behind us, who've remained.
>
> (11.22–24)

And if this coda were not clear enough for those, like me, who were more agitated than attentive, Dante then adds a little postscript in the next line of the canto, immediately after the prayer concludes: "Then praying for themselves and us . . ." (11.25).

Here is Dante's insight, which he is rather directly inviting us to ponder in our puzzlement. Even with his poetic embellishment, Dante is remaining remarkably faithful to the actual petitions of the "Our Father." In fact, it seems as if in fidelity to the prayer itself, Dante had to ask himself something like: "What would it be like for the *Paternoster* to be prayed not here, as we are now, but in purgatory, by those saved and penitent souls?" Dante's insight is that the last petition of the prayer would be *wholly* their prayer offered *wholly* for us.

In one and the same prayer, this penitential community of souls prays both for themselves and for those still on journey in this life, before death. Within the theme Dante is developing, these are not two separate actions— one for them and one for us—but rather two movements of the same action. They seek their own progress as they seek the good of those behind them, "who've remained" (11.24).[6]

According to Dante's account, purgation consists of the chastening of desire, which leads to the redemption of memory.[7] This chastening is much

---

6. Paola Nasti argues that the penitent souls here gathered are practicing, through the communal recitation of the Lord's Prayer, extending personal or even familial concern toward the full range of the ecclesial boundaries, thereby following and enfleshing Jesus's teaching on his true family as recorded in Matt 10:37–39 (Nasti, "The Art of Teaching and the Nature of Love," 231).

7. For more on the themes of desire and memory, see especially Kevin Grove, CSC, and Jessica Keating's respective essays within the present volume.

more a form of disciplining, directing, and reorienting than it is punitive in nature. More to the point, the punitive aspects of penance are all part of a rehabilitative and indeed transformative process through which the souls in purgatory grow to will for themselves the good they most deeply desire.[8] Sin pulls apart what should be united. Penitents' souls are increasing their freedom *from* the sinful inclinations toward self-isolation, while at the same time growing in their freedom *for* the willful participation in this one communal body. Our souls abhor a vacuum: rooting out what is wrong must be matched by practicing what is right.[9]

The vices of those in purgatory are being healed through the remembrance of the needs of others, especially on the first three terraces where the inclinations toward habitual competitiveness are remediated. The penitent souls do not present themselves as having the power to meet those needs on their own,[10] rather they gather up the needs of others in their prayer to their Father as if it were a prayer for themselves: "but free *us* from the one who is our goad" (11.21). They will attain full health when their strength of willing the good of others completely supplants the lingering effects of the competitive tendencies in which they once indulged.[11]

Dante adds words to the "Our Father" with his coda to show us that this prayer is *never* a private prayer. Paradoxically, Dante changes the prayer to make the point that the souls in purgatory do not change the prayer to suit their situation—rather, they allow *themselves* to be changed to pray the prayer aright. This willingness to allow oneself to be changed for the sake of the other may even, in the end, apply to Dante the poet,

---

8. Perhaps the most searing announcement of the point of the purgatorial journey comes from the lips of Beatrice and directed toward Dante when, on the banks of the River Lethe, she questions and accuses him: "What right had you to venture to this mount? / Did you not know that all are happy here?" (*Purg.* 30.74–75).

9. For more on this dynamic of penance and training in holiness, especially in relation to Dante's poem, see chapter 5—"Bodily Memory"—of my own *Work of Love*, from which I have drawn generously for constructing the first portion of the present essay.

10. "May peace, as in Your realm, come down to us. / For we ourselves cannot attain to that, if come it doesn't—not with all our wit / . . . Give us this day the manna each day needs. / Without that, exiled in this grinding waste, / all travel backwards who strive forwards most" (*Purg.* 11.7–9, 13–15).

11. Consider, for example, what the souls doing penance for anger confess about the heavens for which they long, where there is no fear of losing for oneself when involved in sharing with others, as in a monastery: "If love, though, seeking for the utmost sphere / should ever wrench your longing to the skies / such fears would have no place within your breast. / For, there, the more that we speak of 'ours,' / the more each one possesses the good / and, in that cloister, *caritas* burns brighter" (*Purg.* 15:52–57). For the heavenly completion of what is desired and heralded here, see *Paradiso* 19.1–12 and 24.130–47.

whose own pride in his literary powers is as apparent in *Purgatorio* 11 as it is anywhere in the *Commedia*, if not more. Paola Nasti proposes that "Dante rewords the *Paternoster* in order to explain its value to the reader," adopting features of the preaching genre to draw the reader's attention more deeply into its theological and spiritual significance.[12] Furthermore, Vittorio Montemaggi suggests that Dante is opening his reader to join him as he joins these penitent pilgrims, who are praying together for others, thereby learning to "interpret their lives in the light of the Word."[13] In mingling his poetic and pilgrim voice with those performing penance for pride on the first terrace of purgatory and even bending over to adopt their hunched posture when he speaks with them (see 11.73), Dante may indeed be performing his own form of penance, poetically and spiritually, and inviting his reader to do the same.[14]

Salvific Substitution

Seeing the meaning and the fittingness of that tercet-coda was, for me, like suddenly seeing a fifteen-letter word running across the middle of a puzzling crossword. In hastening to heal others in their prayer, these penitent souls are themselves being healed—that is the keyword. The clue for this word was the presence of the "Our Father" not as we pray it here but rather as the souls in purgatory would pray it, prompting the question of how that prayer is the same and yet not prayed just the same way for these penitents. That clue fits in this particular puzzle dedicated to the "Course of Treatment on the Terraces of Purgatory." Sin is division, vices are inclinations to isolation, and so to be healed of the damage sin has done, practicing communion is necessary—that is, opening yourself to the needs of others, allowing their good to become your good, while allowing others to do the same for you.

12. Nasti, "The Art of Teaching and the Nature of Love," 242; see also 239. Nasti draws upon Nicolò Maldina's work to come to this conclusion, see "L'oration Super Pater Noster Di Dante Tra Esegesi E Vocazione Liturgia. Per Purgatorio XI, 1–24." As mentioned in a previous note, a vertical reading of the cantos "eleven" permits one to recognize that Paradiso 11 features Saint Francis, who is for the Dante the greatest interpreter of God's love. In his own form of preaching, Saint Francis inserts commentary between the lines of the "Our Father" to draw his brothers into deeper contemplation of the Lord through this simple Gospel prayer (see Armstrong and Brady, *Francis and Claire: The Complete Works*, 104–6). Dante's own poetic embellishment may be seen as doing something similar, especially as he draws upon biblical imagery (from Exodus, the Psalms, Revelation) to "preach" the "Our Father" in this particular setting.

13. Montemaggi, *Reading Dante's* Commedia *as Theology*, 187.

14. Ibid., 188–89.

The addition Dante makes to the "Our Father" therefore fits the puzzle of the journey of healing on the terraces of the *Purgatorio*.

But still there's another, more important question to pose. *Is it true?* This substitutionary move that the souls in Dante's purgatory make—whereby they pray a petition properly belonging to others as their own petition—is that move true to the logic of the *Commedia* as a whole? Moreover, and more important still, is this true to the movement of the Christian drama of salvation?

To ponder this "substitutionary" move more seriously as pertaining to the "Our Father," we ought to press onwards to this prayer's source. As we know well, the "Our Father" is the prayer Jesus himself taught his disciples to pray (Matt 6:9–13; Luke 11:1–4). Yet, once we pause to consider that these words were on Jesus's lips, we might find ourselves troubled again, in a manner not unlike that pertaining to *Purgatorio* 11. When Dante asked himself, "What would it mean for the souls in purgatory to pray the Our Father?," he stumbled upon the problem of that final petition: "lead us not into temptation but deliver us from evil." If we ask ourselves what it means that Jesus himself uttered the words of the prayer he taught his disciples, we stumble upon the problem of one of the other petitions: "and forgive us our trespasses." Just as it seems that the souls in purgatory would not pray the last petition as their own because they are no longer subject to the possibility of sinning, so it seems that Jesus would not pray to have his trespasses forgiven because he is like us in all ways *but* sin (Heb 4:15). He did not trespass. The easy solution to this predicament is, of course, to say that Jesus was teaching the disciples how to pray but not praying this himself. He would be, in that sense, like a physician who writes prescriptions for those who are sick, while he, the physician, is himself quite well.

If we do not let ourselves out of our own puzzlement quite so easily, though, perhaps we might dare to consider that in teaching these words, Jesus was himself praying these words. If he was praying these words, then he meant everything he said. Dare we consider that Jesus prays to his Father, "and forgive *us our* trespasses?" Actually, this might be a keyword for the salvific theme of Jesus.

The prophet Isaiah knows this theme; he gets the insight. If we listen to Isaiah, we begin to hear what it means for Jesus to pray that problematic petition as his own:

> By his sufferings shall my servant justify man,
>
> taking their faults on himself.
>
> Hence I will grant whole hordes for his tribute,

he shall divide the spoil with the mighty,

for surrendering himself to death

and *letting himself be taken for a sinner,*

while he was bearing the faults of the many

and praying for sinners all the time.

(Isa 53:11–12)

Jesus's care for the needs of us poor sinners is so whole, so complete, so free of impediment and full of desire, that he can say "forgive *us*" and mean it when he asks that "*our* trespasses" be remitted.

What could be more demeaning than allowing yourself to be confused with those who are less than yourself, who have problems you do not have, who are sick with a sickness not your own, a sickness for which they and not you are responsible (see Phil 2:6–8)? Isaiah knows that the Suffering Servant wills the health of sinners so fully that he allows the world to confuse him as one of us. The Suffering Servant is not just a physician writing a prescription; he is the physician who heals by sharing in the illness that is not his own.

If an image rather than words helps us imagine this, then picture Jesus standing on the banks of the River Jordan, waiting in line even, to get down in the water under John the Baptist's hands. How deep is Jesus's concern? Again, so deep that he would even risk being confused with the very sinners he himself saves. He stands among them, waits with them, goes down as they go down in the same muddy waters. If we did not know better, we would think he was just like them. He allows himself to be confused for a sinner. Of course those of us given ears to hear in faith get a coda from the Father delivered in the Spirit—"This is my beloved Son" (Matt 3:17; Luke 3:22; cf. Mark 1:11)—but that does not remove the problem of Jesus being confused with sinners; rather, it makes it all the more startling. He who is without sin goes down with the sinners, in the sinners' place, to pray in solidarity with them and offer himself for them.[15] Such is the mystery of

15. Joseph Ratzinger meditates on the mystery of Jesus's baptism and his acceptance of the plight of the sinners in the following manner: "The act of descending into the waters of this Baptism implies a confession of guilt and a plea for forgiveness in order to make a new beginning. In a world marked by sin, then, this Yes to the entire will of God also expresses solidarity with men, who have incurred guilt but yearn for righteousness . . . Jesus loaded the burden of all mankind's guilt upon his shoulders; he bore it down into the depths of the Jordan. He inaugurated his public activity by stepping into the place of sinners. His inaugural gesture is an anticipation of the Cross. He is, as it were, the true Jonah who said to the crew of the ship, 'Take me and throw me into the sea,' (Jon 1:12) . . . The Baptism is an acceptance of death for the sins of

salvific substitution in the person of Jesus. He speaks in the first-person plural when his petition does not properly pertain to him singularly, because
his pure will to heal those who are sick bears the cost of this humiliation:
"and forgive *us our* trespasses."

It would not be quite right to say that those souls in purgatory who
are allowing the effects of divine forgiveness to become complete in them
do what Christ does or even attempt to—after all, they themselves have no
power to save, and they confess as much (see again *Purg.* 11.7–9, 13–15).
Rather, it is more that they move as Christ moves: they practice hastening
to the needs of others—for the good of others—to the point that they make
room in the first-person plural for that which is not their own to become
their own.[16] Seeking our good heals them because Christ *lets himself be
taken for a sinner* to remedy our sins. They accept his gift in accepting others' burdens as their own.

Some, like Hans Urs von Balthasar, have charged Dante with a much
more serious substitution than the one we just traced—they charge that he
orchestrates a salvific drama that substitutes for the person of Jesus Christ,
who does not appear in the poem in any satisfactory way. As Balthasar
writes, "The cross of Christ, in all its reality, is met nowhere in the *Divine
Comedy*,"[17] and even argues further that Beatrice, for Dante personally, and
Mary, in cosmic empyrean terms, stand "in place of Christ."[18] It is true that
Jesus's name does not appear in *Purgatorio* 11; in fact, the name only appears twice in the whole *Commedia*, both times in the *Paradiso* (25.32 and
31.107), while the name "Christ" appears some forty times but not until
Purgatorio 20.87. Though the "Our Father" in *Purgatorio* 11 presents Jesus's
words, it would be easy enough to conclude that Jesus himself is not sub-
stantially present in that canto or the *Commedia* as a whole. There are symbols of him, allusions to him, but truly, if you go in search of the *character*
Jesus in the *Commedia*, your search will prove rather fruitless. You will find
a lot of Dante, a lot of Virgil, a lot of Beatrice, and a lot of others, but not a
lot of Jesus. That is, unless we change the way we look for him.

---

humanity, and the voice that calls out 'This is my beloved Son' over the baptismal waters
is an anticipatory reference to the Resurrection" (Benedict XVI, *Jesus of Nazareth I*,
17–18). Ratzinger's chapter on the Baptism of Jesus is replete with biblical and Patristic
references, and would serve as an excellent resource for readers who wish to study the
mystery of Jesus's baptism in greater depth.

16. On the theme of making room and yielding space, see Stephen C. Pepper, CSC's
essay in the present volume.

17. Balthasar, *Glory of the Lord III*, 82.

18. Ibid., 104.

The movement we have just observed, where one allows oneself to move from the singular to the plural, opening privatization and isolation to the desire of communion, is not just a remnant of Jesus Christ but he himself, in action. We will come back to this point, but for now we will risk opening our imaginations to the Christic move in *Purgatorio* 11 as pointing to and making manifest the singular theme of Jesus Christ, in whom the whole drama of salvation and also, more specifically, the whole of this poem itself moves. His movement is the order of grace.

The Logos and the *Commedia*

After the "Our Father" is recited in *Purgatorio* 11, the prayer is not mentioned again until *Purgatorio* 26. While the eleventh canto takes place on the first terrace, for the prideful, the twenty-sixth places us on the seventh and final terrace, for the lustful. On this last terrace, Dante enters into conversation with the master of lyrical poetry, Guido Guinizelli, whose style Dante himself sought to emulate and perfect. The following are the last words Guido speaks to Dante:

> Now since you're granted generous privilege
>
> to pass within those cloistered corridors [of heaven],
>
> where Christ is abbot of the brotherhood,
>
> then say a *Paternoster* for me there—
>
> as much, at least, as we, in this world, need—
>
> where no ability to sin is ours.
>
> (26.127–32)

We should notice at least three things about this request. First, Guido echoes what was true of the penitents on the terrace of pride in their present condition—that they are no longer able to sin and thus are being healed of sin's effects. Hence, we are reminded of the oddity of praying the last petition of the "Our Father" in purgatory.

Second, we might venture to contrast how those in the *Inferno* and those in the *Purgatorio*, respectively, ask to be remembered. Those who in the *Inferno* ask Dante to remember them make a request to have their names recalled on earth, on their own terms, pulling others' thoughts into their own closed narratives (see, e.g., *Inf.* 6.89 and 16.82–85).[19] When those

19. One notable and wildly troubling exception to this rule appears at the very beginning of the poem when Beatrice promises to remember Virgil to the Lord in

in purgatory, however, ask either to be remembered in heaven (as is the case here), or to be remembered on earth (see, e.g., *Purg.* 3.112–45; 19.139–41; 26.145–47), they ask to be remembered in prayer so they may move toward that for which they hope and long. The penitents ask that they be remembered in line with their journey toward full health in heaven rather than pulling others' thoughts about them into the sickness of their sin. In this request from another master poet who would likely enflame Dante's pride, we might consider how what Guido asks of Dante is not only for Guido's growth but also a means for Dante's own healing: to pray for the spiritual advancement of one whom he has sought to surpass in worldly accomplishment.[20]

Third and finally, we ought to allow ourselves to stumble on the "Our Father" for a second time, in a new but related way here. In asking for Dante to pray the *Paternoster* in the heavenly realms, we might think "what would *that* be like?" since in the *Paradiso* not even the *effects* of sin remain, and so the prayer offered *there* would be pure praise without any need for one's own healing. While the souls in purgatory have been forgiven of their sins they have not yet been fully healed, while those in heaven have. To pray the *Paternoster* in heaven would mean that the *only* healing that would be sought would be the healing for another who is not yet of full health. Carrying forward the logic of the "Our Father" as prayed in the *Purgatorio*, we would expect that those in the *Paradiso* would pray those petitions for healing *as if* they were their own petitions—again, in the first-person plural. The mystery of that first-person plural is thus amplified when considering the *Paternoster* in the *Paradiso*.

We would be wise to test this theory by listening to how the "Our Father" is prayed in the *Paradiso*. Such an attempt would indeed be wise if such a listening were possible, but therein lies the problem. Even though Guido alludes to such a prayer in *Purgatorio* 26, Dante does not compose a *Paternoster* for the *Paradiso*. At least, that is, if we are looking for those words themselves rather than their movement. So once again, we must change the way we look.

Heaven: "When I again appear before my Lord, then I shall often speak your praise to Him" (*Inf.* 2.73–74). What praise of the damned in heaven would mean and, moreover, what the final status of Virgil is are two issues that exceed the scope of this essay but are subject to further inquiry, even puzzlement.

20. For further and serious consideration of the phases of memory in the three canticles of the *Commedia*—failed memory, redemptive memory, and sanctified memory—see Jessica Keating's essay in the current volume.

Heaven's Harmony

It would not be too simple to say that the *Paradiso* is all about movement. It is about movement become complete, become whole, beyond all impediments. It is about the finale of divine movement taking flesh in the human community.

In the heavenly realms, even without the explicit composition of a *Paternoster* for the *Paradiso*, Dante witnesses that prayer's perfection at the very apex of beatific creaturely life. If we are to see it with him, we have to become sensitive to the most tender of gestures. For when, on behalf of many saints, Saint Bernard offers the final petitionary words of the entire *Commedia* to the Virgin Mary, she embodies the movement of the "Our Father," and it is all in her eyes:

> The eyes—which God both loves and venerates—
>
> attentive to these orisons, made clear
>
> how welcome to her were these holy prayers
>
> and then turned straight to the eternal light
>
> in which (we're bound to think) no creature's eye
>
> inwardly travels with such clarity.
>
> (33.40–45)

Those eyes: they move harmoniously, without sluggishness and with all grace, down to the needs of another and up to the source and summit of Charity that pours itself out for the good of the world. She is by grace what her Son is by nature: the one who welcomes the concerns of others and offers them *as her own in prayer*. The movement of mercy and the movement of praise are united in the complete action of charity, and that is humanity full of grace.

When we contemplate the eyes of Mary at the end we discover anew what those penitent souls were practicing with their *Paternoster* in purgatory. They were practicing the subtlety, the agility, the lightness of that movement of offering themselves in prayer for the good of others, of taking the good of others as their own good.[21] In their economies of competition, those souls had practiced seeing and treating others as rivals in a zero-sum game and so their course of treatment is to practice communion by sharing

---

21. The four properties of glorified bodies that Saint Thomas Aquinas enumerates in *Summa Contra Gentiles* IV.86 are impassibility, subtlety, agility, and clarity. In the grace of Mary's turn from receiving to offering Bernard's prayer for Dante, the properties of humanity in all its glory shine forth.

in mutual concern. What we glimpsed in that keyword in the middle of the *Purgatorio* points to the fulfillment at the end of the *Paradiso*, where humanity is redeemed and sanctified in the light of divine glory. If we allow our initial puzzlement to push us ever further, what we will discover here at the end might also illumine the meaning of the whole journey's beginning, when we set off with Dante in a dark wood in the first cantos of the *Inferno*. In fact, when seen now from the end, we discover in full what we might have known even at the beginning: that the journey did not really begin in the dark wood.

The Beginning in the End

Dante's journey does not begin with Dante because Dante's journey does not begin from his beginning; it begins from the end. Dante's journey begins with the Blessed Mother, who weeps for him. Tears of mercy flow for Dante and he is given a path. That path is opened by the call of the Virgin Mary who beckons Saint Lucy to release the love of Beatrice in search of that lost man in a dark wood (*Inf.* 2.94–114). Along the path this descending mercy cleared, Dante began ascending toward "the end of all desires" (*Par.* 33.47) where he would will to turn in harmony with Love Eternal (33.137–45). Mary weeps for Dante who is drowning in sorrow. Lucy provides the light for his path by summoning Beatrice, his particular love, to go to the gates of hell and pull him from that dark threshold. Skillfully, Beatrice dispatches Virgil who can speak to Dante in verse he admires and so use what compels Dante to lead him toward the movement of love itself.

What Dante witnesses at the portal to divine love in the eyes of the Virgin Mary in *Paradiso* 33 is a theme for the whole journey from start to finish. That merciful gaze and those merciful tears incite Dante's pilgrim steps from the start and, when his journey was offered in the prayer of Saint Bernard, Mary turned to offer all that progress to the source and summit of love: the triune God. Dante's journey begins in being seen mercifully and it culminates when he wills, for himself, to see in like manner.[22]

But this last point—the point about the beginning of Dante's journey—brings us to one last question: *Why do the saints care?* Why did Mary weep for him, why did Lucy light his way, and why, for him, did Beatrice "go to the doorway of the dead" (*Purg.* 30.139; cf. 18.137; *Inf.* 2.116). This is not just my question, but also Virgil's question as recorded in *Inferno* 2, which means that it was Dante's question, too:

---

22. See Balthasar, *Glory of the Lord III*, 48–50.

But tell me [Beatrice] why you take so little care

and, down to this dead middle point, you leave

the spacious circle where you burn to go?

(82–84)

Herein lies the problem: Beatrice wholly desires to abide in the heavenly realm, in the company of the saints, in full union with "the love that moves the sun and the other stars" (*Par.* 33.145). Her proper place is there and yet here she is, when eternal bliss is open to her, standing at the doorway of the dead. Virgil is asking a perfectly rational question: "How could you care so little about where you deeply desire to be that you've come all the way down here? Have you lost your sense? Have you taken a vacation from your holy desire?" Saints desire heavenly ascent and Beatrice has descended.[23]

Let us try to tease out this puzzle as to why the saints care and why Beatrice goes back for Dante by plunging ourselves right back in the middle of the narrative—that is, in that realm of purgation. But this time I do not quite want to look through the window on purgatory that Dante provides; I want to look through another window. One of the clearest visions we can have of purgatory is in the life of a saint, before death. What we see in the complete life of a saint is the penitential journey of ongoing conversion toward the definitive end in Christ. It is not that the saints "before death" are already free of sin like the souls in purgatory, but rather that by virtue of their end we learn to see all their actions and even their failings ultimately as progress in a narrative of salvation. Sins forgiven and repented fuel the journey of holiness as if they were themselves meritorious actions.[24] With this in mind, I want to look upon the life of one of the most recently canonized saints: Teresa of Calcutta.

In a 1962 letter to her spiritual director, Mother Teresa disclosed that

> the physical situation of my poor left in the streets unwanted, unloved, unclaimed—are the true picture of my own spiritual life, of my love for Jesus, and yet this terrible pain has never made me desire to have it different.—What's more, I want it to be like this for as long as He wants it.[25]

---

23. Following Dante, C. S. Lewis takes on this same conundrum in his *The Great Divorce*, 74–75; cf. 66 where Lewis names George MacDonald as being for him what Beatrice was for Dante.

24. Consider the saints' memory, or forgetfulness, of sin in the light of salvation in *Par.* 9.103–9; cf. Augustine, *City of God*, XX.30; and Balthasar, *Glory of the Lord III*, 51.

25. Teresa of Calcutta, *Come Be My Light*, 232.

These are strange, strange words. They are so strange that not a few pan-
icked when these words were made public with her private writings in 2007.
Was she not a saint after all? Surely a saint cannot feel unwanted, unloved,
unclaimed in her love for Jesus. She's supposed to be close to Jesus, growing
closer all the time, making her way up the mountain to him. She could not
have meant what she said.

But what if we suspend our disbelief and consider, at one and the same
time, that she did mean what she said and that she is a saint?

When Teresa penned these words she had spent more than a dozen
years as a Missionary of Charity hastening with the light of Christ to what
she called the "dark holes of the poor."[26] Those in the dark holes *were* unwanted, they *were* unloved, they *were* unclaimed, and she had made such a
habit of hastening to them that, spiritually, she became as they were. She was
being transformed by those whom she loved.

Most of the world did not see that because we only read the coda:
"She's a saint! She's filled with the love of Jesus!" But her prayer itself was
to *move* in Christ, to hasten to those in need and to allow their needs to
become her own. I think she meant what she said, and we only have to hear
her words on her own prospects of being a saint—of being truly holy—to
realize how serious she was: "If I ever become a saint—I will surely be one
of 'darkness.' I will continually be absent from heaven—to light the light of
those in darkness on earth."[27]

For Teresa, the light of heaven would be darkness because she would
not dare imagine herself giving up on those she learned to love in Christ.
Until God brings time itself to an end, Teresa will hasten to those in "dark
holes"—those whom the world leaves as unwanted, unloved, unclaimed—
and she will keep company with them, even though being a "saint of darkness" means we might confuse her for someone who might not be a saint,
or at least not the saint we thought we knew and wanted. The truth, though,
is that she is revealing what it means to be a saint—that a saint is marked by
what she loves, that a saint learns to move as Christ moves, and that a saint
is unafraid to go to the doorway of the dead for the sake of another's good.
Teresa clings to the poor of Calcutta, in the darkness of their isolation, in the
darkness of others' neglect of them.

But why, exactly, does her life give us a window on to purgatory?
Because her life was the time when she practiced becoming the saint she
became. It happened step by step, purging what was wrong with the world

26. Mother Teresa repeatedly referred to the condition, the abandonment, and the
plight of the poor of Calcutta in terms of their "dark holes." See, among others, ibid.,
42–43, 66, 104–21, 168–69.

27. Ibid., 230.

by practicing what is right. Those "dark holes"—the isolation and disregard and abandonment—are the image of the hell the rest of the world has created, and Teresa stands at the doorway of this death to become a light. This is the role she was given and which, ultimately, she herself willed; moreover, she practiced it, purging neglect and forging communion with slow, painful steps. When she was just beginning her ministry to the "poorest of the poor," she wrote this in her journal: "The first step towards the slums is over. It cost a very good deal, but I am grateful to God for giving the grace to do it and also for showing me how very weak I am."[28]

That first step is the one the Rich Young Man of the Gospels failed to take (see Matt 19:16–30; cf. Mark 10:17–31; Luke 18:18–23). Teresa takes it. And she takes the next one and then many more. Even Mother Teresa was healed of her lingering aversion to communion one step at a time.

There is something deeply consoling in knowing that Teresa does not abandon Calcutta for the sake of heaven, that *in her* Calcutta is now made present in heaven just as she toiled to make heaven present in Calcutta. It means that the saints are not on vacation, they have not left us, but rather hasten toward us, filled with desire for our own good. That is holiness: not claiming divine love as a private possession but hastening after the good of the many, of those behind, "who've remained" (*Purg.* 11.24), until the last trumpet (1 Cor 15:52), when time is no more (Rev 10:6).

That is what Beatrice did for Dante. It is what the Virgin Mary does for all pilgrims and would-be pilgrims. It is what saints do and those who desire to be saints must practice. Saints know that ascending in holiness means moving in the descent of mercy. Why? Because Christ says, "I am the way and the truth and the life,"[29] and he never ceases hastening toward us, to give us a home.

The Beauty of Our Common End

Thinking about the ways in which Dante teaches his readers to move as we learn to read the *Commedia*, we know from the start that we must move horizontally, we slowly detect that we should also move vertically, and we learn from either wonder or disorientation that we might also move diagonally, even by way of zigzags. But what I learned beginning from the middle of the *Commedia* itself is that the whole poem moves according to the logic of mercy—moving toward the needs of another to share in the condition of the one who suffers *as if* it were your own suffering. Dante composed the

28. Ibid., 124.
29. John 14:6.

whole poem for this purpose, to use the good that he found to aid those who live all wrong (see *Inf.* 1.8 and *Purg.* 32.103). This degree of truth is first made available on the literal level of the text but deepens considerably in the text's spiritual sense.

With that spiritual sense awakened, maybe we can look up and say one last thing about what this all means for Dante's vision of the saints in heaven. In the Empyrean, Dante sees the saints arrayed together like a rose in bloom. But if Beatrice clings to Dante, and Teresa clings to Calcutta, and each of the other saints clings to those whom they love and who love them, then each petal in that rose is itself a rose. Every saint is a blossom of communion: to see a saint in heaven is to see those whom the saint has hastened to love. The petal that is Teresa of Calcutta is the *whole* Teresa, member of the *whole* Christ.

Divine love is not a private possession; it is the common good. The first-person singular is only ever complete when it becomes the first-person plural, because every "I" is a "we" in Christ, and the whole "we" knows every "I" intimately. To be fully human means to behold each other; what's more, it means being beheld.[30]

Coda

It would have been boring and rather ineffective for Dante to simply tell me all that, even if he did more than enough to lead me to make these connections. The thrill of the discovery was very much tied up in the work of moving within the logic of the poem. In telling of the good that Dante found in his journey, Dante seems to have deemed it insufficient to simply *tell* me, his reader, of that good; instead, he took a chance on me, giving me the chance to discover in delight the intricacies of the journey by allowing me to see it for myself. It is not simply the delight of learning how to read this poem better but of maybe—just maybe—imagining what it would mean to be known in the Father's own knowledge of the saints in his Son, where that knowledge is its own light, unfading, which we call the Holy Spirit. In that light, we belong to one another, together.

To be known among that number, to know each other thus, to desire nothing less, nothing other, and to be transformed in that desire—that is the beautiful end of every new beginning in the human person. The souls in purgatory pray thus, and Teresa hastens to those in dark holes, and Beatrice weeps for Dante at the doorway of the dead, and the Immaculate Mother

---

30. For a beautiful and complex articulation of the mutual indwelling of the saints in their beatific life, see Balthasar, *A Theological Anthropology*, 303–4.

is unafraid in such darkness, untroubled by peril, undaunted in pursuit of those her Son claims as his own. That is the comedy of the *Comedy* and the saints are those who rhyme in meter: they pray with Christ, in Christ, that the whole Christ may become whole. The souls in purgatory learn nothing other than the movement of that prayer and we ourselves make progress even now to the extent that we learn to move in rhythm, by daring to say, "Our Father."

7

Uniting the Eyes

From Fixation toward Fascination in the Easter Tuesday Cantos

Stephen C. Pepper, CSC

P eople occasionally ask me, "Father, why do you like Dante so much? What is it that you find so interesting about him?" On one level, it is a difficult question for me to answer. Why do athletes love their sports? Why do musicians empty themselves into their art? Why does anyone discover the passions of his or her life? It seems to me that a passion is an extension (or a skilled flourishing, perhaps) of one's created being, and when we find something of ourselves buried away within a sport, a song, or a sonnet, there is something very deep in us that says, "Here is a pearl of great worth. Give yourself to this." When I read Dante, I find something of myself within his lines, an anonymous character against the backdrop of his afterlife, and for this reason, I cannot stay away from him. He reflects me back to myself.

On another level, the question lends itself to a rather pithy response. Dante teaches me what is worth being fascinated by.[1] When I pay attention to the things that usually arrest and compel my attention, I have to admit that not all of them fit the standard that St. Paul raises when he says, "Fi-

---

1. The seed for this inspiration came to me during a course on Dante's theology that I took with Vittorio Montemaggi in my last year of seminary at the University of Notre Dame. During one lecture, Professor Montemaggi recalled remarks he once had heard from Robin Kirkpatrick about how Dante shows the good to be more exciting than the bad. From there on out, that idea lodged itself in my own appreciation and appropriation of the *Commedia*.

nally, brethren, whatever is true, whatever is honorable, whatever is right, whatever is pure, whatever is lovely, whatever is of good repute, if there is any excellence and if anything worthy of praise, dwell on these things" (Phil 4:8 NASB). In our fallen condition, the true and the honorable and the right frequently appear to be less alluring than the false and the disgraceful and the unsound. Like Virgil in Dante's dream of the siren on the fourth terrace of Mount Purgatory,[2] however, Dante aims to expose the truth of our false allurements. He illustrates them painstakingly in all of their negative reality. In the next step, moreover, he holds up the good as that which is most truly captivating, because it is a captivation (paradoxically) that liberates. Dante disciplines the imagination in the spirit of St. Paul, and I read Dante because I find such discipline to be not only disorienting but also (and, in this case, for that reason) irresistibly enlivening.

What *should* fascinate us? Moreover, how do we learn, in fact, to be fascinated by that which should fascinate us? These are questions that over-hang the whole of Dante's *Commedia*, but they can be seen to have par-ticular bearing on the Easter Tuesday cantos.[3] The Easter Tuesday cantos mark the eve of Dante's much anticipated reunion with Beatrice. Along with his readers, Dante is standing on the threshold of what Christian Moevs so beautifully describes as the one thing that can bring real change to Dante's life, namely, "Beatrice, the self-unveiling or self-giving of the Real, the *riso de l'universo* ("the smile of the universe"), a cosmic power of attraction or love so intense that it steals the mind and heart from themselves, teaching them the unutterable sweetness that is self-sacrifice, love, the surrender to the ground of one's being, of all being."[4] With the unveiling of Beatrice on top of purgatory, Dante will stand unanaesthetizedly exposed to the *mys-terium tremendum et fascinans* that is God reflected in and as one of God's creatures, and Dante will be invited to recognize himself as one with what he sees. Upper purgatory,[5] then, is immediate preparation for this revelation.

2. Cf. *Purgatorio* 19.1–33.

3. Dante and Virgil emerge from Hell onto the base of Mount Purgatory on the morning of Easter Sunday, 1300, and their ascent of the mountain takes place over the course of four days—that is, the first four days of the Easter Octave. Easter Tuesday arrives to find Dante and Virgil still on the fourth terrace of sloth in canto 19, and it terminates with the setting of the sun across the stairwell that leads from the terrace of lust to the Garden of Eden in canto 27. As such, I speak of the "Easter Tuesday cantos" broadly as the account of Dante's pilgrimage through the upper three terraces of avarice, gluttony, and lust. More precisely, they run from *Purgatorio* 19.34 (when Dante wakes from his dream of the siren) to 27.69 (when that day's sun finally sinks beneath the horizon).

4. Moevs, *The Metaphysics of Dante's Comedy*, 87.

5. I use the phrase "upper purgatory" to designate the three topmost terraces of

Upper purgatory is the final shaking free from all the vestiges of fixated love that keep one locked into the fiction of being on one's own and for one's own in the world. Just so, in leading us up the mountain in his footsteps, Dante tries to shake us free from the drowsy and false contentedness that we can have with the passing things of life, and so help us to see what he sees, to see as he sees, not by mere appearances, but by the fascinating truth of who we most truly are with and in God.

This chapter unfolds, then, not so much as a formal argument about the Easter Tuesday cantos but as a series of reflections about fixated and fascinated loves. I will begin with some biographical notes about how I myself have come to befriend Dante and to regard him as a spiritual master who teaches us how to be in truthful relationship with one another. Next, I will diagnose the postures of fixation in which Dante finds himself in upper purgatory, and I will conclude by tracing his progression to postures of fascination through an interpretation of his experiences among the shades of the terraces of avarice, gluttony, and lust. All of this I attempt in a spirit of deep gratitude to Vittorio Montemaggi and Leonard DeLorenzo, the editors of this volume, and to each of the other contributors, from whose wisdom and insight I continue to profit in my own faltering steps of discipleship.

Befriending Dante

I started reading Dante in the spring of 2006 during a study abroad semester in Rome. It just seemed at the time like an appropriately cultural thing to do. As I expect is the case for many first-time readers of Dante, I found *Inferno* to be a morbidly exciting (even haunting) experience, like a car accident that you cannot tear your eyes away from. *Purgatorio* was not as exciting as *Inferno*, especially given the ethereal quality of the poetry at the end of the canticle, but at least it retained some of hell's graphicness—the eyes of the envious sewn shut with wire, the fires of lust cast fiercer than molten glass!

When I came to *Paradiso*, though, things changed. More specifically, I came to *Paradiso* 2, where Beatrice is explaining moon spots to Dante, and I vividly remember thinking to myself, on a train heading from Salzburg into the Bavarian Alps, "This is not true!" On my own, I could not see past what I judged to be the scientific imprecision of Beatrice's discourse, and distracted to the point of being offended by the sudden change of style and theme in the poetry, I decided to waste no more time with Dante. It is not for nothing that Dante warns his readers at the start of this canto,

---

the mountain, which Dante traverses as a unit in the Easter Tuesday cantos and which Virgil treats as a unit in *Purg.* 17.136–39.

You in that little boat who, listening hard,

have followed, from desire to hear me through,

behind my bowsprit singing on its way,

now turn, look back and mark your native shores.

Do not set out upon these open seas

lest losing me you end confused and lost.

(*Par.* 2.1–6)

Dante was right. I was lost and confused, but you cannot say something like that to a junior in college and expect to be taken at your word! In my pride, I thought at the start of *Paradiso*, "I'm sure that's what all the poets say. I've got this." I was wrong.

Skipping forward a few years to my first year of seminary, I was taking an Old Testament course with Dr. Gary Anderson, Hesburgh Professor of Catholic Theology at the University of Notre Dame. The course included a major research component, and Dr. Anderson, having learned that I had studied Italian at one point in my life, invited me to study the liturgical geography of the *Commedia*. It sounded creatively out of the box, so I agreed to the project. Again, *Inferno* was exciting. *Purgatorio* was compelling. I had to read *Paradiso*, so I willed my way through it. This time, though, something was different. Paradise was inexplicably fascinating. It shone with a light that made me want to enter more and more deeply into it, and from there on out, from reading *Paradiso* all the way through, I was hooked on Dante. In time and with further study, I learned to put into words what I had started to find in Dante that took such hold of my imagination. Simply put, Dante shows us what it is like to *share the same space* as each other.

The blessed of *Paradiso* share the same space as each other. In other words, Dante imagines human relationships at their truest and liveliest as being inherently *perichoretic*, that is, interweaving, moving in and out of and through and around each other, like starlings in an ever-flowing, patterned dance. Human relations are like this because the life of the Trinity is like this. Dante sees this dynamic for himself and imitates it poetically when, finally looking on God in the ultimate canto, he cries out,

Eternal light, you sojourn in yourself alone.

Alone, you know yourself. Known to yourself,

you, knowing, love and smile on your own being.

An inter-circulation, thus conceived,

appears in you like mirrored brilliancy.

(*Par.* 33.124–28)

Trinitarian Being gives rise to and is the model for all human being, so for Dante, "Human relations too . . . [ideally] have about them this same quality of mutual inherence, of one person's entering into the being of another as an inwardly operative principle of affirmation."[6] To be a human person in Dante's view is not to have one's own ontological space in the cosmos. It is the ability to take in and to be taken in by another, who is really the horizon of any "self" worth acknowledging.

Dante plays through this idea of perichoretic relationship across the *Commedia*. We see it *parodied* in hell, for example, in the tempestuous coupling of Francesca and Paolo, which, incidentally, Dante also compares to starlings in flight (*Inf.* 5.73–142), in the contorted wheelings of the Florentine politicians (*Inf.* 16.4–90), and in the serpentine metamorphoses of Dante's larcenous in-laws (*Inf.* 25.35–144). What the damned can only mimic, the redeemed of purgatory can actually *practice*, hence Dante's repeated attempts to embrace his friend Casella at the base of the mountain (*Purg.* 2.76–87), the mutually supportive penance of the shades of the envious (*Purg.* 13.46–72), and the affectionate cross-circlings of the two choirs of the lustful (*Purg.* 26.25–48). Finally, the practice of purgatory gives way to the *performance* of paradise, for example, in the language of "in-you-ing" and "in-me-ing" that Dante invents in order to converse with the troubadour bishop of Marseilles (*Par.* 9.73–81), in the two revolving crowns of souls that settle on Dante and Beatrice in the Heaven of the Sun (*Par.* 12.1–21), and in the voice of the Eagle of Jupiter, which speaks as "I" and "mine" while meaning "we" and "us" (*Par.* 19.10–12). It would not be too far off the mark to say that the *Commedia* is a poetry of perichoresis.

Dante captures in his poetry what, I believe, we can detect in our own life experience, if we pay close enough attention. For example, it would seem that this desire to share space with one another sits at the heart of many of our questions about vocation. Those called to marriage celebrate perichoresis in the most iconic and life-giving way. Man and woman become one; the vocation is not only to share life side-by-side in partnership but also to reflect the Trinity in the total "real presence of one person to another,"[7] which then extends into the paschal mystery of raising children. For those called to priesthood and/or consecrated life, the desire is no different. Priests and religious may not share space in quite the same way as do married couples,

---

6. Took, "Patterns of Collective Being," 412.

7. Ibid., 413.

but the gift of celibacy nevertheless is a focused ability to be stretched in the heart so as to affirm and receive the life of another as the gift that it is, and to reflect Christ uniquely in that moment of encounter. Celibacy, when lived with joy and integrity, foreshadows the sharing of space that takes place in heaven. How is one called to share space with others? In the answer to that question lies the discovery of a vocation.

Human relationships unfold perichoretically not only in the discernment of vocation (that is, in figuring it out and living it well) but also in the practice of mercy. This makes sense on a root level when one stops to consider mercy as a type of compassion, as a feeling-as-you-feel and a seeing-as-you-see in the midst especially of experiences of suffering. On another level, though, as Walter Cardinal Kasper argues, mercy is a mirror of the perichoretic love of the Trinity. The Father models mercy by eternally "giving space to the other [the Son] in himself." The Father "makes room" in himself, as it were, for the Son. The Father "makes room" in himself likewise for creation, and the Son makes room for sinful humanity in the heart of God by going to the cross and laying bare his own pierced heart.[8] At the cross, which the followers of Christ approach in the Eucharist and in each other, we become most truly one with each other, and "in becoming one with the other," as Kasper says, "love creates and grants space to the beloved, in which he or she can become themselves."[9] Human beings imitate the mercy of the Trinity when we take up the crosses of our lives and join others at the feet of their crosses. This mercy, in both its corporal and spiritual works, makes present the eternal, space-sharing love of the Father with the Son in the Holy Spirit.

This lesson in mercy was pressed home on me very clearly one day in my second year of seminary. Throughout that year (which in religious parlance is called a Novitiate), my classmates and I would volunteer on Wednesdays as chaplains at the local hospital, and for several months I was visiting patients in the oncology ward. One day, I received a call to visit a guy named Asher. That is all I knew about him when I knocked on the door to his room. When I entered the room, I found a young man, basically my age, asleep, emaciated, and paralyzed from the waist down by leukemia. His family was there, so I made some small talk and left. The following week, though, I saw that Asher was still admitted, so I decided to make a second visit. This time he was awake, and I was able to get to know him a bit. As we spoke, an interior voice kept creeping in on me that asked, "Why is he in that bed and not you?" The question kept repeating itself; it would not leave

8. Kasper, *Mercy*, 93.
9. Ibid., 92.

me alone. Eventually, it dawned on me, "There is no good reason. Nothing meaningful separates us," and with that, I *knew* (that is, I felt at my core), that Asher and I were *one*. At the foot of the cross of leukemia, I saw myself in the life of another, and the only thing I could do in that moment was to love him. That is what God's mercy shows us when it overtakes us. It lays bare our own pierced hearts. It lays bare the terrifying-yet-fascinating mystery of our own lives, and it teaches us how to share the same space as each other by lifting us together toward "the love that moves the sun and the other stars" (*Par.* 33.145).

Diagnosing Fixation

If human flourishing entails participation in the perichoretic love-mercy of the Trinity, then an obstacle to human flourishing is the failure to share space with one another. Purgatory diagnoses these failures of reason and love and sets out a program of healing. Upper purgatory in particular showcases a series of fixated loves, or as Moevs says, stories of "obsessive and habitual self-identification with the contingent, finite objects of [one's] own experience."[10] The shades of these terraces, far from sharing space in life, sought to consume it by taking into themselves to an immoderate degree the goods of this world (property, food, sex), the reason being that they experienced themselves as other than and as separate from the order of created things.[11] Sharing space takes faith and courage. One must trust that something (or someone) is there on the other side of losing oneself to hold what is most truly "me" together and to return "me" to "myself" in ever-truer form. In the absence of this confidence, the alternative to losing oneself is (seemingly) to take to oneself as the guarantor of one's own safety, identity, and rest.

Dante's experiences in upper purgatory, then, reflect a way of being together that is as yet frustrated in its will and ability to share the same space. For example, the aerial bodies of the avaricious do not move in any meaningful way with each other. They lie strewn and scattered among each other, such that Dante and Virgil have to "pick" their way forward with "scant, slow steps."[12] Human wills are not yet fully at peace in the divine will, and as such, they can still be in competition with one another. Leaving off from questioning Pope Adrian V at the avaricious pontiff's own request, Dante remarks,

10. Moevs, *The Metaphysics of Dante's Comedy*, 88.
11. Ibid., 91.
12. Hollander translation of Dante, *Purgatorio*, 20.4, 16.

> Against a better will, will can't well fight.
>
> And so, against what pleased me, pleasing *him*,
>
> I drew the sponge still thirsty from the stream.
>
> (*Purg.* 20.1–3)

In line with this same passage, human intellects do not as yet intuit each other as they do in the heavenly paradise, so Dante has to thirst for knowledge and, in a way, to beg his daily bread by asking questions from intermediate sources about the novelties of the mountain. Human encounters even seem to be on a lag on these terraces. After the Roman poet Statius intersects and greets Virgil and Dante on terrace five, it takes sixty-five lines for Virgil to get around to asking who he is (see *Purg.* 21.13–81)! Purgatory is practice ground for perichoresis, so it only makes sense that the souls here are still stepping on each other's toes.

In Dante's view, the remedy to fixated love (and the separateness from each other that results) is not solely in loving rightly but fundamentally in seeing rightly. Loving rightly follows from seeing rightly, as Beatrice instructs Dante in the Primum Mobile (*Par.* 28.106–11). Throughout upper purgatory, Dante drops hints that the way he sees is somehow *off*. For instance, he tells Guido Guinizzelli on the terrace of lust, "I make this climb to be no longer blind" (*Purg.* 26.58), and in response to a question about what grace allows them to ascend purgatory, Virgil tells Statius that Dante has to be led up the mountain because his soul's "eyes as yet don't see as our eyes do" (*Purg.* 21.30). Most revealing, however, is Dante's dream of the siren just before dawn on Easter Tuesday morning:

> Now, at that hour when daytime heat cannot—
>
> vanquished by earth, and sometimes, Saturn's rays—
>
> sustain its warmth against the chilling moon . . .
>
> there came, dreaming, to me a stammering crone,
>
> cross-eyed and crooked on her crippled feet,
>
> her hands mere stumps, and drained and pale in look.
>
> I gazed at her. Then, as to frozen limbs
>
> when night has weighed them down, the sun gives strength,
>
> likewise my staring made her free, long-tongued,
>
> to speak, and drew her, in the briefest space,
>
> erect in every limb, giving the hue

that love desires to her blurred, pallid face.

(*Purg.* 19.1–3, 7–15)

It is Dante's own gaze that transforms the cross-eyed siren into an object of appeal. Far from recognizing a beautiful thing as being actually beautiful, dream-Dante exposes a tendency in himself to fabricate beauty divorced from reality, that is, to see by the light of his own projected desire. This would not be as problematic if he was trying to look behind surface appearances so as to evoke some quality of deeper, inherent value in the object of his attention, but that does not seem to be the case here.

The siren quite openly admits herself to be the appeal of surface appearances. She *is* the temptation to claim full content with the passing things of life, and she gives voice to the human tendency to rest in mirages of one's own making (*Purg.* 19.22–24). If this tendency remains unchecked in the waking world, then Dante would be in danger of holing himself up in patterns of apprehension and valuation that no one else can share with him. This way of misapprehending and misvaluing the world of sense experience as a place to stake out one's own security, one's own identity, one's own rest at the expense of genuine, perichoretic human relationship is what makes Dante blind. He sees, as it were, fixatedly. Fortunately, Virgil rescues Dante from the siren, but until Dante confesses his fixations, until he, weeping, admits to Beatrice in Eden, "Mere things of here and now / and their false pleasures turned my steps away / the moment that your face had hid itself" (*Purg.* 31.34–36), her eyes remain veiled from his cross-eyed way of seeing.

There is another way of seeing, which apprehends God in all things and uniting all things, walking not by the light of projected desire but by the light that makes everything else light. This is fascinated seeing. Peter Damien describes what fascination is like for the blessed, who gaze on God directly, by explaining to Dante in the Heaven of Saturn,

Divine light drives its point upon me here.

And, penetrating that in which I'm wombed,

its virtue, joined with my own powers of sight,

lifts me so high above myself, I see

on high the essence where that light is milked.

Hence comes the brightening joy in which I flame.

(*Par.* 21.83–88)

For those still on the paths of salvation, who see God not directly but through the media of created things, Dante himself captures the experience of fascination. As Dante recalls,

Held in her [Beatrice's] look I, inwardly, was made

what Glaucus, tasting grass, was made to be,

consorting with the other ocean gods.

To give (even in Latin phrase) a meaning

to "transhuman" can't be done.

(*Par.* 1.67–71)

Thomas Merton confirms the truth of such experience not only in the poetic imagination but also in the spiritual life when he tells of that now-famous moment on the corner of Fourth and Walnut when he awoke from his own "dream of separateness" and saw all those people on the streets "walking around shining like the sun."[13] Fascination overcomes fixation in this realization that we belong to and are one with each other after all, in the perichoretic love-mercy of the Trinity.

Learning Fascination

There are these moments on a street corner, in a hospital room, on top of purgatory when the grace of fascination lifts us above ourselves in the realization that what is most meaningful is not separateness but communion. This grace, though, is not limited to the extraordinary moments of life. There is a way of seeing (and loving) fascinatedly that pertains to the mundane, and this happens when God is habitually apprehended in the events, persons, and things of everyday life. Thomas Aquinas speaks to this point when he says in *De Veritate* that fallen humanity retains a capacity for seeing God but requires a "triple medium" actually to do so: "creatures themselves, from which [fallen humanity] rises to knowledge of God; a likeness of God, which [they get] from creatures; and a light from which [they receive] the perfection of being directed toward God."[14] Whether or not Dante knew of Thomas's text, I argue that the Easter Tuesday cantos (that is, the accounts of Dante's encounters among the avaricious, gluttonous, and lustful) can be read as a series of meditations on the triple medium Thomas develops, namely, on our value as creatures, on the restoration of God's image and

13. Merton, *Conjectures of a Guilty Bystander*, 156–57.
14. Quoted in Singleton, *Journey to Beatrice*, 19.

likeness in us, and on becoming transparent to the light of grace. By these meditations, Dante moves us, even as he was moved, to see God truly, under the guise of our own lives.

Dante makes the fifth terrace of avarice a focal point for his ongoing meditation in the *Commedia* on our value as creatures. The instant that Dante and Virgil set foot onto this terrace, we see in our imaginations what Rudolf Otto means when he speaks of "creature-feeling," that is, the "feeling of personal nothingness and submergence" that springs from direct (or less indirect) encounter with Divine Mystery.[15] Dante says,

> Now loosed out on to circle number five,
>
> I saw there people all around who wept,
>
> each turned face downwards, lying on the earth.
>
> "*Adhaesit pavimento anima mea!*"
>
> I heard them say this, but sighing deep
>
> so what they said was hardly understood.
>
> (*Purg.* 19.70–75)

The shades of the fifth terrace inhabit literally and wholly what the faithful inhabit liturgically when, for example, on Ash Wednesday they receive the sign of the cross on their foreheads. On the fifth terrace, though, the shades do not simply *remember* that they come from dust; they *adhere* to the dust. They cloak themselves in the symbol of the nothingness out of which God breathes his creatures into being, and they wet the ground with their tears. One detects here an echo of Genesis's second creation narrative, wherein "a mist went up from the earth and watered the whole face of the ground— then the Lord God formed man of the dust from the ground, and breathed into his nostrils the breath of life" (2:6–7 RSV).

In the words of Pope Adrian V, the first penitent Dante meets on this level, the avaricious had "fixed [their eyes] on earthly things" in life and sought their rest among the "lies of life" (*Purg.* 19.118, 108–9). Consequently, God now keeps them bound in a posture of fixation, and Pope Adrian claims that "the mountain has no pain more harsh than this" (*Purg.* 19.117). This is an odd statement. Compared with the weights of pride and the fires of lust, after all, lying prostrate for a few hundred years does not sound terribly agonizing. Perhaps Pope Adrian says as he does, though, for two reasons. First, no pain is more harsh because this pain is intended to heal humanity's most fundamental *temptation*, which, even before denying

15. Otto, *The Idea of the Holy*, 17.

our createdness, is to forget that we spring from nothing by God's creative grace at each and every moment, and in that forgetting to mistake anything else created as something to be grasped at and even enjoyed (in the Augustinian sense of that word). Second, no pain is more harsh because this pain is intended to sharpen our most fundamental *desire*, that is, to see God. In the book of Exodus, Moses asks to see the glory of the Lord. The Lord responds to Moses, "I will put you in a cleft of the rock, and I will cover you with my hand until I have passed by; then I will take my hand away, and you shall see my back; but my face shall not be seen" (33:22–23 RSV). For those who refuse even to see God's back by making gods for themselves out of material reality (that is, for those who refuse to apprehend God through created forms by fixating on the goods of sense experience), God in turn turns their backs to him. In fact, this is an act not of retribution but of mercy. God turns these fixated ones not so much against himself as into the truth of who they really are, *created* forms, beloved *nothings*, who for that reason are free from the compulsion to compete for space (or anything else) in the present order of things.

Inhabiting this nothingness may be the mountain's most painful punishment, but this ontological posture is what makes it possible for these souls to see the light of heaven not only among the stars but also within themselves. When Virgil and Dante are preparing to leave the fifth terrace, an earthquake overtakes the whole mountain. Dante recalls that they were moving on from the shade of Hugh Capet

> when, as though things were crashing down, I heard
>
> the mountain tremble. And I felt the chill
>
> that all will suffer when they come to die.
>
> Delos itself did not so fiercely shake
>
> before Latona made a nest of it
>
> to bring to birth the two eyes of the sky.
>
> (*Purg.* 20.127–32)

Not knowing what is happening, Dante feels as if the mountain is collapsing, and if Mount Purgatory is collapsing, then the end of time has come. Naturally, Dante experiences the sort of fear that Jesus warns will attend that first, unmediated encounter between God and humanity when God comes to judge the living and the dead (cf. Matt 24:29–31). This is likewise the fear that Otto describes as the "wonder that strikes us chill and numb" when we realize exactly what it means to be a creature,[16] and in his memory of that fear, Dante draws an analogy. He recalls Delos, the floating island of mythology, which was subject to severe earthquakes before Latona, the mother of Apollo and Diana, came to give birth on it. The island finds rest when it becomes the nest of "the[se] two eyes of the sky." The classical allusion finds its biblical counterpart in Mary, whose wonder at Gabriel's message manifests her perfect lowliness and, as such, preconditions her *fiat* and disposes her to conceive the light of the world (cf. Luke 1:26–38). Just so, when the human soul shakes in recognition of its nothingness before God, it is then in that moment poised to receive God's creative work. Its nothingness becomes the nest in which God separates the light from the darkness, and it comes to rest in the light of grace that it discovers within itself.

Beyond the fifth terrace's meditations on our value as creatures, the sixth terrace of gluttony inspires reflection on the restoration of God's image and likeness in human nature. The features of this terrace recall the Garden of Eden, the crown of the mountain where humanity first received the stamp of God's image and likeness. Dante thus observes upon his emergence onto the ledge,

> We found there in the middle of the road,
>
> a tree—its fruits, in perfume, good and sweet . . .
>
> and, to the side, where rock walls closed our path,
>
> clear liquids streaming off the towering cliff
>
> sprinkled across the surface of the leaves.
>
> (*Purg.* 22.131–32, 136–38)

In reference to a second such tree further down the path, an unknown voice tells Dante that it has seeded from the original Tree of the Knowledge of Good and Evil, which still grows in Eden. Dante and Virgil (together now with Statius) discover this second tree gathering to itself by some mysterious virtue,

> a group that raised their hands
>
> and called towards the leaves I-don't-know-what,
>
> like silly, over-eager little tots,
>
> who plead—although their target won't respond
>
> but rather seeks to whet their appetite,

16. Otto, *The Idea of the Holy*, 28.

> dangling, unhidden, what they want aloft.

> (*Purg.* 24.106–11)

This grasping spirit, against which St. Paul warns the Philippians (cf. 2:5–11), which in Adam and Eve originally extended too far, too quickly beyond its creaturely limits (thereby disfiguring the divine image and likeness in them), receives here the medicine that transforms the compulsion to consume into the desire to unite.

At this point in his narrative, however, we might ask Dante an uncomfortable question. Adam and Eve disfigured God's image and likeness in human nature when they ate the fruit of the knowledge of good and evil, but in a way, the knowledge of good and evil is precisely what the *Commedia* purports to hold out to its readers. In seeing and naming and speaking with both the truly dead and the truly alive, Dante, as it were, shares with us a fruit that promises to make us like God in giving us knowledge that only God has. How is it, then, that Dante can hold out to us what God first forbade and the terrace still withholds?

One reason why eating the fruit of the knowledge of good and evil results in damage to God's image and likeness may be because, by that act of transgressing their creaturely limits, Adam and Eve sought to know as God knows *while remaining the subjects of their own knowing*. In other words, they postured as true knowers with true knowledge in their own right. Instead of sharing in the knowing of the one subject of all knowing, they tried to objectify that knowledge and to pack it away into their own little subjectivities, falling apart subsequently under the weight of that futile endeavor. The severe fasting that is the penance of the sixth terrace, then, restores God's image and likeness by "milking" its penitents not only of their excessive appetites but also of their false subjectivities. The souls here thirst to be known by each other and to receive the truth of each other's lives. They wear their names, not as expressions of the ego but as revelations of grace. They know good and evil not on their own but in the knowing of God, as the crucifixion of Christ as it plays out in their lives.

Dante extends to his readers the knowledge of good and evil in just the same way, that is, as a participation in the cross of Jesus. That is why the *Commedia* can help to restore the image and likeness of God in us rather than tempting us, in following Dante, to repeat the sin of Adam and Eve. The way Dante suggests this to us, moreover, is by paying attention to his penitents' faces. In particular, he notes what the fasting of the terrace does to their features. When he first catches sight of these souls, he says, "Each one was dark and hollow round the eyes, / pallid in feature, and so gaunt and waste / their skin was formed to show the very bone" (*Purg.* 23.22–24).

Dante cannot recognize even his old friend, Forese Donati, until Forese makes himself known to Dante by his voice. Their faces are unrecognizable as human faces, yet their humanity is writ large on what remains of them. Dante tells us, "The sockets of their eyes seemed gemless rings, / and those who read Man's 'OMO' in Man's face / would clearly have seen 'M' in all of these" (*Purg.* 23.31–33).[17] The fasting, then, parses down in the penitents that which limits their comprehension of the truth of their humanity as something limited yet reflective of the divine.

The "omo" that Dante reads on Forese's face, however, also resonates with the "Ecce, homo!" of Pilate in John's Gospel.[18] Behold, the man! We can presume that Dante intends his readers to say the same thing when we see his gluttons. Behold, *that* man. In their suffering, the gluttonous image God not only in the abstract but also in the vivid concreteness of Christ crucified. Forese admits as much when he tells Dante, "I call it [our penance] pain. Rightly, I should say solace. / For that same yearning leads us to the tree that led Christ, in his joy, to say '*Eli*,' / when through his open veins he made us free" (*Purg.* 23.72–75). These are a rightly sacramental people. In their bodies, they make present the broken body of the savior, and they participate in the saving suffering of the cross. They still reach for the fruit of the knowledge of good and evil, but they themselves also become the fruit that gives knowledge of Christ crucified. Their weeping witness shows that our own participation in the Paschal Mystery is the grace that remakes us in the image and likeness of God.

If the fifth terrace sheds light on our value as creatures and the sixth terrace helps effect the restoration of God's image and likeness in us, then the seventh terrace of lust (the uppermost terrace of the mountain) can be seen to release the light of grace that has been welling up in the penitents and in Dante (and his readers) during the ascent of the mountain. Not only the poetry of this terrace but also the artwork that it has inspired (for example, the watercolors of William Blake) create an impression not so much of pain (although there is pain) as of fluidity, fluency, and transparency. Among the avaricious, Pope Adrian declared that the mountain has no pain more harsh than theirs. Among the gluttonous, Dante emphasized their appalling desiccation. Among the lustful, however, Dante simply notes, "I saw spirits there walking in the flames" (*Purg.* 25.124), and he leaves us to make assumptions about what that must be like. The shade of Guido Guinizelli mentions to Dante that he does "burn" in the fire and that there is "shame"

17. (*U*)*omo* is Italian for "man." It was believed that the structure of the face spells out its own humanity: each eye providing an "o" while the structure of the nose forms the "m."

18. Cf. Gragnaloti, *Experiencing the Afterlife*, 129.

in the self-accusations of this terrace, but Dante's experience of the souls themselves is more akin to how he will experience the blessed in the lower spheres of paradise. The lustful appear as visions in and out of vision, "as fish do going to the water's depth" (*Purg.* 26.135). Their bodies circle and their voices intermingle in an enduring harmony of penance and praise. Dante can drink them in with his eyes and pour himself back into them by his words and gestures (*Purg.* 26.100–107). Far from diminishing these souls in any way, the fire quickens them, like atoms vibrating to their fusing point, and it makes them light and charged enough to translate to their natural place of rest in the shared space of the Empyrean.

The problem with lust is that it self-identifies too quickly with the body (one's own and that of another), thereby obscuring the light that nests in the nothingness of one's created being. Moevs tells us, "To see only the body is to fail to see it as the self-manifestation, in the world, of the ground of all being: it is to fail to recognize Christ, resulting in crucifixion."[19] He notes how Dante in paradise has become transparent to the light of his being, but how in purgatory Dante's body still is prone to "break" and to "eclipse" the light, hence the repeated references throughout *Purgatorio* to the shadow he casts on the mountain.

One could argue, however, that the focus of the seventh terrace has less to do with how Dante still breaks light and more to do with how Dante even now mediates light to those with eyes to see. In order to understand how this might be the case, we have to get into the textual fabric of these cantos. Dante sets the scene with the lustful at a precise time of day, that is, right before dusk,

> The sun was beating on my right-hand side,
>
> its rays illuminating all the west,
>
> changing its face from clearest blue to white.
>
> And I, in casting shadow on the flame,
>
> made fire seem fierier. Then many shades, I saw,
>
> at that one hint, while walking on,
>
> gave thought, and came, because of that,
>
> to say of me their say.
>
> (*Purg.* 26.4–11)

19. Moevs, *The Metaphysics of Dante's* Comedy, 115.

How would these shades be seeing Dante in this scene? They would see him through his shadow on the flames, in his real body, silhouetted by the setting sun.

Each of these details is significant for understanding the spiritual program of the terrace. When we see only a person's body in life, we limit ourselves to seeing and loving shadow versions of each other.[20] Without the (literal) shadow to intervene between them and Dante, though, the lustful would not be able to see Dante truly. The wall of flame and the light from the setting sun (ironically) would work together to cloak Dante in darkness, preventing his interlocutors from taking in the self-communicating features of his face. Instead, Dante's shadow tempers the lights and allows these souls to see Dante truly—through the ephemeral extensions of himself, in his relational spontaneity and immediacy, wrapped in light as in a robe. They see Dante as Dante will see Beatrice in Eden. No wonder, then, that they wonder "as mountain yokels stand—no differently—in dumbstruck stupefaction, staring round, when, red-necked, rough, they make it, first, to town" (*Purg.* 26.68–70)! The object of their previous fixation has become for them the locus for "the self-manifestation . . . of the ground of all being."[21] They see the light of grace that has nested in Dante's nothingness, and by that light, they can recognize themselves as one with what they see.

We ourselves may already have an idea of what it is like to see like this, that is, fascinatedly. Think of Our Lady of Guadalupe, who in 1531, a little more than two hundred years after Dante died and perhaps rejoined the orders of the weeping and singing penitents, appeared to Juan Diego outside of Mexico City and imprinted her image on his tilma. We see her the way that the lustful see Dante. We see her the way that Dante sees Beatrice at first in Eden—through a consecrating veil, in her revealing body, transparent to the divine light of grace, which pierces her through.

As both Montemaggi and DeLorenzo have noted in their essays in this volume, the Virgin is, indeed, where the *Commedia* begins and where it ends, and she is the integration of everything that we have been discussing in this chapter. A humble creature in whose beloved nothingness the light of heaven chose to nest and nurse; a preveniently-restored image of God in whose sevenfold sufferings the solace of the cross draws near to us; a light of grace in whose eyes of mercy we are soaked up and conditioned to see light itself—Mary embodies the triple medium by which God may be seen

20. This is not to posit a duality between the soul that is "real" and the body that is somehow "less real." It is to say, rather, in the spirit of St. Paul to the Corinthians, that the present body still needs to be sown in the grave so as to rise to its fullest, liveliest reality (cf. 1 Cor 15:42–49).

21. Moevs, *The Metaphysics of Dante's* Comedy, 115.

by fallen humanity. Mary exemplifies the life of fascination that perceives God in the ordinary as well as the extraordinary, and she holds us in her view, loosening the knots of fixated attachment that weave their dream of separateness around us, restoring us to each other as brothers and sisters who can share the same space.

Our eyes unite with hers, and after his experiences recounted in the Easter Tuesday cantos, Dante is ready to unite with Beatrice. In that gaze of fascination, we too find the mercy that makes us "pure and prepared to rise towards the stars" (*Purg.* 33.145).

PART 3

Beatitude

8

Geographics of Stars, Metaphysics of Light

Theological Aesthetics and the Form of Human Life in Dante's *Paradiso*

Jennifer Newsome Martin

On Seeing

I grew up on a small farm in North Carolina, past the one stoplight of what could hardly be called a town, past the places where the paved roads all ran out, past even where the gravel roads flattened out into dirt ones. My brother and sister and I grew up on forty acres of fields and creeks among a whole Southern Gothic menagerie: pigs and horses and flocks of quail, honey-bees, a one-legged turkey that would fetch a stick, dogs both wild and tame, black snakes, deer, kittens and cats, foxes, and enough chickens to supply eggs for us and all our nearest neighbors, if there were any close neighbors to speak of. Living so deep in the rural Carolina Piedmont, our nights were not invaded by artificial urban light that would obscure the night sky. So we became well practiced at recognizing and naming the constellations: the Big Dipper of Ursa Major, Orion's belt; the brightness of Polaris, that North star which provided direction and beginning, a place from which we could map the rest of the sky.

I have a memory from one summer night when I was seven or eight, made more shadowy and strange from the decades that have passed since the event that gives it form. My whole family had gathered in a back pasture to watch a near apocalyptic meteor shower. As I watched these stars burn their passes overhead, I remember distinctly feeling a dizzying strangeness, a reversal in perception, a not altogether unpleasant feeling of simultaneous dwindling and expansion where it felt as if the stars were the really real and we creatures sitting there were so fragile, so miniscule and frail as to be nothing at all. When this shock of sheer contingency struck me like a wound as a child, it was suddenly as if the whole world and beyond the world had opened up in an encounter as terrifying as it was beautiful. The impression of that memory I have retained is that I had glimpsed the mystery of something I found then and even now to be utterly in-articulable. The more I saw, the more I wanted to see, and it was as if time had stopped altogether. At the very least, I had seen something beautiful; the experience took me out of myself toward something both known and yet unknown. In his 2002 address to the *Comunione e Liberazione* assembly in Rimini, Pope Benedict XVI spoke to this kind of experience: it is the shock of encounter with the beauty of God, a beauty that "draws us to himself and, at the same time captures us with the wound of Love, the holy passion (eros), that enables us to go forth together, with and in the Church his Bride, to meet the love who calls us."[1]

Dante's *Paradiso* is, at its most fundamental, a text about this kind of wounded seeing that is led toward truer and truer sight, where the subjective and objective converge in an experience of God that cannot be sufficiently pronounced. It is a poem about beauty, and is itself a pedagogy of beauty that leads both the pilgrim and the reader upward, to a more and more expansive vision of God, even if there is an inescapable fissure between what is seen and what can be said or represented properly about it. The text is aesthetic through and through, and not simply because the visionary language and religious symbolism of the poetry itself is beautiful, though it certainly is that. The text is perhaps hyper- or meta-visionary because it details the processes and operations by which human beings see, fail to see, and learn to see. It is aesthetic also because it bears the structure of the revelatory: that which is inside, the mysterious hidden depths, are given expressive form, even if, as Dante ultimately admits when he reaches the Empyrean, the expressive forms—art, poetry, language, even imagination and memory themselves—are ultimately insufficient for the mystery of absolute being that luminously informs them. Much like the apostle Paul's own mystical

---

1. Pope Benedict XVI, "The Feeling of Things," 47.

journey to the "third heaven" reported in language indicating the vastness of distance between the experience itself and the possibility of an adequate retelling, Dante too "was caught up into Paradise and heard things that are not to be told, that no mortal is permitted to repeat" (2 Cor 12:4).[2]

Furthermore, the text privileges such aesthetic concepts as form and proportion. Dante's universe is governed by a deep sense of order and fittingness. Readers of the *Inferno* and the *Purgatorio* can certainly observe the horrific exactness with which punishments or penances are meted out in Dante's ironic calculus, according to which the consequences fit the crime with an aesthetic perfection. Dante's heavens are also—but quite differently—highly proportional and hierarchical, as announced in the very first tercet of canto 1 of the *Paradiso*:

> Glory, from Him who moves all things that are,
>
> penetrates the universe and then shines back,
>
> reflected more in one part, less elsewhere.
>
> (*Par.* 1.1–3)

In this first canto, too, Beatrice reiterates the aesthetic language of form and proportionality: there is a fittingness that governs the order of Dante's universe, an ontological form which comes from God as the creative ordering principle of all things. Beatrice goes on, in an almost humorously patient explanation to her charge about his sudden ascent from the earthly paradise to the heavens:

> At this, in deep, affectionate concern,
>
> she sighed and set her eyes on me,
>
> as mothers do when silly sons rave on.
>
> "There is," she now began, "an ordered ratio
>
> between all things there are. It's this—such *form*—

---

2. For mention of the concomitant phenomena of visionary experience and subsequent forgetfulness or failures of speech in Dante and the visionary biblical literature upon which it is likely based (including the visions of Paul, Ezekiel, Nebuchadnezzar, the disciples at Christ's transfiguration, and John's Apocalypse), see Giuseppe Mazzotta's chapter "Language and Vision," where he argues that "the discontinuity between what is seen and what is said structures the whole movement of the *Paradiso*. Dante's poetic representation is articulated within this gap where vision and words are distinct from each other. Nonetheless, he will attempt to retrieve the original vision in order to generate the vision in his readers" (Mazzotta, *Dante's Vision and the Circle of Knowledge*, 166). All biblical quotations are from the NRSV translation.

that makes the universe resemble God."

(*Par.* 1.100–105)

All of creation is thus ordered to its proper end. Human beings and angels, however, as free agents, can swerve from the Form of their proper end, which is God, and can fail to accord their lives to the form enjoined upon them. Beatrice continues: ". . . a creature which can freely bend / will sometimes, though impelled entirely straight, desert that course and wander off elsewhere" (*Par.* 1.130–32). God as the form of forms, however, attracts to God's Self what is like it, and the journey of the saints—and our own journeys, too—are toward greater and greater approximations of this eternal form. As canto 29 goes on to tell us, "The primal light, whose rays shine out on all, / is taken up in ways as numerous / as there are splendours that it couples with" (*Par.* 29.136–138). We see this hierarchy enacted in the *Paradiso*, as the radiance of the saints is correlative to their degree of beatitude. For instance, consider the paleness of those inconstant saints manifest in the Heaven of the Moon (*Par.* 3.19–30) over against the brilliance of the higher souls like St. John the Apostle (*Par.* 25.100–23), saints who have variously achieved transparence to God such that the luminosity of God's light can illuminate them according to greater proportionality.

In Dante's strange and transcendent visions of the *Paradiso*, the narrative shuttles toward the nearly unbearable luminosity of the sight of God not only accompanied by the distance between what is seen and what can be said but also through the enormous distances of astronomical imagery. Though these dream-visions in and beyond the heavens complicate ordinary modes of perception, requiring both from Dante and his readers a transformed way of seeing, even at its most imaginative or visionary the text never abandons such aesthetic concepts as form, proportion, and perspective. Indeed, Dante's ascent up through the planetary heavens is observed not by the announcement of quantifiable spatial coordinates but rather, significantly, with greater and greater increases in Beatrice's effervescent beauty, until they reach the Empyrean and Dante must admit that her beauty is such that it cannot even be described. Dante's admission of his artistic limits is, however, not a refusal to look, nor, as it turns out, even cause for Dante to abandon the poetic form at the very same time that he is protesting its insufficiency. At the end of the poem, having reached the Empyrean, Dante quite poetically writes of Beatrice:

> The beauty I saw, transcending every kind,
>
> is far beyond us here—nor only us.
>
> Its maker, I think, alone could know its joy.

> From now on, I'll admit, I'm overwhelmed,
>
> defeated worse than all before—in comic
>
> or in tragic genre—by what my theme demands.
>
> As sunlight trembles in enfeebled eyes,
>
> calling to mind how sweet to me her smile was,
>
> itself deprives my mind of memory.
>
> Not since the day that I, in our first life,
>
> first saw her face until this living sight,
>
> has song in me been cut so cleanly short.
>
> It is, however, right that I stand down—
>
> as every artist, at the utmost, does—
>
> and no more trace her beauty, forming verse.
>
> (*Par.* 30.16–33)

If the artist must lay his brushes by, the poet must also put down his pen, and yet he does not, or else cannot. Hans Urs von Balthasar points out in his largely appreciative analysis of the *Paradiso* that the fact that Dante's repudiation of poetry comes precisely in a poetic form foreshadows Dante's later capacity to stand "his ground in the face of the immeasurable. This theme is magnificently realized when, at the very end of his whole journey, Dante prepares to look up into the luminous abyss of the Godhead itself."[3]

In this essay, I will consider further the operation of theological aesthetics in Dante's *Paradiso*, privileging the themes of ocularity and blindness, particularly as correlative to his symbolic presentations of light and darkness. The chapter then explores the concept of "space" in two distinct ways: (a) astronomical or astral space and (b) aesthetic space and the phenomenon of perspective, with special attention to how visual spaces are conceived and configured by an artist, especially vis-à-vis the interplay between the subjective and the objective. The *Paradiso* forces Dante and also the reader herself to adopt a number of dizzying changes of point of view as Dante undergoes his tremendous ascent to God, presenting a number of puzzles in the astral journey about the relationship between the seer and what is seen.

The operation of sight and its failures in the *Commedia* as a whole is a theme so fertile it will be impossible to do anything other than skate along the surface, here providing only an introductory sketch. Like in any

---

3. Balthasar, *Glory of the Lord III*, 79.

mystical allegory of spiritual ascent (for example, Gregory of Nyssa's *Life of Moses*, Pseudo-Dionysius' *Mystical Theology*, or Bonaventure's *Itinerarium*), the themes of seeing and blindness, darkness and light, operate generally on polyvalent levels. There is more than one way to be blind and more than one way to see. For example, when Dante mistakes the giants and the Titans for a city with high towers in the pit of Malebolge in canto 31 of the *Inferno*, Virgil gently chides him, saying,

> I had not held my head turned there for long
>
> when (so it seemed) I now saw many towers.
>
> And therefore, "Sir," I said, "what town is this?"
>
> "Because," he said, "through all these wreaths of shade
>
> you rush ahead too far from what's at hand,
>
> you form of it a blurred and empty image.
>
> You'll see quite clearly when you soon arrive
>
> how greatly distance may deceive the sense."
>
> (*Inf.* 31.19–26)

This particular example of misperception is just a straightforward limitation of the physical senses: the deep circles of hell are too dark, being at the core of the earth and as far as possible from the (physical and metaphysical) light of the Sun, and Dante is simply too far removed from the object of his sight to make out what it is he truly sees. Likewise, near the beginning of the astral journey in *Paradiso* 3, Dante sees on the moon the dimmed faces of those who have broken their vows. His perception is here again deceived. Seeing the pale dimness of these souls' faces, he mistakenly thinks that what he is seeing is merely a reflection—as in Narcissus' pool or, if you will, through a glass darkly—and glances behind him to try to see the genuine article. Here Beatrice smilingly corrects him:

> "You baby!" she said. "Don't worry or wonder,
>
> to see me smile at all these ponderings.
>
> Those feet are not yet steady on the ground of truth.
>
> Your mind, from habit, turns round to a void."
>
> (*Par.* 3.25–28)

At this early stage of the ascent, Dante's capacity for sight is insufficiently developed; he cannot yet see things as they are.

Indeed, as Dante goes on his visual journey through and beyond space, the culmination of which is a transcendent vision of the beauty of Godhead that he can neither describe nor remember, it is important to note that his visions are not always unmediated; on significant occasions, what he does see is not as such but is instead mediated through its reflection in the eyes of Beatrice. In *Purgatorio* 31, for instance, after Dante has drunk from the waters of Lethe so that he would forget and be purified even from the memory of his past sins, Dante has a first beatific vision in the Earthly Paradise. The four cardinal virtues lead him not to look at the thing itself, but rather at its reflection in Beatrice's eyes—in this case it is the christologically inflected twin natures in one person in the figure of the Griffin. Likewise, in the opening canto of the *Paradiso*, Beatrice stares directly into the sun. Though he tries to follow suit, he must look away from the brightness of the vision and see the scene play out instead upon her radiant eyes.

Often, Dante's temporary blindness is the result of an over-saturation of light, an arresting glimpse of glory, a beauty so terrible that it impedes the senses with some degree of violence or at least the persistent possibility of the perceiver's destruction. Dante temporarily loses his capacity for sight on numerous occasions because of this excess of glory: for instance, when the essence of the Holy Spirit is glimpsed between the Sun and Mars; when he sees the vision of Christ triumphant formed in a great constellation in the sphere of the fixed stars in *Paradiso* 23, and again in *Paradiso* 25 when he stares too deeply into the radiance of love that is St. John the Apostle. This text continually reinforces that learning to see aright is a not un-dangerous therapy, a gradual refining or strengthening process witnessed by the reader in changes to Dante's quality of perception by oscillations of partial sight, misapprehension, or outright blindness. The overall trajectory in the *Paradiso*, however, is that the practice of seeing tends to generate more and more aptitude and power to see.

These mysteries of the faith cannot come to Dante in their undiluted strength without the steady work of ascent that would fortify his spiritual senses. In Jupiter, the singular eagle composed of the souls of the just rulers explains to Dante that he can overreach in his quest for greater sight: it is possible to want to see not only too little, but also too much. Evoking God's whirlwind speeches in the book of Job, particularly Job 38, the eagle speaks thusly in response to Dante's question about the nature of divine justice:

> Therefore, the powers of sight that you possess—
>
> which must exist as rays from that one Mind
>
> with which all things that are brimming full—

cannot, in their own nature, be so great

that their Original should not have sight

of much beyond what, there, appears to them.

It follows that the sight your world receives

in sempiternal justice sinks itself

three-fold as deep as eyes in open sea.

Although you see the bottom near the shore,

the ocean floor you *can't*. And yet it's there.

Its depths conceal its being so profound.

(*Par.* 19.52–63)

Likewise in *Paradiso* 21, Beatrice must withhold her smile from Dante in the planetary sphere of Saturn. Here she likens Dante analogously to the ancient character of Semele, who begged to see Zeus in the full splendor of his divinity but when he became manifest she was destroyed by fire, since a mortal form could not look upon him and live (*Par.* 21.4–12).[4]

Eventually, however, as his senses are refined and strengthened Dante is able to behold Beatrice's smile in an unmediated way. Once he has recovered from his swoon at seeing the brilliant splendor of Christ triumphant, Beatrice invites Dante to look upon her as she is:

"Open your eyes and look at what I am!

You have seen things by which you're made so strong,

you can, now, bear to look upon my smile."

I was like one whose waking sense returns

yet strives in vain—his dreaming now oblivion—

to bring once more that vision back to mind,

as I now heard that utterance which deserves

a gratitude that never should be dimmed

from that great book that tells of things long past.

(*Par.* 23.45–53)

Later, in *Paradiso* 30, Dante must stoop to drink from a river of light, a river of divine grace, yet the method of drinking is not with his lips but

4. Cf. Ovid, *Metamorphoses*, III, 235–315.

rather, significantly, with his eyes. Once he has allowed the river of divine grace to sate the thirst of his eyes and wash away the last of his mortal and moral frailty, the scene around him almost magically blossoms into full relief; the colors deepen, his vision sharpens, and he sees—even now in the reflection of God's tremendous light—the mystical rose that is the image of Paradise. There is thus in this text a kind of shattering force that is necessary in Dante's pedagogy of beauty, as pilgrims are purified and drawn up toward true vision, which is less a subjective act which perceives some object "out there" and more a self-forgetful participation in the triune, perichoretic, light of God.

On Space

Dante's praise of the stars orients our eyes to the heavens to consider the phenomenon of space, first astronomical, and correlatively as aesthetic. Even the casual reader can see it: the stars are absolutely everywhere, even in the *Inferno* when they are absent. Virgil, for instance, is able even in the pits of hell to rely on the stars to navigate their journey, reading from their hidden positions the day and the time (*Inf.* 11.112–15). One enormous clue to the fundamental importance of stars in Dante's poem, of course, is that the word *stelle*, or star, is the closing word of all three sections in the *Commedia*.[5] In the *Inferno*, after Virgil and Dante make the treacherous climb over the body of Satan trapped in the ice of the ninth circle of Hell, they emerge from the darkness:

> We climbed, he going first and I behind,
>
> until through some small aperture I saw
>
> the lovely things the skies above us bear.
>
> Now we came out, and once more saw the stars.
>
> (*Inf.* 34.136–39)

And again, at the end of the *Purgatorio*, after Dante drinks from the waters of Lethe and is purified from even the memory of his sin, he writes,

> I came back from that holiest of waves
>
> remade, refreshed as any new tree is,

---

5. For a book length treatment of astronomy in Dante's oeuvre, see Cornish, *Reading Dante's Stars*. For attention to the connection between astronomy (particularly the mythography of Saturn) and Dante's vocation as a poet in *Paradiso* 22, see Mazzotta, *Dante's Vision and the Circle of Knowledge*, 159–65.

renewed, refreshed with foliage anew,

pure and prepared to rise towards the stars.

(*Purg.* 33.142–45)

Finally, at the very end of the *Paradiso*, after Dante has gazed into the mystery of the Godhead in a beatific vision that he can neither articulate nor remember:

All powers of high imagining here failed.

But now my will and my desire were turned,

as wheels that move in equilibrium,

by love that moves the sun and other stars.

(*Par.* 33.142–45)

The stars and the planetary bodies provide both the content and the architectonics of the poem; they are signals of God's grace, expressions of God's glory, intimations of hope, promises of a fuller light. They are symbolic in the *Purgatorio* of the four cardinal virtues (prudence, fortitude, justice, and temperance) and the three theological virtues (faith, hope, and love), the latter of which shine in the night sky to communicate mystically to the purgatorial souls spiritual progress when active progress is not possible (*Pur.* 8.85–93). In *Paradiso* 10, Dante reads in the orderliness of the constellations reflections of the creativity of the divine Trinity, seeing especially in the "equinoctial point" where the celestial equator intersects with the Sun's ecliptic the perfection of creation. It is in the Empyrean that the stars give way to the magnificent, eternal Easter dawn of morning, where, as *Paradiso* 30 describes it, "brightest Aurora who serves the sun / advances and, dawning, the skies, vista / by vista, are closed till even the loveliest is gone" (*Par.* 30.7–9). In short, the *Paradiso* might be considered to be a kind of midrash on Psalm 19:1, "The heavens are telling the glory of God, and the firmament proclaims his handiwork."

The second kind of spatial paradigm in Dante's imagination is aesthetic. How is aesthetic space, like astral space, conceived, ordered, and experienced? How is it, exactly, that human beings see and interpret spaces? This question is, of course, enormously complex, a more sophisticated treatment of which could bring many other disciplines to bear upon it, including the science of optics, art history, anatomy, psychology, and so on. Without dismissing these other discourses, the main interest in the question is fundamentally theological. If it is true that the *Paradiso* is a fundamentally aesthetic or visionary text about the human capacity for and operation of sight, one of the first questions that might emerge is what constitutes the relationship between the seer and the seen. That is, in perception, what are the relative quotients of subjective and objective and how do they interact?

Visual objects present themselves phenomenally, as perceivers look at them. Something definitive and objective is given in the visual field; objects do not spring into existence at the moment of seeing and disappear when we look away, but certainly in perception the subjective element is not absent. Rather, in vision, the objective and the subjective interact in a mysterious way. Consider for a moment the phenomenon of perspective in art that gives the perceiver the illusion of depth even against the flat surface of a canvas. German Renaissance painter Albrecht Dürer (1471–1528) helpfully draws attention to the etymological roots of the word perspective: "*Perspectiva*," he says, "is a Latin word which means 'seeing through.'"[6] Artistic perspective thus allows the viewer in a sense to look through the flatness of the canvas into a space that does not actually exist physically, transforming the opaqueness of the canvas' picture plane into a kind of window.

Standing in the London National Gallery, for example, in front of Jan van Eyck's famous *Portrait of Giovanni Arnolfini and His Wife Giovanna Cenami* (1434)—a relatively early and somewhat disputed study in perspective[7]—it is entirely believable that its viewers might step through the canvas and into the room like Alice in Wonderland going through the looking glass. The eye of the viewer is drawn in, toward the chandelier and the circular mirror which reflects not only the elaborate and richly appointed interior of the room but also two other figures standing in the open doorway. The imperturbable figure of Giovanna Cenami stands right at the edge of the frame, the folds of her emerald gown threatening almost to spill off the canvas into the museum. Neither human figure looks directly out at the viewer, but the lively gaze of the dog is directly oriented toward the perceiver. A pair of wooden sandals is at the bottom left of the frame, as if a visitor has just removed them upon his entrance into the painted space

The manner of configuring artistic space with a central vanishing point (a configuration toward which the van Eyck painting was moving but did not achieve) may be what modern eyes are most accustomed to in art, but it is certainly not necessarily the natural or the only way of conceiving a space. In his classic 1927 text on geometrical or mathematical perspective, *Perspective as Symbolic Form*, Erwin Panofsky explores the development of this manner of perspectival construction from antiquity to modernity,

6. "Item Perspectiva ist ein lateinisch Wort, bedeutt ein Durchsehung" (quoted in Panofsky, *Perspective as Symbolic Form*, 27).

7. Elkins, "On the Arnolfini Portrait and the Lucca Madonna," 53–62.

arguing that the shifts in artistic perspective were actually relative to particular cultural moments that comprise any given *Weltanschauung*, or worldview. In classical antiquity, for example, Panofsky suggests that aesthetic
space was constructed not as unified or mathematical, where figures would
be sized according to the perspective of the beholder, but more distorted
and flattened out, juxtaposed with other figures in a "still unsystematic
overlapping"[8] without great interest in representing bodies and the spaces
between them to scale according to a fixed perspective. That is, there was
no convergence in these antique images toward a single horizon or even
multiple vanishing horizons.

In Renaissance conceptions of aesthetic space, however, when developments in perspective begin to correct the "distortions" of ancient
art, the space becomes rationalized and is made highly mathematical, a
development that is for Panofsky more ambivalent than not, though it is
certainly still instructive. Interestingly, the objective planes of the painting
upon which figures are placed accounts *first* for the eye of the art's perceiver. Indeed, it is this centrally located eye that determines the position
of the figures in the painting, so the lines are correlative to the beholding
subject, who perceives the figures in the painting as "far" or "near" relative
to their particular vantage point. Dürer describes this model as a "planar,
transparent intersection of all those rays that fall from the eye onto the
object it sees"[9]; here the perpendicular lines converge on a vanishing point
based fundamentally upon assumptions of a central, fixed homogenous
position of the eye.

Later developments in Renaissance art, mapped for Panofsky along
scientific, mathematical, and epistemological developments of the time,
culminate in the discovery of the infinite vanishing point, upon which all
of the orthogonals, or perpendicular lines, converge. Panofsky recognizes
this development of infinite mathematical extension in art that resonated
with the Renaissance and early modern over-reaching of the rational as a
detheologization of the universe.[10] He argues, however, that artistic perspective is a double-edged sword, something that opens out onto "the realm
of the visionary, where the miraculous becomes a direct experience of
the beholder, in that the supernatural events . . . erupt into his own, apparently natural visual space and so permit him really to 'internalize' their
supernaturalness."[11] "Perspective," he goes on, "seems to reduce the divine

8. Panofsky, *Perspective as Symbolic Form*, 41.

9. Quoted in ibid., 28.

10. Ibid., 66.

11. Ibid., 72.

to a mere subject matter for human consciousness; but for that very reason, conversely, it expands human consciousness into a vessel for the divine."[12]

These observations raise supremely interesting questions about the phenomenon of sight, here both aesthetic and theological. How, if at all, should an artist account for the subjective perception of the viewer? Should the lines of a painting be dictated based upon where the observer is standing, or generated from within the logic of the painting itself? In short, should aesthetic space be determined by the object or the subject or somewhere in between? On this topic, Panofsky offers a comparison between two similar works of art that depict St. Jerome in his study to elaborate upon this point further. The first is Antonello da Messina's (1430–1479) *St. Jerome in His Chamber*, a painting that is strict, architectural, objective, governed by its own laws of symmetry that do not really account overmuch for the position of the beholder. The vanishing point is placed nearly perfectly in the mathematical center of the page.

The second image is probably the more famous depiction of St. Jerome by Albrecht Dürer, *St. Jerome in His Cabinet*. This painting, in distinction from the first, has a vanishing point that is "eccentric," inviting the spectator into the painting from where he seems to be standing, a bit to the left. As Panofsky puts it, "We imagine that we ourselves have been admitted into it, because the floor appears to extend under our own feet. . . . The entirely eccentric position of the central vanishing point reinforces the impression of a representation determined not by the objective lawfulness of the architecture, but rather by the subjective standpoint of a beholder who has just now appeared; a representation that owes its especially 'intimate' effect in large part to this very perspectival disposition."[13] In a sense, it is the subjective gaze of the perceiver which determines the space.

Despite the admitted anachronism of retroactively importing developments of artistic perspective which came significantly after Dante's immediate context, the invocation of this kind of artistic perspective may be enlightening for a theological—if not historical—reading of Dante's *Paradiso*. The first thing that reading the *Paradiso* allows for in terms of our literary and theological reflections on aesthetic space is a kind of imaginative thought-experiment: what happens to aesthetic perspective when the perceiver standing in front of a canvas moves neither to the right nor the left on a horizontal plane, but shuttles upward at great velocity away from the earth, which in the text's geocentric worldview, was the center of the universe, through the concentric heavens of the moon, the planetary heavens

12. Ibid.
13. Ibid., 69.

of the moon and the planets and the fixed stars, and so on? We glimpse something of this phenomenon on at least two occasions when, between *Paradiso* 22 and 27, Beatrice instructs Dante to cast a retrospective look down toward the earth. In *Paradiso* 22, after Dante has conversed with St. Benedict and before they advance to the fixed stars, Beatrice says:

> "And so, before you further 'in' yourself,
>
> look down and wonder at how great a world
>
> already you have set beneath your feet,
>
> so that your heart may show itself, as full
>
> as it may be, to this triumphant throng
>
> that rings in happiness the ethereal round."
>
> I turned about to look once more through all
>
> the seven spheres and, seeing there the globe,
>
> I smiled to find how small and cheap it seemed.

(*Par.* 22.127–35)

From Dante's heightened perspective, the earth is miniscule, seemingly of little importance, what he calls in the same canto "that little threshing floor that makes men fierce" (*Par.* 22.151; cf. 27.85). With the proper perspective in place, that which might seem in the ordinary course of human lives to be hyperbolically important is appropriately regulated to *adiaphora*, indifferent things that need variously to be sloughed away altogether or else refined on the human pilgrimage to beatitude.

Surely, however, Dante, the esteemed poet who dared soar to the heights of heaven in what Balthasar has called the "inconstant, surging, unstable ocean that is the vernacular,"[14] does not mean to suggest that the earth and the particular people who populate it are of no importance whatsoever. Obviously, history matters for Dante; historical particulars and identities are brought up even into heaven. In *Paradiso* 17, Dante's own great-great grandfather Cacciaguida is able to see from his point of view the whole span or form of Dante's life—past, present, and future—unfolding in earthly history contingently even as it is present with all of historical time in the mind of God as in a single dense point.

Another element of the text that mitigates against the deformative notion that the earth and the bodies within it are nothing is in *Paradiso* 14, when Solomon poignantly tells Dante that the thing that will make the

---

14. Balthasar, *Glory of the Lord III*, 14.

flames or luminous effervescences of the souls even more beautiful is precisely the sublime reunion of their glorified souls with their transfigured, resurrected *bodies*. As Solomon says,

> But when the glorious and sacred flesh
>
> is clothing us once more our person then
>
> will be—complete and whole—more pleasing still.
>
> For then whatever has been granted us,
>
> by utmost good, of free and gracious light
>
> (the light through which we see Him) will increase.
>
> Hence, as must be, our seeing will increase,
>
> increasing, too, the fire that vision lights,
>
> the ray increasing that proceeds from that.
>
> (*Par.*14.43–51)

Bodies, then, especially when transparent to the light of God, are certainly not for Dante *adiaphora*.

The second thing we might notice, especially with respect to the relative quotients of subjective and objective perspective in the *Paradiso*, concerns Dante's perception of the souls of the blessed. In Dante's astral space, the paradisal souls appear variously to Dante as humanoid figures or as in flames or radiances, but they are not always visible and are not subject to the normal laws of mortal perception. Rather, very much like the resurrection appearances of Christ in the Gospels who chooses whether and how his figure is seen, the souls manifest themselves freely to Dante in a volitional and loving act of accommodation to his senses. Indeed, even when the souls manifest themselves in the various heavenly spheres in accordance with the nature and hierarchical level of their beatitude, they are not really there, but reside eternally in the immaterial heaven of the Empyrean. This state marks quite a change from the beleaguered souls of the *Inferno*, who were compelled not only to act out grotesque indignities correlative to their earthly offenses, but, perhaps worse, to enact such nightmarish scenarios necessarily as the objects of Dante's curious gaze. In short, then, what Dante sees in the *Paradiso* is arguably less dependent upon his own perception and more upon the objective reality of the freely given appearing phenomenon.

This transition from the relative privileging of the subjective to the objective also seems to be enacted on a macro-scale in the whole text. The opening lines of each volume—the *Inferno*, the *Purgatorio*, and the

Paradiso—mark a tonal shift, that is, a move from subjective to objective. The famous opening of *Inferno* 1 certainly is marked by the subjective, not least because of its reliance upon first person language. Dante's own perspective wholly determines the scope of the action here:

> At one point midway on our path in life,
>
> I came around and found myself now searching
>
> through a dark wood, the right way blurred and lost.
>
> (*Inf.* 1.1–3)

Likewise, the opening few tercets of the *Purgatorio* see Dante announce his intentions for the second book as he prays to the Muses for poetic inspiration and describes his own perception of the stars, a sweet relief indeed after the darkness of the *Inferno*. In the very first tercet of the *Paradiso*, however, Dante himself is totally under erasure, as the objective givenness of the refracted light of divine revelation takes a full and commanding precedence. The entire "canvas" is determined by the metaphysical light of God that moves and informs all reality. Dante does not insert himself in the same way into the first tercet:

> Glory, from Him who moves all things that are,
>
> penetrates the universe and then shines back,
>
> reflected more in one part, less elsewhere.
>
> High in that sphere which takes from Him most light
>
> I was—I was!—and saw things there that no one
>
> who descends knows how or ever can repeat.
>
> For, drawing near to what it most desires,
>
> our intellect so sinks into the deep
>
> no memory can follow it that far.
>
> (*Par.* 1.1–9)

Even when Dante shifts back into the subjective in the second and third tercets, it is only to make again the admission of the failure of any possible expressive form—knowledge, poetry, imagination, intellect, or memory—to capture, repeat, or even recall with any success the mysterious experience of the beatific vision.

Recall from the discussion of aesthetic space that perspective as correlated to the subject in art is meant to give the impression of depth, the appearance of relative farness and nearness as the viewer stands before a canvas. In Dante's culminating vision of the mystic rose in *Paradiso* 30, however, his limited first-person perspective magnifies, growing more expansive, such that farness and nearness are no longer even relevant categories of vision, lines which recall Piccarda's insistence in *Paradiso* 3 that the blessed do not aspire or strive to rise up through the ranks of heaven, since their will is already at one with the will of God:

> My eyes, despite such breadth and altitude,
>
> were not confused or blurred but took all in—
>
> the kind and sum of this light-heartedness.
>
> Nothing's gained here or lost by "near" and "far."
>
> For where God rules without some means between,
>
> the law of nature bears no weight at all.
>
> (*Par.* 30.118–23)

Indeed, as Christian Moevs details in his elegant text, *The Metaphysics of Dante's* Comedy, the final revelation of the light of God, who is the concentrated actuality of Being itself, dissolves the distinction between subjective and objective, God and self. As he contemplates the mystery of how the finitude of human being might as *imago Dei* come to participate in the perichoretic love of the Trinity, Dante likens himself at this moment to a geometer halted over the impossible mathematical puzzle of how to square the circle. But there is no rational principle to hold onto. As Moevs puts it, "The understanding comes in a flash of illumination or experience, canceling concept and image and with them the last trace of autonomous desire and will, which are now integrated into the harmony of creation, into the experience of self and all things as the self-expression of divine love."[15] Subjective and objective perspectives have here merged mysteriously into one mode of beatified perception.

We see from the *Paradiso*, then, that for Dante it is God, very God, who is the infinite vanishing point of the human life! It would be difficult to over-state the aptness of the analogy as we draw attention to the fact that in the ninth sphere of the *Primum Mobile* in *Paradiso* 28, Dante has a dazzling vision of God precisely as a non-dimensional, infinite point of light:

> Then, as in mirrors, when the light's behind,
>
> we see, although in sight and thought we've yet

---

15. Moevs, *The Metaphysics of Dante's* Comedy, 81.

to grasp the fact, the flame of some twin torch

(so turn around to see if that smooth glass

has told the truth and see it does accord,

as words in song when sung upon their beat),

so too did I—my memory now records—

still looking back towards those lovely eyes,

from which, to snare me, love had made the cord.

And once I'd turned—and once my eyes were touched

by what appears within that scroll to those

who look aright within its turning sphere—

a single point I saw, that shot out rays

so sharp the eye on which it fixes fire,

is bound to close against that needle-strength.

(*Par.* 28.4–18)

In Dante's imaginative vision in the *Paradiso*, the infinite vanishing point is the luminous Godhead, Being itself, in which objective and subjective perspective become unified, a space that is decidedly shared all the way down. Contemplating the increasing hierarchy of the light of the stars, which gives way in the Empyrean to the full light of the light of divine Being, has drawn the pilgrim steadily upward with its undeniable summons to purity, virtue, and vision. In heaven, Dante aligns absolutely the human being's subjective perception with the objective givenness of the Trinity in a non-linear, even non-dual miracle of the perspectival where God is all in all, and there is no longer any need to insist upon his own subjective space at the detriment of others.

Furthermore, that fantastic line "from which, to snare me, love had made the cord" (*Par.* 28.12) sends the reader back to Virgil's early counsel to Dante in *Purgatorio* 18 regarding the summoning force of Love which moves the pilgrim to beatitude. Availing himself of the aesthetic language of "form" that points forward to the *Paradiso*, Virgil says,

The mind, which is created quick to love,

when roused by pleasure into conscious act

will tend towards such things as give delight.

From things that truly are, your *apprehensio*

draws out an image which it then unfolds

within you, so that mind turns round to it.

If mind, one having turned, inclines to that,

this bending is called love—and "nature," too—

bound up in you afresh by pleasure's knot.

(*Purg.* 18.19–27)

Readers of Paul Claudel's long philosophical play *The Satin Slipper* might be reminded here as well of that most striking and visceral image from it, namely, the guardian angel's fish-hook lodged in the human heart that tugs human beings upward toward the beautiful, sometimes quite painfully, with an invisible fishing line.[16] In the play, the angel poses the question to Dona Prouheze:

> If he hears a violin somewhere, or simply two or three times in succession those taps one gives on a piece of wood. . . . You yourself, tell me, is it really true that you have never felt in the depth of yourself, between the heart and the liver, that dull thud, that sharp pull-up, that urgent touch? . . . It was my hook in the very midst of you and I was paying out the line like a patient angler. Look at it twined about my wrist.[17]

In Dante, it is the vanishing point of Primal Love that sends what will become Claudel's fish-hook all the way down to Dante midway through his life's journey, in the reason of Virgil, the compassion of the Virgin Mary, the divine light of St. Lucia, the revelation of Beatrice, pulling him further up and further in. Again, we might invoke Benedict XVI's words: "The beautiful wounds, but this is exactly how it summons man to his final destiny."[18]

To conclude this theological and aesthetic reflection upon Dante's *Paradiso*, we return to the pedagogy of beauty, that is, learning to see aright, as a spiritual therapy. For we poor souls gathered here on earth are not, of course, in heaven yet. Dante, too, had to come down from such great heights and live out the anguished experience of exile from his beloved Florence that his ancestor Cacciaguida had foretold. We conduct our lives not from

16. Balthasar actually puts Dante and Claudel into dialogue, in his suggestion that "only Claudel's *Le Soulier de Satin* again achieves Dante's dimension, in which personal love and the shaping of the universe are mutually conditioned, taking the same path through the hell of the hardest renunciations and the purgatories of expiated infidelity" (Balthasar, *Glory of the Lord III*, 36).

17. Claudel, *The Satin Slipper*, 167–68.

18. Pope Benedict XVI, "The Feeling of Things," 49.

the heights of the heavens, but tentatively, in the reality of a fragmentary vision that is conditioned always by finitude. We might consider, then, in light of Dante's visionary pilgrimage through space and time, adopting the spiritual practice of cultivating our vision according to what we might call an optics of resurrection. In his book *A Theological Anthropology*, Hans Urs von Balthasar alludes briefly to the image of "resurrection eyes," which is an absolutely fascinating concept to layer onto a theological aesthetic reading of Dante. According to Balthasar, "Resurrection eyes are not implanted like a natural organ: they are imparted *through the act of seeing itself*, through the event in which the old tomb is burst and the new truth streams forth."[19] To see with resurrection eyes means to see with an always doubled vision, to see the rays of God in all things; it means to take with equal seriousness physicality and the everyday and that invisible reality which both suffuses and transcends them, to see both form and splendor. It might mean, too, a capacity if not to see at least to imagine the form of the whole coherent narrative of our lives laid out, complete, seen from above, and thus to accord ourselves spiritually to the form which summons us. Moreover, it might mean practicing the *ascesis* of self-forgetfulness by looking with great mercy upon each other as we are, that is, correlated ultimately to the light and love of the God who moves all stars, the one in whom we live and move and have our being (Acts 17:28). We are as St. Paul says we are in the second letter to the Corinthians: "And all of us, with unveiled faces, seeing the glory of the Lord as though reflected in a mirror, are being transformed into the same image from one degree of glory to another . . ." (2 Cor 3:18).

---

19. Balthasar, *A Theological Anthropology*, 289 (italics added).

9

Love's Recollection

Paradiso and Healed Memory

Jessica Keating

I n drawing the gaze of contemporary persons to Dante's *Commedia*, Pope Francis not only invites readers to rediscover the "lost and obscured meaning" of human dignity, but indeed to reclaim the lost and obscured memory of ourselves and each other in the light of mercy.[1] Many of the essays in this volume take up the multivalent theme of memory, remarking on how souls ask to be remembered, how memory functions in the various canticles, and the relationship between speech and memory. The present essay, too, will take up the thick, complex phenomenon of memory in order to see how eucharistic remembering contours the *Commedia*.

Memory is a complex and elusive phenomenon. Despite our best efforts to plumb its depths and to map out its mechanisms and meaning, it continues to evade us—a constant reminder that the human person is not, after all, a mere collector of data, but a perceiver of meaning and mystery. Constitutive of personal identity in community, memory functions even where recollection is not consciously willed.

Children provide a particularly rich example of memory. An older child, say, seven or older, is more or less fully conscious of the phenomenon of memory. In fact, a child of this age delights in hearing stories about what he was like as a younger child himself and in recollecting past events. My

---

1. Pope Francis, "Message of His Holiness Pope Francis for the 750th Anniversary of the Birth of the Supreme Poet Dante Alighieri."

eight-year-old nephew will provide inning-by-inning accounts of baseball games to anyone interested (or willing) to listen. He is also beginning to discover some of the concrete benefits of remembering and forgetting, reminding his parents that they had promised such-and-such a thing, but also forgetting to do chores or to eat parts of his lunch he does not like.

For a younger child memory is not yet tied to time or will, not to mention that memory, as an abstract concept, is meaningless. Young children certainly have memories, but for them past events are unreflectively immediate and present. At this tender age, there is almost no understanding of time's ordering hand. What happened a year ago could just as well have happened five minutes ago, or perhaps five days from now.

For an infant memory is totally nondiscursive; it is absorbed in and as the presence of the other. An infant will not remember the first time her mother smiled at her, even as she inchoately comprehends the smile. She will learn her native tongue from her parents, but will not recollect the experience of learning. Though language is constitutive for realizing human existence and for relating to those around her, she will retain no memory of the transition from babbling infant to articulate child. She will probably not be able to search through the recesses of her memory and exclaim, "Ah, this is when and where and how I learned to say apple!" She will probably not recollect the first time she said, "Thank you," or "I love you." Yet this language, which she learns in the arms of her parents and practices without self-conscious effort at their knees, will shape her personal identity. She does not create this language, her native language, but receives it as gift within the matrix of her family, and it will form her conscious, living memory.

A woman who labors in pain to bring forth her child does not forget the pain of labor, and yet somehow the experience of pain is reinterpreted in light of her love for her child. Her memory of the indignities and pain of childbirth are not annihilated; rather love and joy cover over the pain and transform the indignities into sites of beauty and hope, reshaping and refiguring her vision of the crucible of childbirth.

These observations are fairly general and do not, as yet, take into account the memory of personal sin. Imagine, now, the wound of infidelity. How is the memory of such a transgression both constitutive of and deactivated by the phenomenon of forgiveness? In other words, how does forgiveness reconfigure sin? On the one hand, the event of betrayal must be remembered in order to be forgiven. Amnesia cannot suffice as forgiveness. On the other hand, the memory of transgression cannot be so strong that it makes forgiveness impossible. Forgiveness actually requires some kind of balance, even if it be unequal, between remembering and forgetting, and when the impossible gift of forgiveness does occur, it does not have a unilateral effect. It affects both the one who extends forgiveness and the one forgiven, such that the relationship between the two does not merely return to its previous state; it is elevated and enabled anew.

As a phenomenon of excess, forgiveness does more than disable the effective memory of sin. To be sure, it removes those parts of the self that are dead because of sin, so that we can say the guilt of the offending party is dead. But forgiveness actually does more than remove these effects of sin; it capacitates us anew in the mode of mercy. The one who extends the impossible gift of forgiveness covers over the wound with steadfast love. The one who forgives is re-selfed according to this excessive enactment of love, which exceeds forensic comprehension. The one who receives forgiveness is given back to himself in full, abled anew, freed for communion. When the impossible miracle of forgiveness occurs, it is not merely a formal transaction. It effects something new, something that exceeds human comprehension, but is nevertheless real.

Each of the above examples—the child who learns language, the mother for whom the pain of childbirth becomes a site of joy, the couple whose relationship is reconfigured by forgiveness—demonstrate the delicate interplay between remembering and forgetting as operative within brackets of love. The child who receives the gift of language does so in the context of the primal relationship of love. The woman who forgets the suffering of childbirth does so under the influence of love for her child, whose face effectively revises her memory of what is otherwise a terribly painful event. And the couple that travels the impossible path of forgiveness remembers and forgets according to the excessive phenomenon of love expressed in the event of forgiveness.

At this point, I venture to say three things about memory. First, memory is constitutive of personal identity, and as beings in relation to others, our memories are not solely our own possession. Memory is permeated by the presence of others. Second, memory is not merely the discrete recollection of facts. It is more than a cognitive operation. Human memory does not function in the same way as mechanical memory; rather it is interpretive, malleable, and open-ended. Third, love influences what and how we remember.

Memory in the *Commedia*

Memory contours the entire *Commedia*. Throughout Dante's masterpiece, we encounter the mystery of memory—the fluttering shades of remembering and forgetting. At times Dante remembers that which he wishes to forget. At other times his memory falls short, stumbling on the path of love. Still at other moments Dante's remembering exceeds his poetic skill. Trying to describe the experience of being drawn through the waters of the River Lethe, the limits of Dante's memory and poetic speech intersect: "I can't remember it, still less can write" (*Purg.* 31.97). Indeed, the entire *Commedia* functions in the ambit of memory: Dante is the apocalyptic seer, who sees behind the veil and whose beloved, Beatrice, charges him with remembering his pilgrimage from the ante-chambers of *Inferno* to the heights of the Empyrean in order to "aid the world that lives all wrong" (*Purg.* 32.103). Her command is predicated on self-gift. Whatever we might say about Dante's poetic conceit, Beatrice reminds us that his privileged vision is ultimately not his possession but a gift that has been, from the first, a gift of divine, descending mercy. Remember, Dante's entire pilgrimage occurs precisely because he is remembered—first by Mary, then by Lucy, and finally by Beatrice (*Inferno* 2). If merciful love prompts Dante's journey, his task as poet must participate in the order of that love. He is not prompted to write down that which he has seen and remembered for his own aggrandizement, but on behalf of a world "that lives all wrong."

If Dante's masterpiece is about conversion, then his is a poetics of memory: its deformation, its reformation, and its redemption. Memory not only contours the poem as a whole, but it also shapes the internal workings of each canticle, of each relationship, of each person. Above all, however, the poetics of the *Commedia* is the poetics of divine memory as expressed in the excessive gift of divine mercy. In other words, the poetics of the *Commedia* is eucharistic, which is to say, it is "bound to a memorial of God's mercy that configures or even defines all of one's own memory."[2]

Perhaps this is why the Psalms figure so prominently in the *Commedia*. They are, after all, saturated with images of God's merciful remembering, praising the "God of gods," the Lord of creation and redemption, "who remembered us in our low estate, for his steadfast love endures forever" (Ps 136:2, 23). Psalm 25 petitions God, "Be mindful of your mercy, O Lord, and of your steadfast love, for they have been of old. Do not remember the sins of my youth or my transgressions; according to your steadfast love remember me" (25:6–7). The psalmist implores God to remember and forget according to his merciful love, to remain faithful to the covenant. Indeed, time and again, Israel's patriarchs and prophets ask God to forget the sins that lay behind them—the grumbling in the desert, the idolatry at Sinai, the mistreatment of the poor and the widows and to remember his covenant—and the promise of mercy reaches its apex in Christ: "He has

---

2. Cavadini, "Eucharistic Exegesis," 89.

helped his servant Israel, in remembrance of his mercy, according to the promise he made to our ancestors, to Abraham and to his descendants forever" (Luke 1:55). God's remembering, as articulated in Scripture, is not a static and indifferent act of mental recall or recollection, but the dynamic memory of mercy that touches us in the person Christ.

The *Commedia* invites us into the diminuendos and crescendos of eucharistic memory, to consider what it means to remember and to forget, to be remembered and to be forgotten. The mysterious depth, complexity, and potency of eucharistic memory, which is to say, "formed in the memory of the price of our redemption,"[3] such that one's sight and speech are tuned and united to Christ. Dante dares to imagine the unimaginable reality of memory redeemed, the reality of memory healed and elevated, conformed to the super-saturated gift of divine mercy.

In order to explore the poetics of eucharistic memory in the *Commedia*, I will proceed in three parts. First, I will look at the *Inferno* and the counterfeiting of eucharistic memory. Then, I will turn to the *Purgatorio* and explore the revision and deepening of eucharistic memory. Lastly, I will discuss the actualization of eucharistic memory in *Paradiso*.

Inferno as Anti-Memory

The *Inferno* is inversely referred to the eucharistic memory that is practiced in purgatory and realized in paradise. Hell is the place of counterfeit memory, of anti-memory. The dead remember, but they both remember too much and they remember wrongly, holding onto their memories like dogs possessively guarding their bones and snarling at any hand that dares to reach out to touch them. Indeed, Dante's presence among the dead incites fear, hostility, and pain because for the souls who reside here memory is played in the key of aggression, isolation, rivalry, and pain. Even where the dead are found in pairs and groups, the presence of other souls only serves to form an anti-communion, even to the point of the violent consumption of the other who is present as competitor, rival, and enemy.

In the *Inferno* remembering destroys communion because the memory of the dead is a malignant forgetting of God's mercy. Memory remains incurved, oriented to the past and to the self. All of the senses intersect and disintegrate in this incurving of memory as it descends in utter chaos: the supreme anti-mysticism. The dead reenact their sins eternally, their bodies ironically interpenetrating with increasing violence as a sign of isolation, which culminates in the anti-eucharist of cannibalism. Language becomes

3. Cavadini, "Eucharistic Exegesis," 91.

increasingly jumbled, grating, deceitful and destructive. Sight functions in
the mode of indifference and voyeurism. Space functions in the mode of
disdain and violent encroachment. Memory is stolid, unchanging, and un-
productive, functioning in the mode of anxiety and pain.

The dead are interested in one another as objects of consumption and
utility—as projections of the self. Their interest in Dante is no different. The
dead reduce any suggestion of the positive valence of his presence among
them to his mere usefulness, as they see it. The sodomites, for example,
observing that Dante speaks "at so little cost" and "so well," entreat him to
remember them to the living:

> And so, should you escape from these dark haunts,
>
> and go once more to see the lovely stars,
>
> when you, with pleasure, say that "I was there,"
>
> then do, we beg you, speak of us to others.
>
> (*Inf.* 16.82–85)

Anxious to be remembered in the City of Man, they call upon Dante to
speak of them to others, to act as a kind of intercessor, albeit an inverted
one. These souls do not plead with the poet to remember them at the altar
of sacrifice, but beg to be remembered, that is, praised, in the world.

Even ostensibly pleasant memories make hell's inhabitants miserable.
Recollecting her lust for Paolo, Francesca opines:

> There is no sorrow greater
>
> than, in times of misery, to hold at heart
>
> the memory of happiness. (Your teacher knows.)
>
> And yet, if you so deeply yearn to trace
>
> the root from which the love we share first sprang,
>
> than I shall say—and speak as though in tears.
>
> (*Inf.* 5.121–26)

For the souls in hell, remembering is a source of disorientation, misery,
and restlessness because for them remembering is correlative with forgetting and with hopelessness. This is nowhere more starkly on display than
the traitorous Count Ugolino's massive inversion of liturgical speech and
eucharistic memory:

How hard you are if, thinking what my heart

foretold, you do not feel the pain of it.

Whatever will you weep for, if not that?

By now they all had woken up. The time

was due when, as routine, our food was brought.

Yet each was doubtful, thinking of their dream.

Listening, I heard the door below locked shut,

then nailed in place against that dreadful tower.

I looked at their dear faces, spoke no word.

I did not weep. Inward, I turned to stone.

They wept. And then my boy Anselmo spoke:

"What are you staring at? Father, what's wrong?"

And so I held my tears in check and gave

no answer all that day, nor all the night

that followed on, until another sun came up.

A little light had forced a ray into

our prison, so full of pain. I now could see

on all four faces my own expression.

(*Inf.* 33.43–57)

Ugolino goes on to recollect his sons' offering of their flesh to their father and the death of his son, Gaddo, who "pitched forward" at his father's feet and cried aloud: "Help me. . . . Why don't you help me, Dad!" (*Inf.* 33.69–70). Like the blessed dead we encounter in *Purgatorio* and *Paradiso*, Ugolino remembers details of his life—indeed, he recollects the numbing pain of his and his son's imprisonment and demands that Dante do for him what he would not do for his sons—that is, weep. He remembers right down to the sound of the nails sealing shut the prison door. He recollects the unwelcomed light that forces its way into the cell like an intruder—a light that makes pain visible. He remembers it all. Like a forensic scientist collecting data, he recollects every moment of his misery, which ends in frozen silence.

What is the difference between Ugolino's memory and the memory of those who labor on the terraces of purgatory and flicker and dance like flames in the Empyrean? Ugolino's memory is an anti-memory, a misremembering, just as the liturgy he enacts is an anti-liturgy—the Paschal

Mystery turned on its head, made counterfeit. The language of prayer is inverted, as Ugolino duplicitously seeks to make himself the central reference point of the harrowing ordeal he and his sons undergo. His remembering is a forgetting of the highest order. He talks but he does not confess. He sees his sons, but not as they are in themselves. In the depths of hell Ugolino sees only his expression in the faces of his sons, who act as dark mirrors for their father's pride and anger.

Perhaps this is why the words of Gaddo, which obviously mimic Christ's cry of lament, are impotent. The father refuses to weep; he remains unmoved: "And there he died," Ugolino continues and immediately redounding upon himself, he says to Dante, "You see me here" (*Inf.* 33.70). Insofar as others are present, even his own sons, they are present as objects—always and eternally as reflecting his own face. For Ugolino and all the souls in hell, remembering is forgetting because it is a contracted, impenetrable, self-aggrandizing event.

Purgatorio and the Revision of Memory

In purgatory memory is in the process of being reformed, moving from obsession with oneself to confession. On the liturgically saturated terraces, souls learn how to worship, how to lift the gaze to God and so to one another as mirrors of divine love. The souls doing penance on these terraces are undergoing the process of being re-selfed. Memory, speech, and sight are reconfigured in communion with others. Liturgical speech and practice enable the souls in purgatory to remember aright. In *Paradiso*, Dante will imagine the full realization of memory healed and eucharistically configured. But compare here Ugolino's anti-memory with Virgil's explanation of the burning expansiveness of *caritas* on the terrace of wrath in *Purgatory* 15:

> The Good that—infinite beyond all words—
>
> is there above will run to love like rays
>
> of light that come to anything that shines.
>
> It gives itself proportioned to the fire,
>
> so that, as far as *caritas* extends,
>
> eternal Worth increases over it.
>
> The more there are who fix their minds up there,
>
> the more good love there is—and more to love—

and each (as might a mirror) give to each.

(*Purg.* 15.67–75)

Unlike Ugolino's embittered memory and objectifying vision that allows him to see only himself in the faces of his sons, Virgil's speech describes the expansion of vision correlative with the expansion of love that in paradise allows the blessed dead to confess the truth of themselves as remembered, which is to say, as objects of love.

Purgatory is that process by which souls learn how to assimilate themselves to Christ. Like the souls in hell, the souls in purgatory ask to be remembered, but they ask to be remembered in prayer to either the souls in heaven or to the men and women on earth whose intercessory prayer can speed them through purgatory. In fact, some of the souls Dante encounters in purgatory only escape harrowing of hell because others have interceded on their behalf—they are remembered in prayer and entrusted to the memory of God, which is to say, they are remembered at the altar of sacrifice. Dante's intercessory role in purgatory, unlike hell, functions in the register of liturgical recollection.

The dual aspects of confession are essential to understanding the reformation of memory in *Purgatorio*. Souls confess sin and do penance for them. At the same time, in and through this first mode of confession, they learn what it means to praise God. An essential part of the activity in purgatory is the re-membering—the piecing back together—of the self in the light of God's mercy, which is to say, God's sacrifice of love. Only when they are so identified, will the souls in purgatory fully see rays of truth and speak the burning light of love.

Souls are re-selfed as they progress to heaven, and this re-selfing is fundamentally tuned to the rhythms of liturgical prayer by which they are assimilated into the person of Christ. The reformation of memory in prayer does not imply a simple annihilation of memory, but rather it is the configuring of memory to the redemptive mercy poured out in Christ. The grammar of liturgical prayer is expressive; it lifts eyes heavenward. In *Purgatorio* 8, Dante describes one such scene of prayer. Hearing the evening bell, he gazes at a single soul:

> This soul, first joined his palms and lifted them,
>
> eyes fixed toward the orient, as though
>
> to say to God: "For nothing else I care."
>
> "*Te lucis ante*" issued from his lips
>
> with such devotion and each note so sweet

it made me wander out of conscious thought.

Then sweetly and devoutly, all the rest,

their eyes all turned to those supernal wheels,

picked up from him and sang the hymn in full.

(*Purg.* 8.10–18)

Singing the Ambrosian compline hymn, these souls turn their gaze skyward toward heaven and join in the communal hymn. Gesture, word, and gaze all work in harmony.

Purgatory is a school of prayer. Grounded in the self-giving and self-surrendering of the triune God, prayer continues the process of assimilating souls into Christ, capacitating them for the heavenly liturgy with Mary and the communion of saints. To pray is to be grafted into eucharistic memory, which means being assimilated into the mind of Christ and participating in the kenosis of the triune God.

To learn to pray is to learn to speak and to remember aright. On the terrace of gluttony Dante encounters Forese Donati. His emaciated flesh prevents Dante from recognizing his old friend, rather his voice signals and makes visible the person whose face is obscured and emaciated in longing.

I never would have known him from his face.

But in his voice, all now was shown to me

that had, in feature, been lost and destroyed.

That spark for me rekindled at a stroke

clear recognition of those much changed lips,

and once again I saw Forese's face.

(*Purg.* 23.43–48)

Forese cries aloud at his friend's approach, "For me, how great a grace," and it is the sound of his voice reveals his identity (*Purg.* 23.42). Forese's speech and Dante's sight intersect in the language of prayer, which acts to lift the veil of obscurity. Acquiescing to Dante's request that he tell the *truth* about himself, Forese speaks of his purgatorial sufferings:

"There falls," he said, "from the Eternal Mind

a virtue in that water and that tree

back there—which sharpens me and pares me down.

And all these people, weeping as they sing,

because their gullets led them past all norms,

are here remade as holy, thirsting, hungering.

Cravings to eat and drink are fired in us

by perfumes from that fruit and from the spray

that spreads in fans above the greenery.

Nor once alone, in circling around this space,

is agony and pain refreshed in us.

I call it pain. Rightly, I should say solace.

For that same yearning leads us to the tree

that led Christ, in his joy, to say, '*Eli*,'

when through his open veins he made us free."

(*Purg.* 23.61–75)

Forese makes a daring claim, a claim that inverts *Inferno* 33. For Ugolino, suffering, which is also in the mode of starvation, remains merely the painful event of abandonment. Forese, however understands his suffering eucharistically, interpreting Christ's lament of suffering and abandonment on the cross as a cry of joy. In doing so, he names the central dynamic of purgatory. The intertwining of suffering and joy permeates the logic of *Purgatorio* by which the souls who inhabit the various terraces learn the truth about themselves.

To speak the truth of oneself is to learn how to speak anew. The process of repenting from sin is painful because it requires burning away of those parts of oneself dead in sin. Yet, this pain is simultaneously a solace. Yes, there is penance, weeping, thirsting, and hungering; yet it is by these very means that souls are remade holy. Dante imagines joy as interwoven with the sufferings of purgatory, such that weeping and singing occur simultaneously. Joy is not simply the reward of those souls who grit their teeth through purgatory, rather it is embedded in the very act of penance. Unlike the *Inferno*, where suffering de-capacitates communication and disfigures memory, in purgatory pain regenerates the self, enabling the penitent to re-narrate their biography, to revise their memory in the light of the cross.

An essential part of the purgatorial reconstitution of the self is learning to speak of oneself in Christ, and so Forese must revise his memory as he speaks. Initially describing purgation as pain, he immediately corrects himself, amending his initial locution: "Rightly, I should say solace." He comes to reinterpret himself in light of Christ, who, enduring the sufferings of the cross, cried out *Eli*. We know this as Jesus's cry of abandonment from the Gospel of Matthew: "*Eli, Eli, lema sabachthani?*" "My God, my God, why have you forsaken me?" (Matt 27:46). The lamentation of God-forsaken-ness, inverted by Ugolino, is now reinterpreted by Forese, who declares that this very lament—the lament of abandonment, of being forgotten by God, is also a cry of joy—that the Father's forgetting is also a remembering, a making new. Forese's revision of speech under the cross and in light of the Paschal sacrifice means that his memory is in the process of being penetrated, "in-youed"[4] by the will of Christ, which is always the will of kenotic love. The eucharistic contouring of this scene cannot be underestimated. The souls in purgatory are being fully assimilated to the eucharistic reality. Pope Benedict XVI captures the dynamics of this reality, which seems particularly appropriate on the terrace of gluttony:

> In the normal process of eating, the human being is the stronger being. He takes things in, and they are assimilated to him, so that they become part of his own substance. They are transformed within him and go to build up his bodily life. But in the mutual relation with Christ it is the other way around; he is the heart, the truly existent being. When we truly communicate, this means that we are taken out of ourselves, that we are assimilated into him, that we become one with him and through him, with the fellowship of our brethren.[5]

The Eucharist is only possible because God, who draws us beyond the present and into the future and into the triune mystery of self-sacrificing love, remembers us. God's memory of us in Christ funds our memory of the souls in purgatory. In learning to speak again and to remember anew, these souls are akin to the child who receives the gift of language from her parents. The liturgical language that permeates the *Purgatorio* is the grammar of prayer come to us a gift. This is the prayer we do not possess by ourselves or for ourselves, but which opens new horizons and allows us to see the depth and beauty of reality—to see creation eucharistically.

4. See *Paradiso* 9.80; also 3.79–84; 10.148; 18.112–17; 23.70; 25.130; 28.39; and 30.87. The interpenetration of senses builds throughout the *Paradiso*, as Dante dares to imagine the covalence of sensory perception in heaven where, for example, seeing is a mode of hearing and vice versa. The theme of "in-youing"—in-loving, in-holding, in-willing, etc.—gestures to the reality of being taken up into the mystery of God: of being oneself as beheld, "in-you-ed" by the gaze of Love. What we experience now in the eucharistic presence, Dante imagines in its actualized, heavenly reality. Not only do the senses interpenetrate without losing their distinctiveness (as in *Inferno*), but the saints also participate in the perfection of communion. In heaven distinctiveness is not done away with, rather distance becomes the space of *caritas* that forges a symphony of light.

5. Ratzinger, *God Is Near Us*, 78.

Paradiso and Redeemed Memory

Among the souls in *Paradiso*, Dante encounters the impossible reality of healed memory, and we encounter it with him. The blessed dead in paradise do not find themselves stripped of their historical, personal biographies. Rather, here we encounter souls who are fully given back to themselves in love for love. Memory in heaven is thus abled and disabled in specific ways and the re-collection of the self is the redemption of the particular person with her particular history, actions, and experiences. In the final instance, redemption that does not account for particularity undermines the scandalous particularity of the incarnation.

In the sphere of the moon Dante meets Piccardia Donati, who explains her position in the heavenly hierarchy.

> I am Piccardia—as you'll know I am—
>
> and blessed among the many who are blessed
>
> within this slowest moving of the spheres.
>
> . . .
>
> And though the part allotted us may seem
>
> far down, the reason is that, yes, we did
>
> neglect our vows. These were in some part void.
>
> (*Para.* 3.49–51, 55–57)

She goes on to narrate not only her biography, but also confesses the story of Constance, "who never let the veil fall from her heart" (*Para.* 3.120). The blessed dead tell the truth of themselves in great detail. Piccarda's recollection of herself is keen, astute, yet it is unsullied by grief, guilt, or anger. Rather, her memory, as she is quick to remind Dante, is conformed to charity, which is the mode of heavenly existence.

In the Heaven of Venus, Dante encounters Cunizza da Romano and Folco de Marseilles. Cunizza, with the confident boldness of a child, declares that she forgives herself for her sexual sins, and adds, "It does not brood on me—which will, to humdrum minds of yours, seem hard" (*Para.* 9.36). Folco, who was guilty of sexual vice when he was young and was also involved in the Dominican crusades against the Albigensians, offers the following interpretation of his life:

> I dwelt once on the shores of that great lake
>
> between Ebro and the Magra—whose stream

briefly divides the Genoan and Tuscan realms.

Almost at one same point of dawn and dusk

sit both Boughia and the place I was,

which made its harbor warm with its own gore.

Folco they called me, those who knew my name.

This heaven now bears my imprint, as once I,

on earth, beneath its influence, carried *its*.

For Dido—Belus' daughter—in her love,

harming Creusa and Sichaeus too,

never burned more than I when young, untonsured.

Nor did the Rhodopeaian girl, so tricked

by her Demonphoon, nor did Alcides—

heart around Iole so closely locked.

Yet here we don't repent such things. We smile,

not, though, at sin—we don't think back to that—

but at the Might that governs and provides.

In wonder, we here prize the art to which

his power brings beauty, and discern the good

through which the world above turns all below.

(*Para.* 9.88–108)

Embedded in Folco's narration of his life is a bold claim about the nature of memory of sin, about what is continuous and discontinuous in the memory of the blessed. Sin is both remembered and forgotten. Like Paul, who writes to the community at Philippi that he has forgotten what lies behind and strains forward to what lies ahead, Folco is perfectly capable of recollecting himself and narrating his personal history. Yet at the same time, sin is un-remembered or disabled in such a way that the blessed smile, not upon the sin, but "at the Might that governs and provides." Folco both sees and un-sees sin as the sight of God's providence. Thus on the one hand there is continuity in memory. Yet on the other hand, the blessed dead now remember *more truthfully* because all is recollected within Trinitarian brackets, that is in the dynamism of self-giving and self-surrendering love.

In *Paradiso*, Dante dares to imagine actualized forgiveness, a reality in which "we don't repent such things." As a correlate to sight, memory grows finer and more acute in the realm of heaven. The revision of memory by divine love gives one back to oneself. In the Gospel of Luke, Peter forgets Jesus's prediction that he will deny the Son of God three times, and it is not the cock crow, but Jesus's gaze that prompts Peter's remembrance. "The Lord turned and looked at Peter; and Peter remembered the word of the Lord, how he had said to him, 'Before the cock crows today, you will deny me three times.' He went out and began to weep bitterly" (Luke 22:61–62). Peter is made aware of his betrayal because Jesus turns and looks upon him: Jesus remembers him. At Emmaus, the eyes of disciples are prevented from recognizing the risen Christ until the breaking of the bread. The eucharistic God's memory of us capacitates vision and revises memory. They now recall that their "hearts were burning while he spoke to us on the way" (Luke 24:32).

To be forgiven is not an individual achievement or possession. Forgiveness is a profusion of love, a gift unmerited that does not operate in the realm of merely private consolation, but actually enables one to become a participant in the self-giving and self-surrendering that is the Trinity. Thus the one forgiven is turned outward, ready to give himself over in love. This is precisely why the cross cannot be forgotten and Christ's wounds cannot be elided, and why Hans Urs von Balthasar declares that "without the permanent wounds in the risen Lord, we would never have guessed the depth of the mystery of Trinity."[6] The eternal presence of the cross and of the pierced flesh of Christ are expressive of God's love, and it is precisely this same love which reforms memory. Indeed, it is through Christ's open wounds and the piercing of his Sacred Heart that eternal life is open because his body is eternal life. Thus for Dante the cross is suffuse with Christ who is the Light.

> And here remembering surpasses skill:
>
> That cross, in sudden flaring, blazed out Christ
>
> so I can find no fit comparison.
>
> But those who take their cross and follow Christ
>
> will let me off where, wearily, I fail,
>
> seeing in that white dawn, as lightning, Christ.
>
> From horn to horn, from summit down to base,
>
> there moved here scintillating points of light,
>
> bright as their paths met, bright in passing on.
>
> So minute specks of matter can be seen—

6. Balthasar, *Theo-Drama IV*, 478.

renewing how they look at every glance,

straight in their track, oblique, long, short, swift, slow.

(*Para.* 14.103–14)

The cross blazes out the light of Christ, simultaneously fulfilling and enflaming desire, and attracts the saints of heaven in an encounter that produces an effulgence of light. It is the expressive reminder of love. Unlike Ugolino, for whom even a ray of light brought intense pain, when souls in paradise gaze upon the flaming cross they see divine love, they apprehend the light that draws creation to itself. Under the influence of the excessive gift of love, the memory of sin's effects is disabled.

In the *Paradiso*, knowledge and memory are fully and excessively configured in love. Knowledge is no longer simply discursive; it is intuitive and immediate. Senses interpenetrate. We see speech and hear sight. Division is no more, though distinction remains. So it is for the blessed dead. Memory of the wounding effects of sin—guilt, division, hatred—gives way to admiration, praise, and thanksgiving. Where distance was experienced as division in earthly life, there now exists the interpenetration of love, the "in-youing" of *I* and *Thou*. Where rivalry existed, praise now takes its place. The actualization of forgiveness capacitates the souls for participation in the outpouring love of God, which surpasses speech, sight, and memory. The great love poet finds himself reduced (or is it elevated?) to babbling infant held in the arms of his beloved mother, suckling her breast.

And now my spark of words will come more short—

even of what I can call to mind—

than baby tongues still bathing in mum's milk.

(*Para.* 33.106–9)

All is fresh and full of possibility. The primal relationship of natural love, which creates the "space" for intimacy, the first site of love, communion, and speech, is taken up to express *the* primal relationship. Dante has reached the limits of speech; yes, his words fall short, but he does not fall silent, as do the souls in the pit of hell. Something quite different happens at the heights of the Empyrean. This falling short is at the same time an exceeding, a fullness. For the infant at his mother's breast, all senses interpenetrate. Touch, sound, smell, sight interpenetrate to form a primal comprehension of the beloved, and this primal space of love is where the infant, tongue bathed in milk, first learns to speak.

In the last instance, the blessed dead's participation in the life of God is a phenomenon of excess that exceeds all speech. The eucharistic acclamation, "Lord, I am not worthy but only say the word and my soul shall be healed," is fulfilled. Because Christ "in-yous" in all the dead, they also "in-you" in one another. And yet, this dynamism of interpenetration and self-donation also makes them more uniquely themselves. As angels swarm like bees and the faces of the saints sway to *caritas*, where the voices of children sing bathed in light, prayer becomes the regulative mode of discourse. All is immediacy, gift, and intuition.

The smile of a child's mother (or father) discloses the gift of otherness in the union of relationship. As the child learns her native tongue in the arms of her parents and receives the gift of language from beyond herself, the blessed dead, like babes "still bathing in mum's milk" participate in the eternal circle of divine love—in the giving and receiving of the gift of themselves from beyond themselves. The mother who smiles upon her infant child, whose smile the infant child receives as the gift and sign of another, pales in light of "the love that moves the sun and other stars" (*Para.* 33.145).

Conclusion: Memory as Gift

To be remembered by God is to be mercied, and mercy requires a certain kind forgetfulness—the kind of forgetfulness that covers over sin, that deactivates it. Memory redeemed is eucharistic memory; memory that remembers in the brackets of kenotic love. Eucharistic memory culminates in praise of God. Under the influence of the excessive gift of love, memory of sin is disabled and metaphorically covered over.

The psalmist declares, "Happy are those whose transgression is forgiven, whose sin is covered," expressing the power of God to reconstitute the penitent sinner, to cover over the guilt of transgression, to put it out of sight (Ps 32:1). St. Augustine, in book 10 of the *Confessions*, interprets this psalm, when he remarks on the disabling of the memory of sin. Writing of his past evil deeds, Augustine finds reason to praise God, who has forgiven and covered over his sins in order "to make me glad in yourself, transforming my soul by faith and your sacrament," and he imagines that readers and hearers of his confessions will delight "not because the deeds were evil but because they existed once but exist no more."[7] Clearly, Augustine does not suffer from amnesia with respect to the sins of his past. His memory has not been annihilated; indeed, he expends great effort detailing the sins of his youth in the first half of the *Confessions*. Yet for him, as for the psalmist,

7. Augustine, *The Confessions*, X.4.

these transgressions, though recalled, are no longer operative. They "exist no more." Divine mercy has covered them over, transforming the site of one's sins into sites of God's mercy, such that the evil of sin and the guilt attending transgression are no longer operative. With the psalmist, Augustine's remembering of past sin functions—or does not function as the case may be—according to the intervening and excessive grace of forgiveness, in which God reconfigures the sinner according to gift of mercy.

Forgiveness functions—it heals memory. For Augustine, as for the blessed dead in Dante's *Commedia*, God's merciful memory of us—which involves always a forgetting and a remembering—is not only restorative, though it is that. It also elevates us, capacitating us for praise, and for participation in the eternal giving and surrendering love. In mercy we are given back to ourselves and the flame of memory burns in the eucharistic love that has been leading the way all along. Redeemed memory is eucharistic memory; it is memory that remembers in the brackets of divine memory that is also divine mercy—the love that is always reaching, flaring, blazing out from the throne of the cross, the throne of divine mercy.

10

The *Paradiso* and the Overcoming of Rivalry

Cyril O'Regan

I t has been said so often as to now almost be a truism that from a poetic point of view the *Paradiso* is the least satisfying of the three books of the *Commedia*. The point is not that Dante's poetic skills in verse and image have waned, nor that he is any less able to reproduce, recalibrate, and expand the reflection of Christian culture (high and low) on what it would be like to be for us in the state of blessedness in the company of the saints. It just seems that in the *Paradiso* Dante was simply unable to get the reader to identify with and invent the experience of the bliss of heaven and the beatific vision of the triune God.

There are strong and weak variants of the argument. The stronger argument is that whatever the reason, the *Paradiso* does not satisfy our imaginative expectations either in Dante's own age or thereafter in the way the *Inferno* and *Purgatorio* do. The weaker and more historicist version of the argument has to do with the modern reader who, we are told, inhabits a different world of assumption than premodern readers of the *Commedia* and that while the *Inferno* and *Purgatorio* can be received even without the highly developed medieval world of theological assumption, the *Paradiso* is so tied to this world of theological assumption that it cannot. T. S. Eliot, Dorothy Sayers, C. S. Lewis and others respond to both of these kinds of argument by suggesting that while preferences for one or other of the books of the *Commedia* is a matter of taste and not something that needs to be justified, in their view the spectacle and action of the *Paradiso*, like the *Inferno* and *Purgatorio* on which it builds, is an objective correlative of experience, here the experience of hope in a postmortem existence that would represent the perfection of all that was best in our orientation toward reality in the trial of our earthy life as well as the transformation of all that was inadequate in our orientation.[1] Even more, the *Paradiso* represents the objective correlative of unimagined expansion of the horizon of reality as gifted by a gloriously beneficent divine force who is the origin and end of all that is, from brute matter to immaterial soul.

I think that Eliot, Sayers, and C. S. Lewis are essentially right and that *Paradiso* very much succeeds on poetic terms. This is not to deny, on the one hand, that depiction of the heavenly state may suffer representational disadvantages when compared with the infernal and purgatorial states and, on the other, that there is a lot of theology, even a lot of doctrine presented in the *Paradiso*. Whether real characters or types, the graphic suffering of the damned in hell at once correlates with our real fears of punishment for real transgressions and objectionable modes of being in the world, and correlates well with the highly visual scenarios of punishment laid out in apocalyptic literature—both canonic and non-canonic—which circulate throughout the Western tradition and with which we can assume Dante was familiar.[2] All

1. Dorothy Sayers is, arguably, the most pugnacious of the three in championing not only Dante in general, but the *Paradiso* in particular. This championing is afoot in the introduction to her translation of the *Paradiso* (London, 1962) and in the trilogy of Dante papers gathered together in the 1950s and reprinted in the past ten years by Wipf & Stock. The most important of the three is the third, that is, *The Poetry of Search and the Poetry of Statement*.

T. S. Eliot was a major defender of Dante as the super-eminent poet whose literary value is equaled only by Shakespeare. In many ways, his own reflections on Dante, especially in *The Sacred Wood* (1921) and his famous *Spectator* article of 1929 set the basic terms for Sayers' argument on behalf of a poetry of statement. In addition, in the *Waste Land* as well as his explicitly Christian poetry, for example, *Four Quartets*, the *Commedia* is recalled.

C. S. Lewis became acquainted with Dante in his teens. Not unexpectedly this was the Dante of the *Inferno*. It was only much later, that is, in 1930 that he read the *Paradiso*. If the reading of the *Paradiso* was not exactly a cause of his conversion, it accompanied it. While C. S. Lewis was not as sharp in defending the *Paradiso* as the other two, it was clear to him that the movement of experiences and conversion required an aim, and that his aim could not be other than heaven in which we fully enjoyed God.

2. The scholarly consensus is that Dante had access not only to canonic apocalypses such as Daniel and Revelation, but also some acquaintance either with non-canonic apocalypses of the Enoch and Ezra tradition or imaginative traditions that depended on them. Relative to canonic apocalyptic, there are two formal characteristics and one substantive characteristic that mark off non-canonic forms of apocalyptic. The two formal characteristics are (a) the centrality of a figure who is not yet dead (e.g., Enoch) to breach and traverse the eschatological zone and report back to those on this side

of us know of murderers and people who threw away their lives for a sexual tryst if only by report; and by a certain age we would have needed to have been very fortunate indeed not to have come across personalities marked— if not consumed—by either lust, sloth, vanity, pride, anger, envy, or greed.[3] And with respect to the latter it would only seem right that the punishment would—at least to an extent—fit the crime, or at least some imaginative variation thereof. There is also significant experiential raw material for the *Purgatorio*, as a mixture of suffering and expectation, where suffering is genuinely transformative rather than punitive, and where expectation is hope without doubt, thus hope distilled to a form of waiting. There is some truth to the view that our actual experiences of bliss and beatitude seem less embodied and more tenuous than the experiences of pain described in the *Inferno*, which in large part function as counter-positive projections from the experiences and states of being we escape from, and the experiences of relief and tense expectation in the *Purgatorio*, which are woven so much into the fabric of our lives this side of the eschaton.

Even in cases where the ultimate object of our desire, albeit often ob-scured, is the God who created us and our milieu in the first instance and whom we believe set us once again on a right course after we so inexplica-bly and so needlessly fell, it is incredibly difficult to think a God as to be loved rather than thought when the mirror gives way to direct encounter. And then there is the theological instruction in the *Paradiso*, which if from

---

of death who are struggling in time and who need guidance and reassurance; and (b) a tendency toward prolix depiction of the state of mysterious postmortem existence in contrast with the relative reserve of canonic apocalyptic, even if it is the case that apocalyptic as a whole as a form of apokalypsis or seeing distinguishes itself from the far more significant reserve on eschatological matters exercised by most of scripture. In addition, substantively and somewhat paradoxically, non-canonic apocalyptic, which goes in for spectacle far more than its canonic sibling, seems even more exercised in reforming our pre-eschatological behavior—thus, the fascination with the sufferings of the damned. For good synoptic accounts of Dante's dependence on and use of apoca-lypse, see Herzman, "Dante and the Apocalypse"; and Nohrnberg, "The First-Fruit of the Last Judgment."

3. Dante, of course, was an inheritor of the Christian reflection on the "deadly sins." The deadly sins, whose number had stabilized by his time at seven, were a supplement to sins viewed as particular acts that harmed entirely (mortal sins) or harmed some-what (venial) a believer's relationship with God. Deadly sins concern fundamental dis-positions or deep patterns of behavior that cast a light on the self's most fundamental orientation. From the contemporary perspective we might think of medieval discussion of "deadly sins" as forms of spiritual psychology. This is relatively appropriate since the discussion of deadly sins was generated within a monastic environment in which there was both the time and demand for reflection on the state of the soul before God. The first great synthesizer was John Cassian (360–435). Aquinas is, undoubtedly, Dante's proximate source.

Dante's point of view is the appropriate arena in which doctrine is justified because its truth is directly seen, may ultimately pall. The didacticism puts more than a little strain on all readers, and especially on those who think of instruction and decision regarding truth and between truths to be intrinsically unpoetic. Moreover, the instruction is hardly occasional. To give just some examples: cantos 2 and 29 provide instruction on creation; cantos 7 and 19 certify the fall of the angels, which becomes a theological construct in Augustine; cantos 7 and 14 confirm the rightness of a doctrine of atonement in general and the satisfaction theory of the atonement in particular.[4] Finally, the doctrine to which the *Paradiso* most often returns is that of the Trinity. The orthodox doctrine of the Trinity of three persons and one essence is an object of vindication in cantos 10 and 14, while canto 13 spends some time reproving a slew of Trinitarian heresies. While it is the Nicene doctrine that is vindicated over its various contenders, including contenders denounced at the Fourth Lateran Council,[5] it is obvious that Dante is familiar with the interpretation of the Trinity as grasped under the auspices of knowledge and love, which was rendered by Augustine and Thomas Aquinas.[6] This is just a small sample of the transcendent truth exposed in

4. Dante may have had motives for defending the satisfaction theory of atonement well beyond defending Anselm's particular form of it in *Cur Deus Homo*, written at the very end of the eleventh century. It is an essential element of Paul, even if Christ's substitution for us is not the only element. Still, perhaps more than other biblical soteriological metaphors it suggests God's unimaginable graciousness regarding us and blocks any sense in which we actually earn or deserve paradise.

5. Joachim de Fiore's Trinitarian thought was condemned at the Fourth Lateran Council (1213–1215). The issue, however, was less Joachim's emphasis on the economic Trinity and his specific emphasis on the continuing work of the Holy Spirit. In fact the main concern was with his depiction of the immanent Trinity and the suggestion that there was a divine root to the three persons. For the Council members this view represented a recrudescence of Sabellianism. Of course, as head of the Franciscan order, Bonaventure had to deal with the fallout of a Joachim-like interpretation of Francis and its elitist and sectarian consequences. In fact, Dante could opportunistically take advantage of the pneumatology of Joachim in order to lend authority to his work as authorized by the Holy Spirit in the contemporary period.

6. Aquinas's decisive contribution to the elaboration of the Trinity is to be found in *Summa Theologia*, Par. 1, q. 26–42. Here Aquinas gives an account of the inner workings of the Trinity and especially the persons of the Son and the Spirit according to the model of knowledge, love and their relation. In this respect, he was developing on Augustine's *De Trinitate*. It is only on the basis of the articulation of the immanent Trinity that Aquinas proceeds a discussion of the economic Trinity or the specific missions of the Trinity. In terms of method, Aquinas was following Augustine who, although he invests in a biblical rehearsal before he begins his explicit reflection on the Trinity in *De Trinitate*, proceeds to discuss the Trinity not according to the order of discovery—which would favor speaking first of the economic Trinity—but according to the order of excellence and cause.

heaven, grasped only in faith in this life, refused in hell, and grasped merely inchoately in the purgatorial state.

The comparative representational advantages of the *Inferno* and the *Purgatorio* over the *Paradiso*, therefore, are real, and the *Paradiso* runs the risk of doctrinal overload. But this is only to state the challenges Dante has to face in his depiction of heaven; it does not speak to his failure. First, it is crucial to Dante's eschatological projection that though the world we live in and through which we make our journey is characterized by enormous ambiguity, the Church is expressed through doctrine and precept, and the Church sometimes—but not always through examples—provides reliable guides regarding God and the Christian life. Second, while doctrines concerning God and his creative and redemptive acts are in this life founded on trust rather than apprehension, and thus for the most part will appear external to the believer, they have both their ground and ultimate realization in experience. Crucially for Dante, doctrines and vision are not contraries; the point of doctrines is their service to a vision that is inchoate; the point of vision in the *Paradiso* is that doctrine is a relatively adequate adumbration of a vision which is only fully clarified eschatologically. Understood properly the assertion of doctrines are inevitably accompanied by epistemic provisos, since there is more in the signified than in the signifiers. And while it is true that the heavenly state involves removing the veil of ignorance that is correlative to our sin, there is also a sense in which paradise yields more rather than less mystery in that we come to fully appreciate the manifold gifts that God has bestowed on us throughout our collective and individual histories. Even more importantly we come to understand in paradise that the triune God of Christian faith becomes known as truly mysterious.

Dante seems to want to say that while as a matter of doctrine the Trinity is hedged with the qualifier of mystery, from the point of view of the eschaton this sense of mystery is exposed as merely notional. In the state of rapt attention to the Trinity in heaven, the needle of mystery is moved from notional understanding to real apprehension in that the triune God is revealed to be ontologically excessive. In heaven the knowing of the triune God is ecstatic and the ecstasy is permanent: To grasp the triune God is rather to be grasped by the triune God, to be struck with awe and wonder (*Par.* 33.98–99) and for my mind to have transcended itself (*tutta sospesa*).

As is the case largely with the *Inferno*, the *Paradiso* represents a poetic appropriation, development and extension of the visionary eschatology of *City of God*.[7] Only this time, however, there is an equal dose of *De Trinitate*, especially book 15 where the theme is human beings' participation in the

---

7. John Cavadini makes this point with great force in his contribution to the volume.

triune God who, as the supreme object of our love, is at the same time an unfathomable mystery. One can speak of an Augustinian architecture of the *Paradiso* while also emphasizing Dante's freedom with regard to extending Augustinian themes whether by developing sets of images more fully exposited in other thinkers in the theological tradition such as Pseudo-Dionysius or by means of his own improvisation grounded in his confidence that the tradition allows for bold extension—in poetry if not in theology—as long as it is constrained by a basic Christian grammar.[8] There are any number of important Augustinian themes, but the two I want to attend to here are: (i) heavenly peace and (ii) our participation in self-subsistent beauty which is the goal of all our desire.

In *City of God* Augustine makes it plain that one of the crucial distinctions between the City of God and the City of Man is that peace is a property of the former, enmity the characteristics of the latter. Of course, the latter is not our natural state; our current state is a deviation from what should be and is the result of the fall. The empire's rule of power—variously brutal but almost never just—is the exemplar of the rule of the world which is the rule of Cain. Peace is what is restlessly and relentlessly sought; unhappily in this world treaties are made only to be broken; lying, theft, murder are the symptoms of a chaos in history that seems to have deeper roots than history itself. In the bounds of the world what is almost always sought, and hysterically sought in times of war, is peace which turns out to be at best elusive and at worst chimerical. For Augustine, peace can only be eschatological; it can only be heavenly peace. And peace rests entirely with God who alone can grant it, for what is granted in peace is nothing less than the fully saturating presence of God, who finalizes what begins in Christ, by making community possible.

If the opening cantos of the *Paradiso* suggest that something like Augustine's illuminative view of the intellect that moves beyond analysis and syllogism is illustrative of how we think in heaven (*Par.* 2; 4.125–26), it is equally obvious that Dante takes on board Augustine's view of peace.[9] In

---

8. Against the backdrop of the reflection on doctrine of the Yale theologian George Lindbeck, I prefer to think of doctrine as a grammar rather than a discrete set of conceptual absolutes. The consequence is that a grammar admits a number of formulations or reformulations, while a conceptual construct is invariant. At the same time, I want to underscore that the degree of freedom in formulation and reformulation that Dante allows himself goes far in excess of what one would expect to be authorized by a grammar. Dante understands himself to be literally in an inspired place that if it does not contradict received wisdom, exceeds it in terms of experience and insight.

9. Though Dante shares Augustine's view of peace, it is obvious that he does not adopt Augustine's view of the empire. On these questions, see Hawkins, *Dante's Testaments*, 197–212; Mazzotta, *Dante's Vision and the Circle of Knowledge*, 197–218; and

Paradiso 2 "peace" seems to be woven into the very fabric of heaven. Dante begins an exposition of the Primum Mobile (see *Par.* 2.112) by having as his subject "the sphere of holy peace" (*ciel de la divina pace*). One gets the sense that peace is the glue that holds things together and is the condition of harmony and order. I suppose if we were to speak of the register of "peace" here, we could say that the register is ontological-cosmological.

The second reference to "peace" early in the *Paradiso* seems differ-ent. In *Paradiso* 3.79–85, Dante speaks in a more functional manner about peace. The peaceful life—which is more or less synonymous with the blessed life or life of the blessed (*Par.* 3.79)—is a life in which the will of the creature is completely and finally ordered toward the will of God. As in Augustine, the peaceful life serves a criterion whereby the world—the City of Man— is judged. And while this criterion, as might be expected, gets maximum play in the *Inferno*, where the non-peaceable inhabitants on earth make for non-peaceable inhabitants of hell, even in the *Paradiso* Dante avails of the criterion to judge the behavior of the Church and state on earth.

In any event, "peace" is being spoken of in a different register, one that underscores human beings tuning into or attuning with divine will. What suggests that we are talking about different registers of the same fundamen-tal reality and not two different realities is that in *Paradiso* 3.79–85, Dante underscores the importance of measure or attunement in peace: peace is the reality of harmonious measure in which human beings participate to the degree to which they attune their wills to the divine will. The existen-tial-theological and the ontological-cosmological are, then, two different descriptions of the same reality. The existential-theological presents the condition of the possibility of sharing in peace as an ontological measure, while the ontological-cosmological gets performed in a sense when we have our will attuned to the will of God, but now without effort or strain in this life because we are out of the dark wood where the wild things are.

This also means, however, that peace is constitutive of the sociality of heaven, the true community indicated in part by the Church militant, at once immaculate and subject to sin. This peace, which as Dante later instructs us in the *Paradiso*, is a gift shared with us on earth by Christ, is a peace no longer threatened by the pride in which the self like Lucifer be-comes frozen and immured in ice, the anger that wreaks havoc on others but also the self that is its origin, and the vanity, greed, and envy that make relations of justice and love between selves impossible (see *Inferno* 6). Peace, it should be noted, is not some elixir to drink or divine stuff to eat, and certainly not something to look at. It is the reality of being reconciled to

---

Montemaggi, "Peace, Justice, and Trinity in Dante's *Commedia*."

your brother and sister in relations not only of respect and mutual support, but relations constituted by their glorification and praise.

Nowhere is this reality of peace better indicated than in *Paradiso* 11 and 12. At first blush neither of these cantos comes across as particularly compelling from a poetic point of view. There are no dazzling irradiations of light (*Par.* 32.144), no finalizing of desire (*Par.* 33.142–44), no ecstasies of intellect and love (*Par.* 33.97–99), no synaesthetic mingling of senses already spiritualized, sight and sound especially (*Par.* 7; 14), but also taste (*Par.* 12). Certainly, there are no great images such as for example the great white rose of *Paradiso* 31 to arrest attention and to imprint on the imagination. Cantos 11 and 12 seem to flatten out the poetry by importing the medieval hagiographical conventions, even if the saints are significant: Francis of Assisi in the case of *Paradiso* 11 and Dominic in the case of the following canto.

The heavenly account of Francis's life is intended to sanction Francis's veneration on earth by insisting on its reliability and truth. Francis's conversion is laid out and his vow to Lady Poverty (*Par.* 11.86); his great humility or great lowliness (*farsi pusillo*) is remarked on (*Par.* 11.111), and the gift of the stigmata underlines Francis's specialness (*Par.* 11.108) and his marvelous participation in the mystery of Christ's saving suffering.

The account of Saint Dominic is similar. There is conversion in which the true object of desire is found (*Par.* 12.56). There is approbation concerning the intensity of his vocation (*Par.* 12.74–75), and also an honoring of his love of truth (*Par.* 12.84). Perhaps the single detail that sticks out, even if it does not rise to the level of Francis's reception of the stigmata, is the recalling of how Dominic received his name (*Par.* 12.70). The reception of the name whose root is *dominus* or "Lord" suggests Dominic's proximity to Christ. Disappointingly, hagiographies appear to be transposed from earth to heaven without either correction or addition of new insight that would mark off the difference between taking something on faith or trust and apprehending a reality in heaven.

Yet if the stories are conventional, the speakers are not. Dante springs a surprise. In *Paradiso* 11 Dante has Thomas Aquinas, the great Dominican theologian, tell the tale of the life of Francis of Assisi, and in *Paradiso* 12 Dante has Bonaventure, great Franciscan theologian and in his later life head of the Franciscan order, who actually writes the biography of Francis, tell the story of Dominic the founder of the Order of Preachers to whom Thomas Aquinas belongs. We might be tempted to assume that Dante is relieving the earnestness of heaven by the levity of a joke. Perhaps in a wonderful subversion of our expectations—expectations which the first ten cantos have generated or at least reinforced—Dante is suggesting that heaven is a hoot because now we get to role-play. This would at once trouble more or less absolute distinctions between the high dignity that seem called for by Dante's eschatological explorations, Boccaccio's subversive humor, delightfully postmodern, and deliciously scoop twentieth-century psychologists who are inclined to overplay their originality. Of course, none of this is going on. What *is* going on is that Dante understands that *Paradiso* 2 and 3 simply provided the protocols of peace, and what is now required is an example of what peace between individuals and groups actually looks like in heaven.

In the quadrate of Aquinas and Dominic and Bonaventure and Francis there are obvious differences between Dominicans and Franciscans both regarding their spirituality (Dominic and Francis) and their theology (Aquinas and Bonaventure) that need to be reconciled. For us, given our historical location, these differences seem very trivial, indeed, but were taken quite seriously by medieval Christians and even more seriously by the two religious orders. Dante wants us to grasp, however, the prospect of commitment to particular inflections of Christian faith and practices as potentially providing the seed of disparagement of others and in the last analysis a justification for the violence that we might visit on them. The reconciliation imagined in *Paradiso* 11 and 12 vindicates plurality and difference, while removing the tendency of both to engender antagonism.

For Dante, however, the peace of heaven is a great deal more than a hyperbole—if somewhat staged—display of mutual tolerance of difference. In peace of heaven—or the peace that *is* heaven—there is no holding back in terms of vouching for and celebrating the other. With a psychological acuity that leaves us twenty-first-century know-it-alls ashamed, the vouching and celebrating has to begin with the proximate other, the other that is on an everyday basis in your business. Aquinas and Bonaventure avail full-bore of the Franciscan and Dominican hagiographical traditions to ratify the founders of the Franciscan and Dominican orders respectively, precisely the orders to which they do not belong, precisely the ones that have proved not sufficiently attractive to enter and with which they are in competition. Both theologians empty themselves of particular interest in or allegiance to a particular form of Christian spirituality and theology to praise and exult the exemplar of a rival form, perhaps *the* rival form. It is in this kenosis—which mirrors the self-giving of God which finds its supreme expression in Christ—that the other before Bonaventure and Aquinas is to be spoken of. It is only in and through this setting aside of interest that one recognizes the other and in that recognition praises.

Meister Eckhart (1260–1328), who is writing roughly at the same time as Dante, and also in the wake of Aquinas,[10] would call this *Gelassenheit*, a letting be that indicates a transcendence in time of time, of our normal ways of relating, even our normal ways of virtuous relating. What Eckhart thinks is episodically available here and now is eschatologically available *in toto* and eternally in heaven. In addition, unlike Dante, Eckhart does not look at the challenges presented by human creatures who compete for space, attention, honor, and compete with others who want what I have, who want what I desire, who are indifferent concerning my flourishing, and may wish to frustrate my desires and who might wish my discombobulation, if not my ruin. It is precisely these creatures that I have to "let be," that I have to fore-give—to allow them to be without judgment—before as well as after the fact. In heaven, the overall structure is "letting be" before the fact, to allow Dominic and Francis everything they could possibly be. Of course, relative to the lesson that we here on pilgrimage are supposed to draw, we are talking about fore-giveness after the fact for having a different—potentially competitive—excellence. If to let be is to allow the recognition of the potentially rivalrous other to happen, this recognition is fully actualized in praise. And this praise extends to the speakers, who are saints, as well as the saints whose lives of heroic sanctity are laid out. For example, Bonaventure, the second of the two speakers, introduces his honoring of Dominic's life by praising Aquinas, the great Dominican theologian (*Par.* 12.32–33). It is safe to assume that praise is a closed circuit and that were Aquinas allowed to speak again, he would have returned the appreciation in kind.

If to recognize and lavish praise on another is heaven's way of constituting community—at the same time noticing how Dante deconstructs traditional epics of Homer and Virgil which praise their group but which produce imprecation for other groups who are rivals or potential rivals—then it turns out that narrative is crucial. To speak about someone rather than something is to tell the story of their life. Of course, this is generally important in the *Commedia*, given its Augustinian-Thomistic view of life constituted by individual decisions and patterns of decisions with eschatological or eternal significance. To speak about a person who is a saint—one who ran the good race enabled by the grace of God—is to be constrained to

10. Meister Eckhart, who was a student of Albertus Magnus as Aquinas was, was a High Scholastic whose most original thought was in the vernacular German. He departed from Aquinas in a number of ways. One of the most important is that he considered the attitude of "detachment" as more primary than the theological virtues of faith, hope, and charity. In addition, he thought that the attitude of radical openness or *Gelassenheit* was the condition of an experience of an event of divinization that blurred the boundary between the creator and the creature. In contrast, Dante clearly works within the broad Augustinian-Thomistic parameters of the creator-creature distinction.

praise. Although the point is implied, perhaps it might help to draw attention to what is not the real object of praise, that is, a set of general attributes or virtues which the saint possesses and those who are less perfect than the saint—say you and I—do not possess. Dante does not neglect to speak to the virtues displayed in the lives of Francis and Dominic, humility in the case of the former, the love of truth in the case of the latter. Yet for Dante, to use a Newman-like expression, the life's the thing. It is this that is the object of the glorification.

Only purged of our own individual and group interest—possible only in heaven—can we see a life for what it is, which is to say what it is meant to be. This eschatological seeing would have been impossible without the example of Christ whose generosity fully renders who God is. Nonetheless, what Dante depicts as the overcoming of rivalry in *Paradiso* 11 and 12 provides the measure of our relation to the enfleshed particular other, potentially or actually a rival, while each of us makes our way through the dark wood and remember—or more often forget—the very dangerous and hungry animals among whom we live and accompany us on our way and even more the very dangerous and hungry animals that we are. We are enjoined to participate in the peace that is as surely eschatological as it is heavenly, in which we come to see a unique story and a unique way of desiring and seeing that gives glory to the God of splendor who from the start of the poem we come to know is lavish in the creation of otherness and difference. I suppose the converse also holds true, that is, that one truly gets a glimpse of heavenly peace if and only if we learn to recognize the other as a unique and irreplaceable life and an irreplaceable form of desiring and seeing.

Heaven is the place and state in which the community that is longed for in history is realized, with the added benefit that now we are talking about a community that will not be lost. Throughout his great epic Dante avails of Augustine's contrast between the two cities, marking the former with violence (*Inf.* 6; 15, *inter alia*) and the latter with peace. Dante is clear that if violence is expressive of wrath—as Homer and Dante would have us believe—it is undergirded by the root dispositions of vanity and pride and left unchecked by lust, avarice, sloth, and envy (see, for instance, *Inf.* 7). Violence is both cause and effect of the breakdown of community. It is at once a thing in itself (*Inf.* 12) and the result in history of practices such as lying (see for instance, *Inf.* 11; 18; 19) which breaks the bond between people conditioned by their reference to truth and ultimately to the Truth which is the triune God.

History is chiaroscuro, the intermingling of light and dark, of love, hope and peace lost yet aspired to and occasionally exemplified. Whereas the contrast between the temporal and the heavenly kingdom therefore is less than absolute, the contrast between hell and heaven truly is. This is where if Dante does not exceed the possibilities of Augustinianism, he certainly seems to develop Augustine's thought. Hell focuses, condenses and eternalizes the dark side of the kingdom of man and demonstrates what the breakdown of community looks like. Hell lays out in detail the diabolic coincidence of the opposites of self-incurving and the loss of identity: all the souls of the damned incurve and are void of regard of any other soul; all of the souls of the damned are crushed into abominable collectives which represent the parody of community in the strict sense whose image is the community of the tri-personal Trinity. It is not accidental that in his observations of the appearances of different groups of souls as he descends the circles of hell, Dante introduces them by means of such words as "flocks," "herds," "packs," "bands," "swarms," and "broods." More specifically, however, hell is violence to the nth-power, primarily violence with respect to others (*Inf.* 6; 7), demons with respect to damned souls, demons with respect to each other (*Inf.* 22), damned souls with respect to each other (*Inf.* 7; 11). Of course, there is also violence with respect to oneself (*Inf.* 13), and intended—but ultimately useless—violence toward God and especially Christ who deserves the title of "Prince of Peace." Community, for Dante, supposes the eradication of all violence. Reciprocally, the eradication of all violence supposes mutual recognition, the absence of self-loathing, and the ability to glorify, which begins by giving glory to what is supereminently worthy of glory, the triune God and Christ, and by derivation Mary and all of God's saints.

I have mentioned Christ already as the giver of peace, and given the foundational nature of peace in heaven, Christ clearly has something to do with participation in the triune God whose glorious dance in *Paradiso* 32 and 33 is the goal of all our desire. I promise to say something about the very important connections between the peace of the saints—which is a community—and both Christ and the triune God before I close. In the case of the latter, I will reflect on the possible relation between peace and beauty as satisfactions for a perpetual thirst which Dante—after Augustine—says in *Paradiso* 2.19 is "inborn." But before I go into any of this, I would like to draw Dostoevsky and especially *The Brothers Karamazov* into our discussion about the relationship between original and renewed seeing and peace.

The fact that Dante is reporting back to us from the other side of the eschaton and that Dostoevsky does not pierce the eschatological veil might suggest that these two great writers cannot be brought together. But this difficulty turns out not to be decisive. As well as making a truth claim about reality with his fundamentally Catholic eschatological architecture, Dante's depiction of the state of souls in the afterlife is intended to provide a model for action, disposition, and way of being in this life and indicate their momentous consequences. The *Paradiso* and *The Brothers Karamazov*, therefore, can talk to each other.

For Zosima, the monk who is the vehicle of Christian spirituality in *The Brothers Karamazov*,[11] the alienation between human beings, which is ground as well as consequence of the pride, vanity, anger, lust, envy, and gluttony exhibited by the characters inside and outside the monastery, is to put them beyond the love of Christ, which alone can heal them. But this love is among other things a form of seeing, a seeing of the heart (*cardiognosis*), an eschatological form of seeing corresponding to the protological and unfallen form of seeing that we human beings have lost and whose loss we reproduce from generation to generation. To see through a person, to apprise the root, and grasp the entire life is to "let be"—to see in the mode of fore-giving—to give back a life that has been interrupted or that has been arrested entirely. Not everyone will be a saint, and almost all are in need of repentance to live again. One of Zosima's points is that there can be no community (*sobornost*) without this new form of seeing which is the principle of the overcoming of rivalry that wreaks havoc throughout the novel: Dmitri and Fyodor Karamazov, Ivan and Dmitri Karamazov, Father Ferapont and Zosima, the duel of the young Zosima and the captain, the enmity between Nastasha and Catherina, the warping distrust between Catherina and Ivan, the envy and hatred between a conniving Ivan and Smerdyakov, etc. However enmity comes into being, whether it is greed that rules Fyodor Karamazov, the lust as well as anger that governs the wild actions of Dmitri Karamazov, the vanity of the younger Zosima, pride in the cases of Ivan Karamazov, Smerdyakov, and Catherina, enmity is always a multiplier and violence is always on the horizon. Enmity is also a multiplier of the ugliness of our lives from which we so want to be delivered. This is the acknowledged ache of the dissolute such as Dmitri and a prostitute such as Grushenka, and the unacknowledged ache of Ivan. It is not an accident that Dostoevsky who is a genius at detailing the living hell of our ugliness speaks not only of the truth and peace that is Christ but insists that beauty saves the world. For him peace and beauty implicate each other as they had in a different Christian dispensation in Dante.

11. I speak in this way of Dostoevsky's great 1880 masterpiece mindful of the fact that the Christian interpretation of this text has been often challenged and routinely ignored in both the commentary tradition and in the history of reception by major twentieth-century writers. The fact is, however, that its Christian intent is everywhere and can only be ignored on the apriorist assumption that a great work of literature in modernity cannot be aligned with Christianity.

It would not be an exaggeration to say that Zosima's major project in life after his conversion is the making of saints, for in his sense only saints will save the world, make possible the kingdom of God, and only a community made up entirely of saints can keep the kingdom of God from being overtaken by the ideologically twisted and violent kingdom of the world. Of course, the character who Dostoevsky thinks has the greatest plasticity, the one whose eyes of the heart are already open, is the youngest Karamazov, that is, Alyosha Karmazov. He sees into the heart of each of the persons who are at war with each other, divines traces of original or eschatological goodness, and inhibits those habits in a person that make for isolation and enmity. Alyosha is Dostoevsky's idea of a saint as a life on this side of death, who struggles with temptation and failure, but whose life's task is allowing others to be others, thereby allowing them to be perpetual beginnings and thus be the rivets of community.

After this Dostoevsky excursus let me return to the *Paradiso* and particularly to the role of Christ in the construction of the community of saints. In the *Paradiso* Christ appears in the center of the white rose to the extent to which the raised host is associated with the rose (*Par.* 30). The rose, then, is the heavenly Eucharist which contains even the angels. The Eucharist, which is the heavenly form of the saving sacrifice, is in turn the condition of the heavenly community, and represents an answer to the anti-eucharistic mode of existence and behavior of the *Inferno* which makes community impossible.[12] In the *Paradiso* it is Beatrice who instructs Dante in the saving sacrifice of Christ (*Par.* 7.115–20). The Christ, who atones for us not only makes satisfaction for the sins for which we do not have the means of satisfaction, he is also the condition for our unity or our eucharistic fellowship.

There is nothing moralistic about Dante's reflection on atonement. There is no logical necessity for Christ to save us; its mode is that of aesthetic rightness which belongs to the economy of grace.[13] The aesthetic hint is important. The *Paradiso* begins and ends on reflection of light which gives

12. Here I am again mindful of John Cavadini's essay in the present volume.

13. One might think of Dante here as taking advantage of the opening in medieval theology provided as early as Anselm in *Cur Deus Homo* concerning "reasons of convenience" or what I would call "aesthetic rightness." Dante is not accepting Anselm's distinction between "reasons of necessity" and "reasons of agreement." Instead he seems to be suggesting that in the economy of grace nothing that happens is necessary, nor is anything that happens simply contingent. To the contrary everything that happens can be subsumed under aesthetic rightness. It should come as no surprise that in the earliest cantos in *Paradiso* Dante avails of the Neoplatonic definition of God as *bonum diffusivum sui* which seemed to suggest that the world is because God has a certain kind of character rather than that God in order to be God necessarily had to have a world, indeed precisely the world that is in existence.

itself.[14] Clarity together with proportion or measure, according to Aquinas, makes all things beautiful.[15] But in heaven each soul is a scintilla of light from the light of lights and ordered toward the other lights. Each soul, awaiting its resurrection, flares and flames in a uniquely individuated way as it finds its model in the uniquely colored light of the Trinitarian persons (*Par.* 33). I am making the case here that Dante the artist, who seeks beauty and who is familiar with the medieval aesthetic theories, sees through the eyes of Augustine, Pseudo-Dionysius, and Bonaventure the beauty of creation, incarnation, and the triune God.[16] What Dante adds is the confirmation in paradise of a light ordered toward God as true and good because it participates in the self-subsistent truth and goodness of the triune God. But such a soul—on the verge of resurrection—is rightly seen as beautiful. But to see the soul as beautiful requires a reformed mode of seeing, a mode of seeing conformed to the seeing of Christ's mercy and self-giving. If this seeing and this beauty is the eschatological truth of the kingdom of God, then this means that the road to salvation involves seeing in this reformed way. The kingdom of God is not only the kingdom of peace, but also the kingdom of the beautiful. Beauty and peace are both realities we have longed for; both have their ground ultimately in the light of lights; each is implied in the other insofar as clarity and proportion are the means for the kinetic community which, on earth as in heaven, finds its meaning in praise. Praise happens because souls in heaven looking forward to their resurrection see all the way through the one who is the subject of their regard. From this seeing follows a thanksgiving that is not servile, but is an ecstatic response to heavenly beauty in which mortal beauty inheres.

What Dante tries to do in the *Paradiso*—and in my view succeeds in doing—is to demonstrate that peace is the powerfully positive reality, not war whose economy is destruction, and that beauty in the full and strict sense is not an adornment but the infinitely valuable object of desire, which precisely as such is not an object of possession. As suggested already, one can say that for Dante peace rests on a graced "letting be" of the other, which not only gives the other room, but sings the other's uniqueness and difference. Only in this way is the community of saints formed who sing the triune God, whose self-sufficiency is an endless dance at which we are far more participators than spectators. One dizzies at the whirling of the triune God, who is the merry-go-round moving beyond the speed of light.

14. Light is also connected with beauty in *Paradiso* 5 and 13, 31, 32.

15. For a wonderfully accessible account of the aesthetics of Aquinas, see Eco, *The Aesthetics of Thomas Aquinas*, 64–121; esp. 65–66, 91–92, 114–15.

16. See my essay "Theology, Art, and Beauty," 245–71; esp. 446–52.

How dynamic is that; heart in the mouth thrill to the exponential power! In speaking of the triune God as the final object of desire in *Paradiso* 33 (esp. lines 46–48) Dante can speak to the end or conclusion of all desire. This is to speak in the manner of Augustine's *De Trinitate* and in consequence of the entire Western tradition.

It would be a mistake to think, however, that no changes are rung on the triune God which is the ultimate object of the beatific vision which makes each of us complete. The first change is that Dante seems to emphasize the imbrications of the persons and in effect literalizes the metaphor of dance that is at the basis of Eastern Christianity's underscoring of perichoresis.[17] The second change afoot is that while our desire is satisfied, to the extent to which our knowing and our loving are ecstatic, he seems to be anticipating the worry that the Christian view of the beatific vision remains unpersuasive because hopelessly safe and static, and in consequence, if the *Commedia* in general and the *Paradiso* in particular are intended to translate the mysteries of Christian faith into the language of experience and thereby become Christianity's consummate apology, the creeping sense that the beatific vision as the final end of human life is boring has to be deconstructed. This I believe is what is going in *Paradiso* 33 when the mind achieves its final end. Desire turns out to be satisfied, but not satiated. Satiation is an impossibility in heaven since mind has to be in ecstasy in order to correspond to the dynamism of the endless Trinitarian dance. In correcting for a deficiency in imaginative projection that is the function of the contrast between earthly restlessness and its overcoming in heaven, Dante inflects the Latin theological construction of beatific vision with the Greek view of *epekstasis*, that is, eternal becoming. Dynamism in the full and proper sense, that is, dynamism that is not movement for movement sake, and change for change sake, is consistent with satisfaction as long as the satisfaction concerns the infinite rather than the finite, the infinite which is the height, breadth, and depth, the infinite that cannot be exhausted, and which leads the ecstatic from glory to glory.[18]

17. Not to deny that hints of this more communitarian view of the Trinity do not make their way into the Western Christian tradition. This is especially true in the case of the twelfth-century theologian Richard of Saint Victor. But it is also true of Bonaventure, who is an important figure in the *Paradiso*. More than Aquinas, the emphasis in the Trinitarian thought of Bonaventure falls on the communication of the persons with each other.

18. Gregory of Nyssa, the fourth-century Cappadocian theologian, is famous for having articulated the notion of *epekstasis* or "eternal becoming" as a mark of the eschatological beatified state. Despite Gregory's attempt to suggest that the notion had biblical roots, by and large Western theology followed Augustine in thinking of eternal life as rest. While it is often supposed that the two figurations are contraries, this might

Though it is true that Dante avails of all the aesthetic gilding at his disposal, one would do him wrong if one thought that the *raison d'être* of heaven is that it offers us something spiritual in contrast to the carnal. It is easy to see why this might be so. Beatrice is the lure, and it is the sublimation of Dante's love for her that has allowed him to see and pass beyond flesh to embrace spiritual and non-corporeal reality. Dante avails of Platonism, its contrasts, and its metaphysical staircases to make an important point. We are through and through creatures of desire, who, it turns out, haplessly do not know what we desire. "Desire" translates *eros* and fully captures its meaning. But the better word for us is "want." It is grittier, more urgent, and goes deeper to the bone. We *want* and we do not know what we want; sometimes in order to keep going we even want "want." In the overwhelming ugliness of our lives, the frailties of our physical condition and station, a social status that mocks us or encourages us to wear masks, the invisibility we endure, the hatreds we tolerate, the obsessions we cannot get rid of, the lies we cannot put off, the resentments we harbor, the dreams that have been shattered, the prize that will never be ours, the glory that will never come our way, and the love that will never be returned—indeed, our relations are ugly.

We need beauty, perhaps beauty above all, perhaps beauty that incorporates the good and the true.[19] Dante tells us we need it. First, however, we have to discover that we want it. We might discover we want it in any number of ways. Yet discovering it through encounter with a beautiful and delicate girl-woman (Beatrice) is as good as any. What needs to be broken, however, is the link between desire and possession. Possession runs the risk of reinscribing the ugliness of pride and vanity, and our insecurity of having such a possession, for surely what I have is wanted by others as I want what

---

be a stretch. First, in the case of both Nyssa and Augustine, eternal becoming and rest are contrastive terms. It just so happens that Nyssa thinks that this life is constituted ultimately by paralysis rather than true dynamism, whereas Augustine tends to characterize this life as aimlessly dynamic. A more comprehensive phenomenological description of the kind implied in Dante would take account of both. Second, although for the most part Augustine does emphasize rest in the beatific life, he is by no means univocal. There are places in both his sermons and his commentary on the Psalms where he suggests dynamism in which we continue to search into the mystery of the triune God.

19. For the most part medieval articulations of the transcendentals, which provide the horizon of experience rather than being proper objects of experience (unless mystical or eschatological), left out beauty. The usual group was Unity, Being, and Goodness, and this despite the fact that Plato, who was the arch-philosopher of the transcendentals, and Plotinus his most illustrious student, greatly elevated beauty. Of course, so also did the early Augustine and even more importantly Pseudo-Dionysius. Eco gives a satisfying account of Dionysian and Augustinian traditions in Eco, *The Aesthetics of Thomas Aquinas*, 1–61; and Eco, *Art and Beauty in the Middle Ages*.

they have.[20] More, each of us waits on the other to discover what they desire and desire it also. Beatrice is not, nor can be an allegory; which is not to say that she cannot be surpassed. In the *Paradiso* she is surpassed first by Bernard of Clairvaux, famous for his commentary on the Song of Songs, and then by Mary whose compassion and tenderness she exemplifies. Of course, Mary is the penultimate form of "letting be" which exemplifies and attends Christ's amen to the Father, and which is subject and object of praise in *Paradiso* 33.

Beatrice has to be surpassed, because all possession has to be surpassed, indeed, all self-possession. Only then am I a gift to you, only then do I see you as a gift. Only then will I be able to respond to you as the unrepeatable singularity you were and are. I respond to you as an irradiation of light, which light will shine in and through your transfigured body after the final judgment and resurrection. If I find myself with you, if I find myself dispossessed, and ecstatically oriented to you, I can only lavish my attention on you and be prepared to praise. But first I have to gasp—the gasp will return the time of the resurrection—and exclaim: you are beautiful! As we whirl in our own exuberant dance around the center of the light of lights, each of us is a light to see and a light to be seen. We sing each other; we find at once the paradoxical coincidence of full transparency and depth, the joy of knowing and being known indistinguishable from loving and being loved. Each of us is beautiful and our rapture will never cease in the kingdom of peace, where there is no shadow of rivalry, and everyone is beautiful and the giver and the receiver of praise.

20. I would be remiss not to invoke the name of René Girard who not only is the name above all contemporary names when it comes to analyzing rivalry and its origins, but who might be cast as a postmodern Augustine. He is difficult to ignore especially since in addition to being a philosopher, anthropologist, an aficionado of the history of religions, and sometimes biblical exegete, he is also a literary critic who has written interesting pieces on both Dante and Dostoevsky. Still, he is but atmosphere to the present essay, since though he has written on Dante and Dostoevsky, these pieces are not as focused on rivalry and overcoming it as this essay. Girard produced an interesting essay called "By Love Possessed," which reflects on Francesca in the *Inferno*, in which lust is mediated by a book. The other rivalries of the *Inferno* are not recalled. Nor does he discuss anywhere—as far as I am aware—how Dante depicts its overcoming in the *Paradiso*. Girard, who is a champion of the literary merits of Dostoevsky and insistent on the fact that he is a Christian author and magnificently so in *The Brothers Karamazov*, focuses a great deal on "the underground man" as providing the basic outline of all alienated figures in Dostoevsky's corpus. But he does not give a detailed examination of either Zosima's or Alyosha's performance of peace in *The Brothers Karamazov*. See in particular Girard, *To Double Business Bound*, 36–60.

Afterword

Robin Kirkpatrick

Regnum celorum violenza pate
da caldo amore e da viva speranza
che vince la divina volontade

(*Par.* 20.94–96)

In the Name of Mercy

Pope Francis, in proclaiming the Jubilee Year of Mercy, spoke warmly of how the theme he then proposed is treated by Walter Cardinal Kasper in his *Mercy: The Essence of the Gospel and the Key to Christian Life*. In a similar way, the Holy Father recommended Dante's *Commedia* as appropriate reading for the Year of Mercy. There is certainly much to be said for bringing Kasper and Dante together in discussion of the papal concern. This will provide the starting point for the present afterword, on the basis of which we will then reflect on how every one of the ten essays contained in the present volume contributes, each in its own way, to a new understanding of how theological and poetic considerations intersect in a contemplation of divine mercy. In the light of such reflection we will then return to Dante's text itself, allowing the present volume to end with a renewed invitation to turn our detailed attention to the text that inspired it in the first place.

It may well indeed seem surprising to speak at all of the *Commedia* and mercy in a single breath. Dante is represented all too often as the merciless author of the *Inferno*. The result is that readers, hallucinated by the awful vision of hell, are deprived of the unparalleled vivacity of thought and imagination which open before us once this *cantica* (representing no more than a third of the whole poem) gives way to the *Purgatorio* and *Paradiso*. Reading the *Inferno*, Dante scholars sometimes speak of the poet's "fearful art of justice." But work like that present in this volume helps one to see the liberating art of mercy in Dante's work.

Kasper speaks of mercy in relation to God's very name; mercy is central to the revelation of who God is. Drawing on Hebraic conceptions of *hesed*, he writes:

> The most important expression for understanding mercy is *hesed*, which means unmerited loving kindness, friendliness, favour and also divine grace and mercy. *Hesed* therefore goes beyond mere emotion and grief and human deprivation; it means God's free and gracious turning towards the human person with care.[1]

Implicit in this contention, there is an important adjustment to the notion of justice. Too easily, one supposes that mercy is merely a relaxation of the rigorous demands imposed by an absolute principle of justice. But this cannot be the case with the God of mercy. In that perspective, justice undoubtedly remains a virtue; and law also—as the application of justice in the political and ethical sphere—is still a human necessity. But with *hesed* in mind—or divine action as traced through the Old Testament—we shall quickly come to see that "God's justice is not a punitive justice but rather a justice that justifies the sinner."[2] Justice aims to set us right—or "justified"—on the page of God's revelation. It might indeed be said that merciful forgiveness is best understood as "fore-given-ness." It is a mercy that we exist at all. Our Creator brings us into being *ex nihilo*. And that gift of existence, given freely before all others, is subsequently sustained in every manifestation of divine mercy. Mercy calls us to reenter the providential narrative: the meaning of mercy can only be ascertained from the entirety of the biblical history of salvation; "mercy is ultimately grace for conversion."[3]

For Dante, too, mercy is best perceived in the gradual unfolding of his narrative; and in the final section of this essay I will attempt to sketch out something of this process as it passes through the *Purgatorio* to those cantos in the *Paradiso* that concern the virtue of justice. I confess at the outset to one particular and long-standing bias, which is that by "narrative"

1. Kasper, *Mercy*, 43.
2. Ibid., 79.
3. Ibid., 54.

and "process" I do not mean merely the progress of some fictive avatar, commonly known as "Dante-the-Pilgrim." I am concerned, rather, with the ways in which Dante, through the words he himself writes, progressively engages with the Logos of his Creator. This is, in part, simply an invitation to read the *Commedia* in a way similar to that in which one reads Augustine's *Confessions*. But there are at least two issues on which Dante's poetic *agon* displays characteristics and intensities entirely its own. One of these is a matter of language and terminology. The other is matter of history, even of politics and economics.

In regard to language, Kasper again proves illuminating. Kasper is well aware of how many terms—all with nuances of their own—can be used in speaking of mercy. These include, in English, "compassion," "sympathy," and "pity." And there can here be a truly jubilant sense of the manifold ways in which mercy may express itself.[4] Yet, especially in the Romance languages, there is also a difficulty in this. In the *Inferno*, some of the most intense moments of linguistic drama occur when Dante confronts the ambiguities of the word *pietà*. The possibilities of a purely seductive use of *pietà* are registered in the Francesca-episode of *Inferno* 5. Equally, in *Inferno* 20.19–30, Virgil's (arguably mistaken) attempt to repress Dante's moment of sympathetic distress underlines, for the reader, the need for an unremitting vigilance in the analysis of lexical detail. This is particularly true because *pietà* in the vocabulary of the courtly love tradition that Dante inherits can carry erotic connotations, signaling a moment in which a lady may at last begin to yield to her lover's enfeebled beseechings.

Something of the same could be said of *mercy* itself (where in Occitan *merce* can plead for the overthrow of *razo*). But it is here, too, that political and economic considerations begin to enter. After all, *mercy* is semantically connected to words for "reward" and akin, etymologically, to *commerce*. For Dante, the disasters that beset him in his own historical circumstances could be seen directly as a consequence of the commercial appetitiveness that fueled the economic expansion of his native city. His poem stands clamorously against these dire developments. And it is undoubtedly true that he establishes a notion of justice—particularly of Imperial Justice—which aims, in the interest of proportionate distribution, at the repression of any taint of partiality or greed. At the same time, he also deploys the resources available in the tradition of love-poetry—or of a love-poetry that speaks of fine or refined desire—to refresh our understanding of relationship as founded most freely and most truly on good will and gift.

---

4. See translator's preface to ibid., xi–xii.

The epigraph at the head of this essay points to a deliverance which is brought about when God's own will is freely overthrown. The final section below will return in more detail to the context of this liberating paradox. But, before that, it is important to explore how all of the essays in this volume serve as a *vade mecum* to illuminate the ways in which Dante's narrative of mercy itself advances, literarily, theologically, and spiritually.

Speaking of Mercy

Consider first, on the basis of the reflections above, Cyril O'Regan's authoritative contribution. Approaching the *Commedia* with Augustinian eyes, O'Regan identifies desire as the crucial dynamic in the human self as revealed especially in the *Paradiso*, where the enjoyment of heavenly peace as "the goal of all our desire" is seen to be realized through "our participation in [*God's*] self-subsistent beauty" (184). But this realization involves a radical detachment or redirection of the will away from those objects which, in both the erotic and economic spheres, might generate cupidity:

> What needs to be broken . . . is the link between desire and possession. Possession runs the risk of re-inscribing the ugliness of pride and vanity, and our insecurity of having such a possession, for surely what I have is wanted by others as I want what they have. More, each of us waits on the other to discover what they desire and desire it also. (195–96)

But remarkably the "other" who opens Dante's eyes to glory of such dispossession is Beatrice. In contemplating the beauty of Beatrice, from the *Vita nuova* onwards, Dante has gradually come to recognize that she, as a living and particular creation, is the point at which his desires and the desires of his Creator may properly coincide. And, as O'Regan makes clear in his conclusion, the language in which this new recognition will be expressed is the language of praise. This is crucial for an understanding of Dante's theology—or his sense of worship—and equally for an understanding of his poetics. As early as chapter 18 of the *Vita nuova* Dante had spoken of his own poetic style as the "praise-style"—*lo stile della loda*. To readers who confine themselves to the venomous poetry of *Inferno*, this will seem an implausible suggestion. But the *Paradiso*, engaging with the reality of God and the reality of Beatrice, demonstrates *in excelsis* what the praise style truly is: an expression of delight in the existence of the Other. There can be no question of possession here. The praise style aims, in purely disinterested love, at celebrating the existence of the Other and communicating its value to all who are willing to hear.

Though the *Paradiso* is the exultant apex of Dante's theological poetry, the *Purgatorio*, as seen in this volume through readings offered particularly by Kevin Grove and Chase Pepper illustrates how precise and, in narrative terms, how carefully graded Dante's vision of religious experience always is. In some ways the *Purgatorio* is the most original *cantica* in the *Commedia*. The emphasis here—in the middle phase of the three—falls not upon absolute states, be they of damnation or beatitude. Imagining, without precedent, a mountain landscape which often anticipates in its invention and daring the effects of modern magic realism, Dante produces a connected narrative in which the strivings of the human will and the offerings of grace interrelate in constantly changing configurations of action, moral and divine. In Kasper's terms, purgatory can be seen as a sign of the "infinite mercy and forbearance of God."[5] But the peculiarly Dantean inflection is to see God's forbearance displayed in a realm where the human creature is called to collaborate fully and freely but progressively in the working out of its own salvation. Penitence here is not miserable self-recrimination but rather a liberated and liberating awareness of the work that, in active creation, we may perform in bringing our Creator's design to fruition.

Grove speaks of Ash Wednesday and the penitential signing of the forehead, as Pepper also speaks of dust. But in both cases the purpose is to recall the miraculous nothingness out of which Adam was delivered into the fullness of his original life. And, both authors likewise speak in tones as much of exhilaration as consolation (entirely consistent with Dante's own) of how a re-creative act of forgiveness in Christ irradiates the liturgical act of penance.

Grove then proceeds to delineate a conception of Truth as the recovery, not of some dogmatic orthodoxy but a joyful living in one's own true existence, which should be as fundamentally harmonious with Christ's body as it is with the living truth of God: "This journey [*through purgatory*] is meant to make [Dante] True" (55). So Dante writes of himself that on reaching the Earthly Paradise at the summit of the mountain he is "free, upright and whole" (*Purg.* 27.140). There is, however, a devastating proviso here, entered by Beatrice who, in a moment of the highest penitential drama once Dante has entered the Earthly Paradise, confronts her *fedele* with abrasive vigor and directly challenges her lover's right to be there. In Grove's words, "Beatrice is saying that Dante's life of sin has made him false, a lie to his own self. It is not who he is; it is not who he was created to be; it does not

5. Kasper, *Mercy*, 109.

set him free but it ensnares him" (55). Yet Beatrice's words, terrible as they seem, are also an act of mercy—or in Dante's own phrase of *pietade acerba* (*Purg.* 30.82)—a phrase which incidentally wholly transforms any suggestion drawn from the courtly code that a Lady is required to be, erotically, complaisant, toward her servant. Here Dante is reduced to nothing, but this is the re-creative nothing that replicates the act of divine creation.

"Nothingness" is a powerful central theme in Pepper's essay where he speaks of "humanity's most fundamental *temptation*, which, even before denying our createdness, is to forget that we spring from nothing by God's creative grace at each and every moment, and in that forgetting to mistake anything else created as something to be grasped at and even enjoyed (in the Augustinian sense of that word)" (130–31). Purgatorial suffering, in this perspective, is the rediscovery of "the light that nests in the nothingness of one's created being" (135). But in reentering this state of total dispossession, the soul on Pepper's account is equally preparing for paradise, so that, as he puts it, purgatory is the practice ground for the perfect *perichoresis* of heaven. In that dance, which draws us into relationship with the action of the Trinity we shall enjoy, "interweaving, moving in and out of and through and around each other, like starlings in an ever-flowing, patterned dance. Human relations are like this because the life of the Trinity is like this. Dante sees this dynamic for himself and imitates it poetically when finally looking on God in the ultimate canto" (123).

Though it is a great virtue of this volume that it emphasizes so strongly the merits of the *Purgatorio* and *Paradiso*, it is nonetheless salutary that John Cavadini's essay should recall the horrors in hell from which mercy redeems us. It is striking that this essay speaks so incisively of irony—and above all of the irony which from Augustine onwards has seen us, in a state of sin, delude ourselves as to the real way in which we might achieve or prepare to receive the happiness that God desires to bestow on us. Sin on this account is a vortex of falsehood which pulls us ever downwards to the depths that Dante horrifically envisages in *Inferno*: "The lower you get in hell, the closer you get to the act of lying which is constitutive of the 'city of this world,' which persuades people to join, and which creates the community that is no community. . . . There is no circle that punishes 'liars,' because the entirety of hell is founded on a lie" (139). Nor is Cavadini talking here of any trivial mendacity but rather, as he starkly recognizes, of a radical lie against all that is most human and indeed divine, which is horrifically expressed in the cannibalism envisaged particularly in *Inferno* 33—an atrocity that, mercilessly, be-lies eucharistic communion

Much of Dante's *Commedia*, in the interplay of part with part, is sustained (to use Cavadini's terminology) by a form of beneficent irony in which the horrors envisaged so pointedly in hell are parodic anti-types of the truths he will subsequently rejoice in. Indeed as early as *Inferno* 1 (line 8) Dante girds himself to speak of the "good" that he found in hell. So it is that Cavadini's reading *ex negativo* of community and also of "Eucharistic Vision" moves in counterpoint with the subtly graduated recuperation in the second and third *cantiche* of a sacral imagination. This development is followed with insight, confidence and beauty in essays by Leonard DeLorenzo, Jessica Keating, and Jennifer Newsome Martin.

DeLorenzo focuses on the central cantos of the *Purgatorio*—which are also the central cantos of the whole *Commedia*—and rightly discerns there the originality that underlies Dante's conception of sin and also of love that in purgatory begins to be seen as a characteristic of human existence infinitely truer than sin. Strikingly, Dante insists that the harm we do in sinning is no way harm that affects our Creator, since God transcends the reach of any mortal injury; and that no one would intentionally harm themselves. So sin must be an offence against our *neighbor*. In DeLorenzo's words,

> Pride is born of your wish to keep others down so that you may excel *by comparison*. Envy is spurning the success of others because you are concerned that you will not be as praiseworthy *by comparison*. And anger arises from that urge to cause someone else harm as retribution for a grievance you see as done to yourself—in other words, anger is lashing out at others because you have learned to see them as harming you (your status, your security, your prospects for self-promotion) *by comparison*. (103)

But Dante's narrative in the *Purgatorio* operates less by judgemental comparison than by an oscillation between an awareness of vice and an awareness of virtue. So, as DeLorenzo shows, the proud are redeemed from all the effects of sinful divisiveness by the recovery of community: the penitential act is here a communal act involving, as in the liturgy, a recitation of the Lord's prayer, subtly rewritten to allow a modulation of pronouns from singular to plural and to promote adaptations that establish an embrace between living and dead. Citing *Purgatorio* 11, DeLorenzo declares that the penitent proud "move as Christ moves: they practice hastening to the needs of others—for the good of others—to the point that they make room in the first person plural for that which is not their own to become their own. Seeking our good heals them because Christ lets himself be taken for a sinner to remedy our sins" (110).

The community envisaged here is shown, by Keating to be animated in Dante's understanding by a eucharistic rhythm:

> The *Comedy* invites us into the diminuendos and crescendos
> of eucharistic memory, to consider what it means to remember
> and to forget, to be remembered and to be forgotten. The mys-
> terious depth, complexity, and potency of eucharistic memory,
> which is to say, "formed in the memory of the price of our
> redemption," such that one's sight and speech are tuned and
> united to Christ. (165)

An essential part of the activity in purgatory is the "re-member-ing"—
the piecing back together—of the self in the light of God's mercy, which is
to say, God's sacrifice of love. In this light, memory is properly seen to be
more than reminiscence (as it might be on a modern understanding). It is
the vitally active recovery (as in Augustine) across space and time of what
existence truly is. Indeed, as in the Psalms God's own memory is invoked
as that which sustains and safeguards his chosen people. So Keating concludes, "To be remembered by God is to be mercied, and mercy requires a
certain kind forgetfulness—the kind of forgetfulness that covers over sin,
that deactivates it. Memory redeemed is eucharistic memory; memory that
remembers in the brackets of kenotic love. Eucharistic memory culminates
in praise of God" (177).

Martin's essay offers a brilliantly focused understanding of how memory is in a sense most vigorously alive when it is incised by visual or visionary impressions. Thus, for Martin,

> Dante's *Paradiso* is, at its most fundamental, a text about this
> kind of wounded seeing that is led toward truer and truer sight,
> where the subjective and objective converge in God. It is a poem
> about beauty, and is itself a pedagogy of beauty. . . . The text is
> aesthetic. . . . [It] is hyper- or meta-visionary because it details
> the processes and operations by which human beings see, fail to
> see, and learn to see. (142)

Such a reading justifies and refreshes the familiar contention that Dante is
a "visual" poet. One also welcomes Martin's insistence that the *Commedia*
is a processive and progressive work in which the poet himself demonstrably expands the visual compass of his own poetic repertoire. Moreover, the
reader, too, on Martin's account might be called directly to engage in an
exercise of moral optics, "practicing the *ascesis* of self-forgetfulness by looking with great mercy upon each other as we are, that is, correlated ultimately
to the light and love of the God who moves all stars" (160).

Eucharistic memory, communal action, visual imagery and solemn
process are all collected together under the great attention that Matthew
Treherne devotes to liturgy. Treherne here notes the originality that Dante

displays, especially in the *Purgatorio*, choosing to punctuate his narrative throughout with explicit reference to liturgical practice. Nor is this simply to say that the text derives a religious coloration from such references. Rather, as readers, we are invited to engage directly in the performance of psalmody and prayer. Treherne notes that preachers, within years of Dante's death, had begun to incorporate references to the *Commedia* into their homilies. And, as modern readers of the poem, we are also located in the "middle way" of a communal narrative that stretches far into the past and—with hermeneutic promise—far into the future. In that regard, there are exact parallels to be drawn between our participation in the liturgy and, correspondingly, in Dante's own work:

> Liturgy shows us one way out of the dark wood: living liturgical-
> ly, with others, inhabiting and performing a place in providen-
> tial history. We arrive at any moment in the condition of being
> midway . . . it is an invitation for us, as we read, to reflect on how
> new beginnings must be grounded in this moment" (97).

The primal narrative that sustains and justifies the common work of both liturgical practice and of Dante's poetry is the narrative of providence—understood as both fore-given-ness and forgiveness. So Christian Moevs speaks powerfully of Dante's poem as an *iter mentis in Deum* which is, simultaneously, a journey toward the true ground of human selfhood: "a journey into the self, a search for the source or being or ground of the finite self, of the finite ego or thinking mind, a search that leads the mind into stillness, into unlimited consciousness and love" (65). The power of this understanding to illuminate particular passages in Dante's poem is evident, for instance, in Moevs's discussion of Dante's encounter with Adam in *Paradiso* 26 where he comes face to face with our archetypal progenitor. The realization here is that "if we awaken or surrender to the truth of our own being, we will know ourselves as manifestations, as embodiments" of the divine reality (68). In that episode, we see the purest example of mercy in its power to recreate what was, originally, created out of nothing. But we also see *caritas* in its ultimate form. Indeed, immediately before his encounter with Adam, Dante had been examined by St. John in the virtue of *caritas*. And the fullest expression of charity is to be experienced in our rejoining that totality of human intercourse and unity that divine love originally intended us to enjoy.

Recognition in *caritas*—and a full and free enjoyment of that—are the guiding themes of Vittorio Montemaggi's essay: "One of the most fruitful ways of thinking about the *Commedia* as a whole is to think of it as a journey towards the possibility of that spontaneous moment of recognition" (24). On this understanding, recognition is the mode of perception whereby

individual meets individual in the fullest realization of our common humanity. The communal work of liturgy has, certainly, a place in promoting
and reestablishing that realization. But, above all, Montemaggi—along with
Dante—acknowledges the supreme importance of Our Lady as being the
focus through which our prayers and worship must all happily be projected:
"To ask what accounts for the possibility of Mary ushering Dante into full
divine union . . . is to ask ourselves about nothing less than the meaning
of Dante's *Comedy* as a whole. A simple set of gestures which finds its full
meaning in all the human encounters that have preceded it on Dante's journey" (24–25). This understanding is especially clear in *Paradiso* 32 and in
the great prayer to the Virgin which, at the opening of canto 33, precedes
the infinite vision of God. Here, before absolute mystery displays itself, we
are invited to contemplate the play of recognizably human gestures—even
smiles—and to participate in a supplication that acknowledges our depen-
dency and interdependency. A community gathers here that reflects the
fullest expression of Marian compassion. And that compassion—following
Montemaggi—must mean a liberation into the grace, luminosity and joy
that, through Christ, human beings are once again capable of revealing.

Mercy as Divine Redress

Whether taken individually or as a collegial chorus, the essays discussed
here can be trusted to lead one through the sequences and choreographic
(or perichoretic) intersections of thought and form that characterize the
narrative-structure of Dante's *Commedia*. To speak for myself—though distinctly under the influence of all that I have read in the foregoing pages—I
return in conclusion to Cardinal Kasper's principles and in particular to
two sequences in the *Commedia* where the relationship between justice, creation, and mercy is represented in and through the narrative in an especially
dynamic form.

The first is canto 9 of the *Purgatorio*, where Dante passes from the
ante-purgatory to purgatory-proper. This threshold is alive with terrors and
tensions. Yet in passing over, Dante envisages the merciful assurance that he
will eventually proceed to heaven. The second is a sequence in the *Paradiso*
running from canto 18 to canto 20 that includes the lines here quoted as an
epigraph and opens with a celebration of the virtue of justice. There will, of
course, be space here only to hint at the richness of thought and imagination displayed in these cantos—though, needless to say, the essays so far
discussed suggest many ways in which this sketch might be expanded.

The Mercy of Repentance

Purgatorio 9 displays characteristics essential to almost all narrative writing, where predictable advances in a journey are rarely smooth or easily achieved. Here Dante's progress toward a (quasi-liturgical) resolution is complicated by intense moments of disorientation and surprise. There is a stair to be climbed and a threshold to be crossed, but how this is to be accomplished—or even *why* it should be—is by no means apparent. The scene is set on the first of three dark nights that Dante has to pass on Mount Purgatory. At lines 10 to 12 he falls asleep, but this is an uneasy sleep: he is "overcome" by tiredness, and "bows down" to the earth under the burden he has inherited from Adam—*che meco avea di quel d'Adamo*. There is a note here of unrelieved penitence, as might also be heard in the dust and "nothingness" of Ash Wednesday.

Then into this vacancy there erupts a dream so vivid and surreal as to be described more accurately as a nightmare. It seems that, for all his slumbering weight, Dante is being carried aloft into the very realm of fire by an Eagle flying on wings of heraldic gold—or better say that this is a rape, since at lines 23 to 24 his plight is compared to that of Ganymede, helpless in the talons of Jove. The "nothingness" here is that of a self totally dispossessed of self.

Eagles in the *Commedia* are always likely to be symbols of Imperial Justice; and it would be simple enough at this point to begin an allegorical exegesis of the episode. This might, helpfully, conclude that Dante is now in the grip of a transcendent power that will restore him to himself in the perspective not of punishment but (in Kasper's terms) of redemption and re-creation. This style of reading, however, would hardly offer an adequate response to the visionary intensity of the scene—sharp enough to deliver a visual "wound." Nor would it account for the dramatic complexity that is generated at lines 43 to 57. Now Dante wakes from his dream and the fire of his nightmare is, first, discovered to be simply the natural warmth of the dawning second day. Furthermore, Virgil is still at Dante's side as a comforting presence. But Virgil at this point opens yet another dimension, miraculous rather than either terrifying or even natural. He explains that Dante has indeed been lifted up to the steps of purgatory. The agent, however, was not a fiery eagle. It was, in truth, Saint Lucy—Dante's matronal saint and embodiment of True Light—who came to carry him upwards.

Here, as before, an allegorical reading would provide a short-hand explanation of the episode, whereby Imperial Justice was revealed ultimately to be a manifestation of love or visionary revelation or, indeed, of mercy. And the notable fact that Virgil—as a representative of Rome—is still there and able to narrate the actions performed by the unseen saint immediately suggests that the relationship between justice and mercy is dialectical rather than exclusive. For all that, if one wishes to stress how re-creative, and indeed truly gratuitous, the actions of mercy—and love and revelation—must always be, then one needs, as reader, to trust the "aesthetic pedagogy" of this moment and allow the imagination to expand into a seemingly ungraspable disruption.

Dante has now to climb the three steps—at the summit of which sits an angel—and enter the gate of purgatory. This may seem an encouraging prospect, requiring only a firm tread on the designated path, culminating in a well-qualified entry into the security of the purgatorial community. Indeed, one familiar interpretation of the sequence associates the three steps with the three stages of the Sacrament of Confession—and the number three, especially in Dante's work, is always likely to carry connotations of Trinitarian perichoresis.

Yet, again, the imagination delivers a more complex understanding than paraphrase ever can. Steps and doors and thresholds are motifs that, as archetypes, reach deep into our psychic memory, recalling rites of passage, as if—here as throughout *Purgatorio*—Dante were recognizing that the self could arrive at health and maturity only through ordeal. The steps themselves—and even the angel—act in this moment with a hyper-visual intensity as disconcerting as, earlier, the appearance of the Dream Eagle had been. The first step is of white stone so perfectly polished as to reflect back to Dante an image of himself dazzlingly—and intolerably—perfect: *ch'io mi specchiai in esso qual io paio* ("that I as I appear was mirroired there," *Purg.* 9.96; "mirroired" [*sic*]: one notes here the elisions playing around and dissolving the first person pronoun *io*). The second step wholly erases that image, being rough, black and, significantly cracked in the outline of a cross, by horizontal and vertical fissures (line 99). The third step is constructed of brilliant porphyry and this brilliance carries nerve-racking tensions of its own. At line 102 it is said to be as red "as fresh blood spurting from a severed vein" (*come sangue che fuor di vena spiccia*), as though new life were displayed through the stinging vitality of a wound.

Nor does the danger or awareness of vulnerability diminish as Dante advances into the angel's presence. On the contrary, this angel, draped in a cloak the color of penitential ash, carries a sword glittering as brightly and with as much menace as did the incandescent eagle. This sword glitters so brightly that it dazzles Dante's eyes (lines 79 to 84). Yet just as the eagle is, in truth, the light and grace of Saint Lucy, so the action of the angel is as gentle and reassuring as the touch of a feather (lines 112–14). Seven wounds in the form of the letter *P* are inscribed on Dante's brow. This letter could signify

Peccata—or Sin—but just as easily "penance" or repentance. In any case this wounding comes with the merciful baptismal promise that the letters will be progressively "washed" from Dante's forehead as he climbs up the mountain. The door of purgatory now opens. The sound it makes is a rusty roar (compared at lines 136 to 138 to the opening of the treasury in ancient Rome). But also, through the din, Dante hears—as an expression of the incalculable mercy that accepts our conversion—the singing of the *Te Deum*, where human voices join with the whole of Creation in praise of the Trinity.

The Triumph of Mercy

The interplay registered in canto 9 of the *Purgatorio* between the eagle and Saint Lucy points to a dialectic between the principles of justice and love which, as I have argued elsewhere,[6] can be seen as the fundamental feature of both narrative and theological action in the *Commedia*. A sustained illustration of this interplay could be found in the relationship, throughout, of Virgil and Beatrice. The depiction of Virgil may be taken to encompass considerations not only of Imperial Justice but also of ethical purpose and of linguistic practice. Correspondingly, Beatrice would manifest what it means to live in the light of revelation and of God-given glory or beauty. In saying this, I do not—yet again—wish to imply any form of allegorical identification. And if I were to pursue this insistence to a conclusion I should turn to the drama of the Earthly Paradise episode where, as Virgil falls silent, Dante's poetry enters a phase in which the dominant factor in the action is an attempt to register in language powers of seeing which are beyond the scope of discourse. There are, however, essays in this volume that already pay searching attention to this crucial moment of crisis. So simply as to further underline how justice and mercy may be seen to be related (as they are in *Purgatorio* 9) I would only note that Virgil's sustainedly rational support for Dante's endeavours is here shown to yield before the *pietade acerba* ("bitter pity" [*Purg.* 30.81]) of Beatrice's searching gaze. "Pity" here—as I suggested earlier—is far from being the erotic sentiment stressed in the Francesca episode. But since the *Vita nuova* Beatrice's presence has always inspired the possibility of new life. So now *pietade*—or compassion or mercy—offers, though seemingly bitter, a new life of incalculable dimensions.

A similar pattern and a similar process may be traced in cantos 18, 19, and 20 of the *Paradiso* which, beginning in celebration of the virtue of justice, engage directly with the realities of divine creation and resolve (around the lines given as an epigraph here) into a contemplation of mercy

6. See, for instance, my *Dante's* Inferno: *Difficulty and Dead Poetry.*

as the primary characteristic of divine love. One might begin with the consideration of divine justice that dominates canto 19. Here, with a certain severity of tone, all justice is seen ultimately to derive from and be dependent upon the justice of God. Justice is one of the infinite and essential principles that operate in the creation of the world. This does not exclude the idea of regulation and restraint. So attention is given to the "compasses" that God employs in the act of creation. But even here these compasses may be seen as determining the hierarchy and proportions which allow created things to exist freely and in harmony:

> Colui che volse il sesto   The One who turned his compass
> a lo stremo del mondo, e dentro ad esso   around the reaches of the Universe
> distinse tanto occulto e manifesto   and marked, within, things clear and
>   dark to view

(Par. 19.40–42)

Two things follow from this. One is, happily, that all human conceptions of justice derive from, and are sustained by, the primal justice of our Creator (Par. 19.58–66). This frees us from any suggestion that justice might ever be reduced to the laws that human beings can—sometimes arbitrarily—devise for their own social or political purposes. Justice is, rather, given to us freely as a constituent aspect of our existence as creatures.

The second consequence is, at first sight, more restrictive: our Creator is transcendent and infinite, so the justice of this Creator must infinitely exceed all human comprehension (Par. 19.43–45). Logically, therefore, we cannot submit divine justice to the test. The attempt to do this would amount to a self-contradiction, since any conception of justice that we entertain derives from the eternal—and transcendent—idea. This restriction applies even to such profoundly troubling questions as, for instance, why the noble pagan should be deprived, though perfect in virtue (or indeed justice), of the joys of heaven (Par. 19.79–81). Yet stern as this prohibition is—at least as voiced in canto 19—it need not be taken to imply conclusively that noble pagans—such as Virgil—are damned beyond redemption. It is, rather, to insist that, in the perspective of eternal justice, human considerations of justice must wait for the further unfolding of the Infinite Mind. We need to recall, perhaps, that the sin of Lucifer was to fall and be degraded, becoming merely "Satan" (Par. 19.46–48) because even as being the highest creature in the universe, he would not "wait for light" (non aspettar lume). The question of the noble pagan, forbidden as it may be, is not unlike the apple that tempted Adam. Or better say that the question is legitimate but must be allowed to wait, dangling unanswered on the tree, until the light of mercy brings it to maturity.

Justice, then, though crucial, is part of an eschatological narrative unfolding toward Judgment Day through phases that (returning to Kasper) one may regard as restitutive and re-creative. Certainly this is the case of Dante's own narrative. In this regard (and many others) one should not expect to abstract from his work single or supposedly definitive propositions. Rather, one must attend to the (perichoretic) interweave as his poem travels from point to point. And cantos 18 and 20 echo with tonalities in significant contrast with those of canto 19.

In *Paradiso* 18 when Dante first encounters the souls of the just they are shown to be participating communally in a sort of calligraphic choreography, where thousands of dancing lights flow through the heavens in form of visible vowels and consonants. These lights settle momentarily and spell out a sentence drawn from Solomon's *Liber Sapientiae*: "*Diligite Iustitiam qui iudicatis terram.*" Then, finally, they assume the shape of a golden eagle, as the M of *Terram* extends into wings and projects an avian neck and beak. The profile of the eagle, as always, recalls symbolically the justice of Imperial Rome; and the fact that Dante envisages how this eagle grows from the lexical conceit of the opening dance only serves to emphasize that language itself—as also in Dante's figuration of Virgil—is fundamentally associated with the principles of justice. At the same time, the picture of dynamic movement that Dante here imagines leads one to understand justice as more than a matter of principle or proposition. Justice is, rather, a true virtue and to be celebrated as such. Which is to say (as canto 19 also emphasizes) that justice is no mere instrument of control but a mode of being that flourishes in human nature when human beings are truly displaying the character that, as creatures, they were formed properly to display. It is through such virtue in all its facets—linguistic as well as legislative—that we participate directly and justly in the life of the Logos.

The celebratory key of *Paradiso* 18 returns, more triumphant still, in canto 20. And it is here—particularly around the *Regnum Celorum* verses at lines 94 to 99—that justice reveals itself to be, as in *Purgatorio* 9, the lovely mask of even lovelier mercy. Already at the opening of the canto, the just souls are transfigured—beyond words or even aquiline formation—into free-flowing lines of musical sound:

udir mi parve un mormorar di fiume	I heard, it seemed, the murmur of a river,
che scende chiaro giù di pietra in pietra,	falling from rock to rock in limpid streams
mostrando l'ubertà del suo cacume.	that show the swelling richness of its source.
E come suono al collo de la cetra	Compare: guitar notes sound from where the fret
prende sua forma, e sì com' al pertugio	gets pressed—as, likewise, at its apertures
de la sampogna vento che penètra,	a reedy flute when pierced by breaths of wind.
così, rimosso d'aspettare indugio,	So here, the moment of delay now done,
quel mormorar de l'aguglia salissi	that murmur, as in hollow columns, rose
su per lo collo, come fosse bugio	through all the length of that great Eagle's neck

(*Par.* 20.19–27)

Here, the communal relationship of one self to another immeasurably surpasses the necessary disciplines of lawful regulation, and thrives, rather,
in that free—or gratuitous—enjoyment that art and beauty freely offer us.
(Theologians might speak at this point of *convenientia*.)

And this new understanding is finally carried home by a miraculous
transformation in the symbolic significance of the eagle. In *Paradiso* 20
we are now asked to look not at the choric form of the eagle but, specifically, at its eye. Here, as one among a group of five, Dante sees, at the pupil
King David. One notes that David explicitly is designated not as King but
as the Psalmist—*cantor dello Spirito Santo* (line 38)—thereby suggesting
that David's need for and longing for divine justice was translated into a
waiting upon the Lord, expressed "conveniently" in song after song. But the
underlying modulation here is registered in Dante's new attention to the
eye as the organ of vision. And the difference that this makes is precisely
consistent with that which, in *Purgatorio* 9, appeared when the Eagle of Jove
was revealed to be Saint Lucy. For the eagle is the bird not only of Empire
but supremely of Saint John. Eagles in medieval lore are capable of looking
directly into the sun without their eyes being consumed (*Par.* 20.31–33).
Saint John similarly looks deep into the mystery of divine revelation and
participates, through the splendor of its truth, in the life—always new, always renewed—of the Logos processively making known its creative love.

This is the context in which we are called to contemplate the mystery,
expressed almost as a paradox, that is addressed in the two *terzine* around
which *Paradiso* 20 spirals:

Regnum celorum violenza pate
da caldo amore e da viva speranza,
che vince la divina volontate:

Regnum celorum will submit to force
assailed by warmth of love or living hope,
which overcome the claims of God's own will

non a guisa che l'omo a l'om sobranza,
ma vince lei perché vuole esser vinta,
e, vinta, vince con sua beninanza.

not in the manner that men beat down men
but win because will wishes to be won
and, won, wills all with all its own good will.

(*Par.* 20.94–99)

At the opening of the justice-sequence, the words across the heavens had been "Love Justice . . ." Now justice resolves into *caldo amore*. To be sure, the meaning of love will continue to evolve in the course of the *Paradiso* (not least when in *Paradiso* 26 Saint John examines Dante on the meaning of *caritas*). But love at this point is synonymous with mercy. God's sovereign love here wills itself to be overcome, and this act of apparent self-contradiction replicates the paradoxes of creation *ex nihilo*. The violence of "selfhood" resolves into joy at the very existence of self, one's own self in the company of all others that God has created. And from this point Dante's poem will advance towards a final understanding in which the community of self-hood, redeemed from self-hood, will gather under the aegis of the Blessed Virgin as Mother of Mercy.

Mercy and love, then, are alike conditions of a new life in which human beings participate, as being "fore-given," in the constant rediscovery of the originary gift. And if we seek a model for how we might view this form of life then Dante's own art will provide it, as displayed in the lines quoted above—or indeed in the whole narrative of the *Commedia*. The poet's words dance, interweaving in alliteration, from one line to the next, confident that at the end of every three-lined verse a rhyme will arrive which is both a conclusion and an impulse, pointing beyond itself to meanings and sources of pleasure that are always delivered anew.

Bibliography

Anselm. *Anselm of Canterbury: The Major Works.* Edited by Brian Davies and G. R. Evans. New York: Oxford University Press, 2008.

Aquinas, Thomas. *Summa Contra Gentiles.* Complete English ed. London: Aeterna, 2015.

————. *Summa Theologica.* Complete English ed. Westminster, MD: Christian Classics, 1981.

Armstrong, Regis, and Ignatius Brady, trans. *Francis and Claire: The Complete Works.* Classics of Western Spirituality. New York: Paulist, 1982.

Auerbach, Erich. *Mimesis: The Representation of Reality in Western Literature.* Translated by Willard R. Trask. Princeton: Princeton University Press, 2013.

Augustine. *The Confessions.* Translated by Maria Boulding. New York: Vintage, 1998.

————. "Exposition on Psalm 75." In *Expositions of the Psalms,* translated by Maria Boulding. Hyde Park, NY: New City, 2002.

————. "Sermon 272." In *Essential Sermons,* translated by Edmund Hill and Boniface Ramsey. Hyde Part, NY: New City, 2002.

————. *The Trinity.* Edited by John Rotelle. Translated by Edmund Hill. Hyde Park, NY: New City, 2012.

Baldwin of Canterbury. *De Sacramento Altaris.* Edited by Jean Leclerq. Paris: Les Éditions du Cerf, 1963.

Baldwin, Paul. "Historic Discovery: Physicists 'Prove' God Didn't Create the Universe." *Express,* March 10, 2015. http://www.express.co.uk/news/science/612340/Origin-of-the-universe-riddle-solved-by-Canadian-physicists-and-er-it-wasn-t-God.

Balthasar, Hans Urs von. *The Glory of the Lord: A Theological Aesthetics.* Vol. 1, *Seeing the Form.* Edited by John Kenneth Riches. Translated by Erasmo Leiva-Merikakis. San Francisco: Ignatius, 2009.

————. *The Glory of the Lord: A Theological Aesthetics.* Vol. 3, *Studies in Theological Style: Lay Styles.* Edited by Joseph Fessio. Translated by Brian McNeil. San Francisco: Ignatius, 2004.

————. *Theo-Drama: Theological Dramatic Theory*. Vol. 4, *The Action*. Translated by Graham Harrison. San Francisco: Ignatius, 1994.

————. *A Theological Anthropology*. Eugene, OR: Wipf & Stock, 2010.

Barański, Zygmunt G. "La Lezione Esegetica Di Inferno I: Allegoria, Storia, E Letteratura Nella Commedia." In *Dante E Le Forme Dell'allegoresi*, edited by Michelangelo Picone, 79–97. Ravenna: Longo, 1987.

Barnes, Bernadine. "Metaphorical Painting: Michelangelo, Dante, and the Last Judgment." *Art Bulletin* 77 (1995) 64.

Barolini, Teodolinda. *The Undivine Comedy: Detheologizing Dante*. Princeton: Princeton University Press, 1992.

Benigni, Roberto. "'Il Nome Di Dio È Misericordia': L'intervento Integrale Di Roberto Benigni in Vaticano." *Repubblica Tv - La Repubblica.it*, January 4, 2016. http:// video.repubblica.it/vaticano/il-nome-di-dio-e-misericordia-l-intervento-integrale-di-roberto-benigni-in-vaticano/224673/223934.

"'Blessing and Distribution of Ashes,' Ash Wednesday." In *The Roman Missal*, 71–72. Totowa, NJ: Catholic Book, 2011.

Bonaventure. *The Journey of the Mind to God*. Edited by Stephen F. Brown. Translated by Philotheus Boehner. Indianapolis: Hackett, 1993.

Brilli, Elisa. *Firenze e il profeta: Dante fra teologia e politica*. Rome: Carcocci, 2012.

Bruni, Leonardo. *Della Vita, Studi E Costumi Di Dante*. Florence: Sansoni, 1917.

Cavadini, John. "Eucharistic Exegesis in Augustine's Confessions." *Augustine Studies* 41 (2010) 87–108.

————. "Spousal Vision: A Study of Text and History in the Theology of Saint Augustine." *Augustinian Studies* 43 (2012) 127–48.

Chester, Ruth. "Virtue in Dante." In *Reviewing Dante's Theology*, edited by Claire Honess and Matthew Treherne, 2:211–52. Bern: Peter Lang, 2013.

Claudel, Paul. *The Satin Slipper; or, The Worst Is Not the Surest*. Translated by John O'Connor. New Haven: Yale University Press, 1931.

Cornish, Alison. *Reading Dante's Stars*. New Haven: Yale University Press, 2000.

Dante Alighieri. *Convivio*. Translated by Christopher Ray. Saratoga, CA: ANMA Libri, 1989.

————. *Inferno*. Edited and translated by Robin Kirkpatrick. New York: Penguin, 2006.

————. *Paradiso*. Edited and translated by Robin Kirkpatrick. New York: Penguin, 2007.

————. *Purgatorio*. Translated by Jean Hollander and Robert Hollander. New York: Anchor, 2003.

————. *Purgatorio*. Edited and translated by Robin Kirkpatrick. New York: Penguin, 2007.

————. *Vita Nova*. Translated by Andrew Frisardi. Evanston, IL: Northwestern University Press, 2012.

Dean, Anne. *David Mamet: Language as Dramatic Action*. London: Fairleigh Dickinson University Press, 1990.

DeLorenzo, Leonard J. *Work of Love: A Theological Reconstruction of the Communion of Saints*. Notre Dame: University of Notre Dame Press, 2017.

Dostoevsky, Fyodor. *The Brothers Karamazov*. Translated by Richard Pevear and Larissa Volokhonsky. 12th ed. New York: Farrar, Straus and Giroux, 2002.

————. *Notes from the Underground*. New York: Dover, 1992.

Dreher, Rod. *How Dante Can Save Your Life: The Life-Changing Wisdom of History's Greatest Poet*. New York: Regan Arts, 2015.

Durand, William. *Rationale Divinorum Officiorum*. Edited by Anselme Davril and Timothy M. Thibodeau. Vol. 3. Corpus Christianorum Continuatio Medievalis 140–40B. Turnhout: Brepols, 1995.

Eco, Umberto. *The Aesthetics of Thomas Aquinas*. Translated by Hugh Bredin. Cambridge: Harvard University Press, 1988.

———. *Art and Beauty in the Middle Ages*. Translated by Hugh Bredin. New Haven: Yale University Press, 1986.

Eliot, T. S. *Four Quartets*. New York: Harcourt, 1971.

———. *The Sacred Wood and Major Early Essays*. Mineola, NY: Dover, 1997.

———. *The Waste Land*. Edited by Michael North. 1st ed. New York: Norton, 2000.

Elkins, James. "On the Arnolfini Portrait and the Lucca Madonna: Did Jan van Eyck Have a Perspectival System?" *Art Bulletin* 73 (1991) 53–62.

Esposito, Enzo. *Dante E Il Giubileo*. Florence: Olschki, 2000.

Freccero, John. *Dante: The Poetics of Conversion*. Edited by Rachel Jacoff. Cambridge: Harvard University Press, 1988.

———. "The Significance of Terza Rima." In *Dante: The Poetics of Conversion*, edited by Rachel Jacoff, 258–73. Cambridge: Harvard University Press, 1986.

Girard, René. *To Double Business Bound: Essays on Literature, Mimesis, and Anthropology*. Baltimore: Johns Hopkins University Press, 1978.

Gragnaloti, Manuele. *Experiencing the Afterlife: Soul and Body in Dante and Medieval Culture*. Notre Dame: University of Notre Dame Press, 2005.

Grove, Kevin. "Desires, Counsels, and Christ: The Christology of Aquinas's Treatment of the Evangelical Counsels." *Jaarboek: Thomas Instituut te Utrecht* 35 (2016) 49–73.

Guardini, Romano. *Dante*. 4th ed. Brescia: Morcelliana, 1999.

Hawkins, Peter. "Dante and the Bible." In *The Cambridge Companion to Dante*, 2nd ed., edited by Rachel Jacoff, 125–40. Cambridge: Cambridge University Press, 2007.

———. *Dante's Testaments: Essays in Scriptural Imagination*. Stanford: Stanford University Press, 1999.

Heidegger, Martin. *The Phenomenology of Religious Life*. Translated by Matthias Fritsch and Jennifer Anna Gosetti-Ferencei. Bloomington: Indiana University Press, 2010.

Heisenberg, Werner, and Peter Heath. *Across the Frontiers*. New York: Harper & Row, 1974.

Herzman, Ronald B. "Dante and the Apocalypse." In *Irenic Apocalypse: Some Uses of Apocalyptic in Dante, Petrach, and Rabelais*, edited by Dennis Costa, 398–413. Saratoga, CA: Anma Libri, 1981.

Hollander, Robert. *Allegory in Dante*. Princeton: Princeton University Press, 1969.

Honess, Claire, and Matthew Treherne, eds. *Reviewing Dante's Theology*. 2 vols. Oxford: Peter Lang, 2013.

Jelenko, Jane, and Sara Marshall. *Changing Lanes: Road Maps to Midlife Renewal*. Los Angeles: Random, 2008.

Kasper, Walter. *Mercy: The Essence of the Gospel and the Key to Christian Life*. Translated by William Madges. New York: Paulist, 2014.

Kermode, Frank. *The Sense of an Ending: Studies in the Theory of Fiction*. New York: Oxford University Press, 1967.

Kirkpatrick, Robin. *Dante's* Inferno: *Difficulty and Dead Poetry*. Cambridge: Cambridge University Press, 2008.

———. *Dante's Paradiso and the Limitations of Modern Criticism*. Cambridge: Cambridge University Press, 1978.

———. Introduction to *Paradiso*. New York: Penguin, 2006.

Le Goff, Jacques. *The Birth of Purgatory*. Translated by Arthur Goldhammer. Chicago: University of Chicago Press, 1984.

Little, Stephen. "The Sacramental Poetics of Dante's *Commedia*." PhD diss., University of Notre Dame, 2009.

Lombardi, Elena. "Augustine and Dante." In *Reviewing Dante's Theology*, edited by Claire Honess and Matthew Treherne, 1:179–208. Oxford: Peter Lang, 2013.

Luzzi, Joseph. *In A Dark Wood: What Dante Taught Me about Grief, Healing and the Mysteries of Love*. New York: HarperCollins, 2015.

Maldina, Nicolo. "L'oration Super Pater Noster Di Dante Tra Esegesi E Vocazione Liturgia. Per Purgatorio XI, 1–24." *L'Alighieri: Rassegna Dantesca* 53 (2012) 89–108.

Marchesi, Simone. *Dante and Augustine: Linguistics, Poetics, Hermeneutics*. Toronto: University of Toronto Press, 2011.

Marshall, Andrew G. *It's Not a Midlife Crisis, It's an Opportunity*. London: Marshall Method, 2016.

Mazzotta, Guiseppe. *Dante, Poet of the Desert: History and Allegory in the Divine Comedy*. Princeton: Princeton University Press, 1979.

———. *Dante's Vision and the Circle of Knowledge*. Princeton: Princeton University Press, 1993.

Meister Eckhart. *Meister Eckhart, Teacher and Preacher*. Edited by Bernard McGinn. New York: Paulist, 1986.

Merton, Thomas. *Conjectures of a Guilty Bystander*. New York: Doubleday, 1989.

Moevs, Christian. *The Metaphysics of Dante's Comedy*. New York: Oxford University Press, 2005.

Montemaggi, Vittorio. "'E 'n la sua volontade è nostra pace': Peace, Justice and the Trinity in Dante's *Commedia*." In *War and Peace in Dante: Essays Literary, Historical and Theological*, edited by John C. Barnes and Daragh O'Connell, 195–225. Dublin: Four Court, 2015.

———. *Reading Dante's* Commedia *as Theology: Divinity Realized in Human Encounter*. New York: Oxford University Press, 2016.

Montemaggi, Vittorio, and Matthew Treherne, eds. *Dante's* Commedia: *Theology as Poetry*. Notre Dame: University of Notre Dame Press, 2010.

Nasti, Paola. "The Art of Teaching and the Nature of Love." In *Vertical Readings in Dante's Comedy*, edited by George Corbett and Heather Webb, 1:223–48. Cambridge: Open Book, 2015.

Nohrnberg, James C. "'The First-Fruit of the Last Judgment: The '*Commedia*' as a Thirteenth Century Apocalypse." In *Last Things: Apocalypse, Judgment and Millennium in the Middle Ages*, edited by Susan Janet Ridyard. Seewanee, TN: University of the South Press, 2002.

O'Regan, Cyril. "Theology, Art, and Beauty." In *The Many Faces of Beauty*, edited by Vittorio Hosle. Notre Dame: University of Notre Dame Press, 2011.

Otto, Rudolf. *The Idea of the Holy*. Translated by John W. Harvey. New York: Oxford University Press, 1950.

Pagels, Heinz. *Cosmic Code: Quantum Physics as the Language of Nature*. New York: Bantam, 1983.

Panofsky, Erwin. *Perspective as Symbolic Form*. Translated by Christopher S. Wood. New York: Zone, 1991.

Pelikan, Jaroslav. *Eternal Feminines*. New Brunswick, NJ: Rutgers University Press, 1990.

Planck, Max. *The New Science*. 3 works in 1 volume: *Where Is Science Going?*; *The Universe in the Light of Modern Physics*; and *The Philosophy of Physics*. New York: Meridian, 1959.

Plato. *Republic*. Edited by G. R. F. Ferrari. Translated by Tom Griffith. Cambridge Texts in the History of Political Thought. Cambridge: Cambridge University Press, 2000.

Pope Benedict XVI. "The Feeling of Things, the Contemplation of Beauty." In *The Essential Pope Benedict XVI: His Central Writings and Speeches*, edited by John F. Thorton and Susan B. Varenne, 47–52. San Francisco: HarperSanFrancisco, 2007.

Pope Francis. "Extraordinary Jubilee of Mercy: Holy Mass and Opening of the Holy Door." Homily, December 8, 2015. https://w2.vatican.va/content/francesco/en/homilies/2015/documents/papa-francesco_20151208_giubileo-omelia-apertura.html.

——. *Lumen Fidei*. San Francisco: Ignatius, 2013.

——. "Message of His Holiness Pope Francis to the President of the Pontifical Council for Culture for the Solemn Celebration of the 750th Anniversary of the Birth of the Supreme Poet Dante Alighieri." May 4, 2015. http://w2.vatican.va/content/francesco/en/messages/pont-messages/2015/documents/papa-francesco_20150504_messaggio-dante-alighieri.html.

——. "Misericordiae Vultus." Papal Bull, April 11, 2015. https://w2.vatican.va/content/francesco/en/apost_letters/documents/papa-francesco_bolla_20150411_misericordiae-vultus.html.

Pope John Paul II. *Vita Consecrata*. Washington, DC: United States Conference of Catholic Bishops, 1996.

Ratzinger, Joseph. *God Is Near Us: The Eucharist, the Heart of Life*. 1st ed. Edited by Stephan Otto Horn and Vinzenz Pfnur. Translated by Henry Taylor. Ignatius, 2003.

"The Rite of Penance." In *Rites of the Catholic Church*, 1:519–629. Collegeville: Liturgical, 1990.

Sayers, Dorothy. *Further Papers on Dante: His Heirs and His Ancestors*. 2 vols. Eugene, OR: Wipf & Stock, 1957.

——. *Introductory Papers on Dante: The Poet Alive in His Writings*. Eugene, OR: Wipf & Stock, 2006.

——. *The Poetry of Search and the Poetry of Statement: On Dante and Other Writers*. Eugene, OR: Wipf & Stock, 2006.

Schrödinger, Erwin. *Mind and Matter*. Cambridge: Cambridge University Press, 1958.

Scott, John. *Understanding Dante*. Notre Dame: University of Notre Dame Press, 2004.

Singleton, Charles. *Journey to Beatrice*. Cambridge: Harvard University Press, 1958.

Soskice, Janet. "Monica's Tears: Augustine on Words and Speech." *New Blackfriars* 83 (2002) 448–58.

Tagore, Rabindranath, trans. *Songs of Kabir*. York Beach, ME: Samuel Weister, 1977.

Tolle, Eckhart. *A New Earth: Awakening to Your Life's Purpose*. New York: Plume, 2005.

Took, John. "'S'io M'intuassi, Come to t'inmii' (Par.IX.81) Patterns of Collective Being."
    Modern Language Review 101 (2006) 402–13.

"Top 40 Signs of a Mid-Life Crisis." *Mynewsdesk*, July 8, 2013. http://www.mynewsdesk.
    com/uk/crown-cosma-clinic/pressreleases/top-40-signs-of-a-mid-life-
    crisis-885103.

Van Dijk, Stephen J. P. "The Bible in Liturgical Use." In *The West from the Fathers to the
    Reformation*, edited by G. W. H. Lampe, 220–52. Cambridge History of the Bible.
    Cambridge: Cambridge University Press, 1969.

Virgil. *Aeneid*. Translated by Frank O. Copley. Indianapolis: Bobbs-Merrill, 1965.

Wittgenstein, Ludgwig, and Peter Winch. *Culture and Value*. Chicago: University of
    Chicago Press, 1980.

Wittgenstein, Ludwig. *Tractatus Logico-Philosophicus*. Translated by D. F. Pears and
    B. F. McGuinness. London: Routledge & Kegan Paul, 1974.

Wybrew, Hugh. *The Orthodox Liturgy: The Development of the Eucharistic Liturgy in the
    Byzantine Rite*. London: SPCK, 2013.

Index